The Simple Guide to Commercial Diving

by
Steven M. Barsky
&
Robert W. Christensen

Hammerhead Press
Ventura, California
www.hammerheadpress.com

© 2004 Steven M. Barsky and Robert W. Christensen. All rights reserved.

No part of this book may be reproduced or transmitted in any form or by any means electronic or mechanical, including photocopying, recording, or by any information storage or retrieval system, without permission in writing from the publisher.

Original photography and illustrations by Steven M. Barsky unless otherwise noted. Design and typography by Hammerhead Press.

Printing history: First printing 2004

Printed in the United States of America by Ojai Printing, Ojai, California.

ISBN Number: 0-9674305-4-2

Library of Congress Control Number: 2004114014

⚠ WARNING

Commercial diving is a potentially hazardous occupation that presents many dangers that far exceed the risks in sport diving. Commercial divers work in industrial environments that frequently involve heavy construction, the threat of electrical shock, and the risk of pressure related injuries due to differences in pressure between the diving environment and pipelines, dams, and other structures that may be operating at a higher or lower pressure. These are not the only construction related risks, but are just a few of the more common ones.

It is not uncommon for commercial divers to work in environments where the underwater visibility is zero. This increases the risk of a diving accident tremendously, since the diver is unable to see imminent hazards that pose a threat to his health and safety.

All of the usual risks in sport diving, such as drowning or arterial gas embolism, are present in commercial diving, but some of these risks are multiplied many times. Although the incidence of decompression sickness has been greatly reduced in the commercial diving industry, explosive decompression is still a risk on certain types of commercial dives.

In addition to the physical risks in commercial diving, there are also serious emotional risks. The commercial diving lifestyle is difficult and not conducive to a happy family life. Many commercial divers suffer through the pain of divorce and the difficulty of maintaining long-term relationships due to the frequent travel and long hours required by the profession of being a diver.

This book is not intended to be used as a basic manual in the fundamentals of diving and survival underwater. Its purpose is to acquaint the prospective commercial diver with the job environment, the profession, and some of the challenges and risks people face in pursuing this type of work.

Other Books by Steven M. Barsky

Published by Best Publishing
Careers in Diving (with Kristine Barsky and Ronnie Damico)
The Simple Guide to Rebreather Diving
The Simple Guide to Snorkeling Fun
Small Boat Diving
Spearfishing for Skin and Scuba Divers

Published by Hammerhead Press
Diving in High-Risk Environments, Third Edition
Dry Suit Diving, Third Edition
California Lobster Diving (with Kristine Barsky)
Investigating Recreational and Commercial Diving Accidents (with Tom Neuman, M.D.)

Published by International Training, Inc.
Deeper Sport Diving with Dive Computers
Easy Nitrox Diving
Underwater Navigation, Night, and Limited Visibility Diving
Wreck, Boat, and Drift Diving

Published by Scuba Schools International
The Dry Suit Diving Manual

Table of Contents

Foreword	X
Acknowledgements	XII

Chapter 1 - Introduction to Commercial Diving — 1
Inshore and Offshore Divers — 1
Women Face a Special Challenge — 3
Greater Risks than Sport Diving — 4
Commercial Diving Millionaires? — 4
Why Be a Commercial Diver? — 5
True Tales of Commercial Diving from the North Sea — 6

Chapter 2 - Training to Be a Commercial Diver — 9
Desirable Mechanical Skills — 9
Rigging — 9
Welding and Cutting — 10
Pipefitting/Plumbing — 11
Engine Mechanics — 11
Photography and Videography — 12
Technical Report Writing — 12
Electronics and Computers — 13
Diving Skills — 13
Other Skills — 14
Confidence — 14
Everyone Has Different Talents — 14
Commercial Diving Schools — 15
Attending Commercial Diving School — 17
True Tales of Commercial Diving from the Santa Barbara Channel — 19

Chapter 3 - The Physiology of Commercial Diving — 21
Fitness to Dive — 21
Decompression Dives are Common in Commercial Diving — 22
Diver Heating is a Major Issue — 24
Saturation Diving Poses Its Own Set of Challenges — 25
True Tales of Commercial Diving from the North Sea — 26

Chapter 4 - Modes of Diving — 29
Scuba Equipment — 29
Surface-Supplied Air Diving Systems — 30
Surface-Supplied Mixed-Gas — 33
Bell/Saturation Diving — 33
Annual Testing — 33
True Tales of Commercial Diving from the Gulf of Mexico — 35

Table of Contents

Chapter 5 - Risks in Commercial Diving — 37
- Drowning and Asphyxiation — 38
- Pressure Related Injuries — 38
- Squeezes — 38
- Decompression Sickness — 39
- Differential Pressure — 39
- Marine Life Injuries — 41
- Underwater Explosions — 41
- Polluted Water — 42
- Industrial Accidents — 43
- Emotional Stress — 45
- True Tales of Commercial Diving from Alaska — 45

Chapter 6 - Commercial Diving Equipment — 47
- Personal Diving Equipment — 47
- Diving Helmets & Full-Face Masks — 47
- Diving Helmets — 47
- Full-Face Mask — 49
- Harness and Bail-Out System — 49
- Commercial Diving Weight Belt — 50
- Thermal Protection — 51
- Wetsuits — 51
- Dry Suits — 51
- Hot Water Suits — 52
- Knives — 53
- Gloves — 53
- Heavy Hardware — 54
- Air Compressors — 54
- Manifold — 54
- Communications Box — 55
- Umbilical — 56
- Decompression Chamber — 57
- Stage — 58
- Mixed-Gas Diving Equipment — 59
- Mixed-Gas Diving Manifold — 59
- Helium Unscrambler — 60
- Open Bottom Bell — 60
- One-Atmosphere Suits — 60
- Bell/Saturation Systems — 61
- Diving Bell — 61
- Entrance Lock — 63
- Saturation Chamber(s) — 63
- Environmental Control System — 63
- Control Van — 64
- Bell Launch Systems — 65
- Dive Support Vessels — 65
- True Tales of Commercial Diving from the North Sea — 66

Chapter 7 - Employment as a Tender — 69
Who Do You Want to Work For? — 69
Preparing Your Resume — 70
Finding a Job — 70
Interviews — 72
Pay Rates and Work Schedules — 73
On the Job — 74
Don't Gripe — 75
Always Be Available for Work — 75
Developing Your Confidence and Attitude — 76
Crew Sizes and Assignments — 76
Tender's Responsibilities at the Start of a Job — 76
Dressing and Tending the Diver — 77
Other Tasks for Tenders — 78
Setting Up and Running an Underwater Cutting System — 78
Running the Decompression Chamber — 80
Treating a Diver with Decompression Sickness — 83
Diving as a Tender — 83
Packing Up the Job — 83
Tools for Tenders — 83
Breaking Out — 86
True Tales of Commercial Diving from the California Coast — 87

Chapter 8 - Working as a Commercial Diver — 89
Safety Gear — 89
Just Say No – Sometimes… — 91
Standing by to Dive — 91
Communicating with Topside — 92
Entering the Water — 92
Using the Down Line — 92
Managing Your Diving Hose — 93
ROVs — 94
Working in Black Water — 94
Bell and Saturation Diving — 96
Emergency Procedures — 99
Loss of the Topside Breathing Gas Supply — 99
Recovering an Unconscious Diver — 99
Lost Bell — 100
Evacuation by Hyperbaric Lifeboat — 100
Reporting Decompression Sickness — 101
Responsibility for Paperwork — 101
Your Mobile Office — 102
Moving Up — 102
Interfacing with the Client — 102
True Tales of Commercial Diving from the North Sea — 103

Chapter 9 - Working with Tools Underwater — 105
Use the Right Tool for the Job — 105
Using an Ascender — 105
Lines for Tools — 106

Table of Contents

Hand Tools	106
Hammers	106
Wrenches	106
Hand Powered Hydraulic Cable Cutters	106
Come-Alongs and Hoists	107
Pneumatic Tools	108
Hydraulic Tools	108
Burning Gear	109
Working Underwater with a Crane	112
Welding Underwater	112
Water Blasters	114
Jet Nozzles	115
Explosives	115
Digital Still Cameras	116
Underwater Video	118
Non-Destructive Testing	119
True Tales of Commercial Diving from the North Sea	121

Chapter 10 - Rigging for the Commercial Diver — 123

Safe Working Loads	123
Fiber Rope	123
Manila	124
Polypropylene	124
Nylon	124
Whipping	125
Splices	126
Knots	127
Hitches	127
Wire Rope	128
Wire Rope Eye Splices and Slings	129
Rigging Tools	130
Rigging Hardware	130
Hooks	131
Chain	131
True Tales of Commercial Diving from the Santa Barbara Channel	133

Chapter 11 - Working as a Diving Supervisor — 135

From Diver to Management	135
Talents of the Diving Supervisor	135
Company Politics	138
Moving Into Management	138
Careers Beyond Diving	138
True Tales of Commercial Diving from Alaska	139

Chapter 12 - The Future of Commercial Diving — 141

Helping to Ensure Your Employment	141
Your Future	142
True Tales of Commercial Diving from the Gulf of Mexico	143

Bibliography	145
About the Author - Steven M. Barsky	146
About the Author - Robert W. Christensen	148
Appendix	150
Field Neurological Exam	150
Index	152

Foreword

In 1974 I enrolled in commercial diving school in Santa Barbara, California. I had only the vaguest notion of what commercial diving was about, and no background in any of the trades generally considered to be essential to a career in commercial diving. My only practical skills at that time were that I could write and I had a limited knowledge of photography.

I was completely lost for the first few weeks of the course and thought for sure that I would be a complete failure as a diver, but for some reason I stuck it out. Quitting is not generally in my nature and that is one of the more important personality traits required of successful divers.

In my mechanical drawing class they showed us mechanical drawings of three-dimensional shapes and we had to figure out what they looked like in real life. I was baffled. In our welding class the instructor made the statement that if you had two perfectly machined surfaces and placed them against each other they would "weld." I had no idea what he was talking about, since I had never welded and had no knowledge of the trade.

Luckily, I was in the care of three exceptional divers who took an interest in me and encouraged me to continue. They were Ramsey Parks, Jim Parker, and Bob Christensen.

Ramsey Parks was the director of the program, a former Los Angeles County lifeguard, sailor, and savvy heavy gear diver. Jim Parker was a diver, a welder, and a draftsman who helped design many of the early saturation diving systems for SubSea International, one of the largest commercial diving firms in the late 70s through the early 90s.

Bob Christensen had been a diver in the Underwater Demolition Teams (UDT), and a heavy gear diver in Alaska and off the coast of California. Bob also participated in the early experimental saturation dives for Ocean Systems (another large diving firm) and made chamber dives down to 650 feet of seawater (FSW). Bob is probably the most intuitive mechanic I have ever seen in action, and he gave me extra assistance in developing my meager mechanical skills. Without the extra attention I received from Bob, it's doubtful I would have been successful as a commercial diver. He's been an important mentor to me throughout my life.

Although the physical skills I learned at diving school were crucial to my success, particularly for someone like myself with a limited mechanical background, the people skills I learned at diving school were equally important. Understanding the politics of the offshore environment and the diving industry are crucial to your success as a diver.

Immediately following my graduation from commercial diving school in 1976, and the completion of my master's degree, I went to the North Sea to work for SubSea International. It was the height of the North Sea oil boom and my timing could not have been better. Divers were in demand and within a year I had completed my apprenticeship and became a diver. The skills that I had learned in diving school were all directly applicable to the work that I did. Things that did not make complete sense in the classroom jumped into focus, sometimes painfully so, as soon as I began to work in the field.

One of the fortunate things that happened when I worked for SubSea is that Jim Parker, one of my instructors from Santa Barbara, was on sabbatical and also working for SubSea in Scotland. We ended up on the same job, which was a blessing for me because he would frequently pull me aside and explain to me what I needed to do to get along with the other members of the dive crew. Without Jim's help and words of wisdom, it's doubtful I would have "survived" my first year in the offshore environment.

I continued to work in the offshore industry for seven years, before returning to Santa Barbara to work for Diving Systems International (today known as Kirby Morgan Diving Systems, Inc.), the leading manufacturer of commercial diving helmets and masks in the world. Although I no longer work as a commercial oilfield diver, I work as an underwater photographer and filmmaker. I am still involved in the commercial diving industry and consult to commercial diving firms and manufacturers of deep sea diving gear. I also participated in the development of standards for polluted water diving for the Association of Diving Contractors International.

Although the world has changed greatly in the last thirty years, and divers have better equipment than they ever did in the past, the fundamentals of commercial diving and the physics that control what happens underwater have not changed since the first helmet divers went underwater in the late 1800s. Water is still wet, knots must still be tied properly, diving helmets still need non-return valves, and proper decompression procedures must be followed. As we've gained knowledge based upon improvements in diving science, better tools, and regrettable accidents, we've adjusted how things are done, but the basic practice of commercial diving remains unchanged.

This book is a result of many years of experience working underwater in the marine environment. As much as Bob Christensen and I hope that you'll learn about the practical skills of working in the underwater world, we also hope that you'll understand the importance of how to get along in the offshore environment. We wish you the best of success in your career as a commercial diver.

Steve Barsky
Ventura, California

Acknowledgements

Writing a book is always a time consuming project. Aside from the writing, we probably spend the most time trying to secure photographs we don't have and finding qualified people to help us by reviewing the book. These two tasks always seem to take the most time away from the creative process, so it's a joy when we find people who are willing to pitch in and help immediately.

On this particular project, we were especially fortunate to receive tremendous assistance from a number of special people, and we would like to thank them here.

• Don Barthelmess is a professor at the Santa Barbara City College Marine Technology program and a good friend. A former commercial diver, submersible pilot and ROV operator, Don has a broad knowledge of the diving industry. He has always assisted us whenever we've asked for help. Don participated in some of the photos seen in the book and took the time to review the manuscript and make suggestions.

• Greg Bryant has done so many things in his life it would be difficult to list them all here. A licensed engineer, Greg has been a commercial diver, a commercial diving instructor at Santa Barbara City College, worked on films like James Cameron's *The Abyss*, and today, consults full-time to the film and television industry. Greg read the manuscript for us and provided many important comments and suggestions.

• Bob Evans is a prolific inventor, an artistic photographer, and a close friend. Bob is the inventor of the Force Fin, which has powered us on many of our dives. He provided several of the photos used in the book.

• Bev Morgan is one of the greatest diving inventors of all time, a phenomenal photographer, and a good friend. Bev was gracious enough to allow us to use his photographs of heavy gear divers throughout the book for the chapter "opener" image for the start of each chapter. We're especially appreciative of his contribution.

• Ella Jean Morgan is the Dean of Academic Programs at the College of Oceaneering. She has an extensive teaching background in the diving field. Ella Jean assisted us with arrangements for shooting photos at the great facilities of the commercial diving training facilities at the College of Oceaneering.

• Mark Perlstein has been a friend for many years and although he is not a commercial diver, he took the time to read the manuscript and give us his comments as a sport diver would perceive the topic. This was especially important information that helped to improve the book.

• Jon Sears has been a friend for many years and is one of the most successful commercial divers we know. A diver for almost all of his life, Jon attended Santa Barbara City College with Steve Barsky and together they worked in the North Sea for SubSea International. Jon went on to work for Oceaneering International and has risen through their ranks to the management

level. Jon critiqued the book for us and gave us numerous valuable ideas for ways to improve our work.
- Doug Smith, formerly with Broco, helped us with photos from the Broco archives of underwater explosives in use.
- Ed Stetson is another good friend who also read the book from the sport diving perspective. Ed has been teaching diving for many years and has always been a positive influence in the diving community in Santa Barbara.
- Geoff Thielst was a commercial diving student of Bob Christensen's and a fellow diver with Steve Barsky at SubSea International. Today, Geoff is an instructor at Santa Barbara City College for the Marine Technology program during the school year, and manages diving projects during his summers. Geoff took the time to review the manuscript for us and provide us with his critical comments.

Companies who assisted us with photographs include the following:
- Amron International
- Chicago Pneumatic
- Gerber Knives
- Kirby-Morgan Dive Systems, Inc.
- MSA – Thanks to photographer John Talent.
- Ocean Technology Systems

A special thanks goes out to our wives, Kristine Barsky and June Christensen, who have always supported our work and our lives, in addition to pursuing their own careers.

Finally, we would like to thank the many divers we have known and worked with over the years, who have shared their experiences and knowledge with us. Diving is definitely a field where no one person knows all of the answers, and that certainly includes us. Without the sharing of experiences and knowledge in this business, there would be many less than successful dives.

Steve Barsky
Bob Christensen

© Bev Morgan. All rights reserved.

Chapter 1
Introduction to Commercial Diving

Nobody will pay you to make bubbles!

Although most sport divers have heard of commercial diving and probably have seen photos of divers working underwater, few people who have not worked in the industry have a good idea of what commercial divers actually do to make a living. Some people think that it's treasure hunting, and in rare situations some divers actually get to do this type of work. Other people believe that it involves the salvage of large vessels, and there are some companies that do these types of dives. However, neither of these jobs make up the meat and potatoes of the work that most divers perform.

In this book you will get an idea of the training you need to be a diver, the types of work that commercial divers do, the tools they work with, and the attitude you need to be a successful diver. If you get bored with the information you find here, or don't think you want to work as hard as we have described, or don't have the type of attitude you need to be a diver, then you should probably look for another profession.

Inshore and Offshore Divers

Divers who work to collect seafood are generally not considered to be "commercial divers," nor are the people who clean the bottoms of small boats, scuba instructors, or professional underwater photographers. Basically, there are two main types of commercial divers; those who work "inshore" and those who work "offshore." The distinction primarily affects the water depths in which they dive, the locations where they work, and the type of diving support equipment they use,

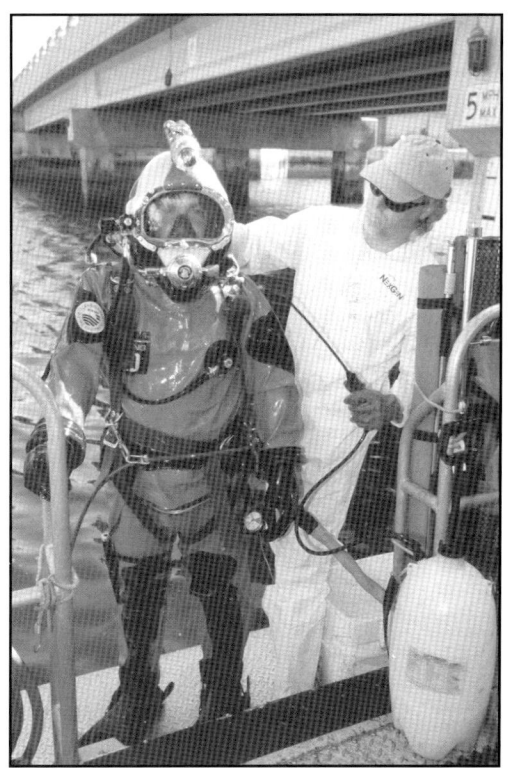

Inshore commercial divers work on bridges, in harbors, on shallow dams, on sewer outfalls, and many other types of jobs.

because the tools they use to get the job done are essentially the same.

Inshore commercial divers tend to work on shallow dams, in harbors, on sewer outfalls, and service municipal drinking water tanks. There is also a significant amount of work done in the repair of ships. Most of their diving is performed at depths that do not exceed 150 FSW (feet of seawater).

Introduction to Commercial Diving

Almost every major port has multiple commercial diving companies who help to keep harbor operations going.

Many divers work inside potable (drinking) water tanks performing inspections.

Commercial divers work in many phases of the offshore oil industry. As a diver you may spend months of your time on offshore barges, rigs, and platforms.

Most inshore commercial diving companies are relatively small, and do not usually employ more than 15 or 20 divers. Their work is normally performed locally, within their home state or geographic region. Inshore divers may work from a barge or other vessel, but in many instances their base of operations may be a pier, a dock, or even off the beach. In many cases, the inshore diver is able to return home each night and his work does not usually take him away from home for more than a few days at a time.

Offshore commercial divers usually work in the offshore oilfields around the world, performing work during all phases of the life of an offshore oil producing facility. They may be involved during exploratory drilling - platform and pipeline installation – platform and pipeline maintenance, repair, and inspection – and platform and pipeline salvage and decommissioning. They may work in shallow waters just below the surface, or in seas in excess of 1000 feet deep.

There are a number of large offshore commercial diving companies that have the equipment and manpower to perform work at just about any depth. These companies frequently send their divers around the world, where they spend their time working from ships, barges, rigs, and offshore platforms. Divers who work for companies like these may spend 30 days or more offshore at one time, working seven days a week, twelve hours a day.

If you are a person who is unduly modest, or needs lots of time alone, you will probably not enjoy working in the offshore environment. There is almost no privacy in the offshore oil patch.

The Commercial Diver's Lifestyle

If you are considering a job as a commercial diver, it's important to realize that you are committing to more than a career, but a lifestyle as well. While inshore divers may stay in the business for many years, most offshore divers find that after six to ten years in the business, the lifestyle tends to get rather tiresome. While it sounds like fun, traveling around the world, the offshore environment is demanding and difficult, both emotionally and physically.

Most commercial diving firms want their divers to be on call at all times, which means that you must live with a cell phone or pager at all times. If you want to be successful you must make yourself available for work, whenever the call comes in, whether it's the middle of the night or on the weekend.

All divers must work odd hours and for long stretches of time, and this makes family life and normal relationships extremely tough to maintain. It is rare that a diver does not miss important family events or dates with a loved one. In fact, most divers end up missing more social events than they would care to recall. As the old saying goes, there's a reason the yellow pages list "divers" right before "divorce" in the phone book.

Women Face a Special Challenge

While there are more women who are working in commercial diving today than at any time in the past, the cold hard truth is that commercial diving is still a male domi-

Female divers often face challenges that male divers don't encounter. They may need to come up with innovative ways to complete a job due to their smaller physical stature.

nated field, and probably will be for many years to come. We don't mean to imply that women are incapable of doing the work, but the fact of the matter is that women face special challenges in working as a diver, particularly in the offshore environment, where subtle, unspoken sexual discrimination may still exist.

Since many older divers, and diving services customers, tend to think of commercial diving as a "macho" profession, a woman diver may be put in a position where she may be challenged and feel the need to prove herself. Also, since many women are physically smaller than their male counterparts and may lack the upper body strength and leverage to do certain jobs, they may need to be more clever about how they perform certain underwater tasks.

Introduction to Commercial Diving

Greater Risks than Sport Diving

Another important consideration for anyone considering commercial diving as a career are the risks involved in the profession. There are numerous risks in commercial diving, many of which expose the diver to situations that may cause death or produce long-term disability.

Aside from the usual physiological risks in diving, there are many risks that are unique to commercial diving, due to the nature of the industrial environment where the diver works. For example, most sport divers don't ever worry about the possibility of someone dropping a heavy object on them while they are underwater, but in the commercial diving world, this is a potential threat on many jobs. There are also other risks, such as electrocution or explosions that are virtually unheard of in recreational diving. Additional risks will be discussed throughout the book.

Commercial divers must also constantly weigh the fact that normal risks in diving are usually greatly amplified in commercial diving. For example, while it is highly unusual for a scuba diver to die from decompression sickness (DCS), this is a danger on some deeper commercial dives. Similarly, the threat of hypothermia (extreme body cooling) is also much more serious in certain commercial diving situations.

Commercial Diving Millionaires?

Given all of the risks in commercial diving, you would think that the profession would be highly paid, and in some cases you would be right. However, the average commercial diver is NOT highly paid, although he can make a great deal of money in a short period of time.

The problem most divers face in earning a good salary involves several issues. First, not everyone in the profession starts out as a diver. Most people begin their career as an apprentice, or "tender," a position which is not highly paid and usually does not provide a great deal of opportunity to dive. Consequently, it usually takes most people several years to gain enough experience on the job to make a good wage.

Another issue that most divers face is the irregular nature of the work. Divers work for diving companies who are hired by municipalities, hydroelectric firms, or oil companies to perform specific jobs. If the diving company does not have a job, it does not hire divers to do the work.

In some years, there is more work than any of the diving companies can do, and you can make a good living. Unfortunately, there are other periods where there is little or no work for divers, and unless you have some other job you can do, you may go through an extended period with little or no income. Some people, especially if they have a family, may have a difficult time handling this uncertainty.

You must be a good money manager in order to survive during the downturns in the profession, if you want to succeed in the industry. This is a challenge for many divers and not everyone can cope with the lean times that face every diver.

The average commercial diver is not highly paid, although there is the potential to make good money if you put in the time.

Why Be a Commercial Diver?

Given all the negative factors associated with a career in commercial diving, you might wonder why we would bother to write a book about the profession. There are numerous reasons why people choose to be commercial divers. In many cases, it boils down to a yearning for adventure, the opportunity to travel, or satisfaction doing a difficult job. If money is your sole motivator, it is doubtful that you will last very long as a commercial diver.

There are many days offshore that are deadly dull, but there are also special moments that are filled with magic. It is awe inspiring to stand on the bottom in 200 feet of water and look up and see a massive offshore platform towering above you. To look out the porthole of a diving bell and see the water teeming with sharks is definitely a real rush.

If it is travel you want, commercial diving provides the chance to visit many different parts of the world. Between the two authors, we have worked in Alaska, California, Holland, Louisiana, New England, Norway, Scotland, and Texas. Although the opportunities for U.S. citizens to work in Europe and other countries are much more limited today, there are still many diving jobs taking place in Africa, the Middle East, the far East, the Indian Ocean, Mexico, and South America. Any place there is water and civilization in close proximity, you will generally find divers at work.

If you are successful and become a proficient diver, you will be in great demand. Your success as a diver will be partly dependent on your ability to do the job, but also dependent on your ability to get along with other people. If you are difficult, arrogant, unfriendly, or unreliable you will not do well in a profession where you are cooped up on a ship for long periods of time with other people. The most successful divers not only have talent, but also are people who others want to be around.

There is a great deal of satisfaction to be derived from being a diver, particularly in situations where you have been flown in from a great distance to perform a particular job that few others can do. The work is almost always challenging, usually as much mentally as

If you like a challenge, commercial diving is a good career.

physically. It's an especially good feeling when you complete the work successfully and board the helicopter to return home! If you like to solve problems and figure things out, this is a career that you will probably find very rewarding.

Introduction to Commercial Diving

True Tales of Commercial Diving from the North Sea

I finished commercial diving school on a Friday in June of 1976 and the following Sunday I boarded a plane for Aberdeen, Scotland. I arrived at the offices of SubSea International on Monday morning at 7:00 A.M. and waited for the first people in the office to arrive. When I entered the office I saw my name on a magnetic board along with the names of all of the other offshore crew and the jobs on which they were posted. Tenders' names were in green, divers' names were in blue, and supervisors' names were in red.

After filling out a couple of forms, the operations manager suggested that I get some sleep and report to the harbor at midnight where a supply ship was being outfitted with a saturation system to conduct a long term inspection job. My assignment was to help install the diving system and then sail with the ship to work as a tender on the project.

I arrived at the ship at midnight and reported to the diving supervisor. My assignment that night was to supply diesel fuel for all of the welding machines and generators being used to keep the job running. Since there was no diesel fuel outlet on deck, and none on the dock, my only choice was to carry two five gallon buckets down two narrow flights of stairs to the engine room, fill the buckets, and carry them back up to the deck.

The temperature on deck was in the low 50s, but the temperature down in the engine room felt like it was 85. A round trip to fill the buckets, carry the fuel upstairs, fill a machine, and head back below took over half an hour. After the second trip, I was bathed in sweat. By the time I finished fueling the last machine, it was time to start filling the first one again.

The deck of the ship was strewn with spools of wire rope, piles of equipment, the welding machine, the generators, and anchor winches. There was standing water on the deck, from some unknown source, six inches deep. At about 5:00 A.M. I was crossing the deck carefully when I looked up to see the diving supervisor and several of the divers deep in conversation as they surveyed the operation deciding what needed to be done.

While looking at the divers, I tripped over a two-inch anchor cable, slipped, and landed in the water, on my back. Diesel fuel poured out of the buckets and covered me with an oily, smelly film. I could see the supervisor and divers shaking their heads and I was sure they were thinking that I was a loser. It certainly wasn't the most auspicious beginning to my career, and I was definitely embarrassed, but I learned that the crew was very accepting of most mistakes, provided you worked hard and contributed to the team.

Steve Barsky

Opposite Page: The "Forties Field" in the North Sea was one of the first producing oil fields in this part of the world. This platform is located in 400+ feet of water. Much of the installation work was performed by commercial divers.

On the rear of the ship below the platform, is a saturation system inside the dark containers.

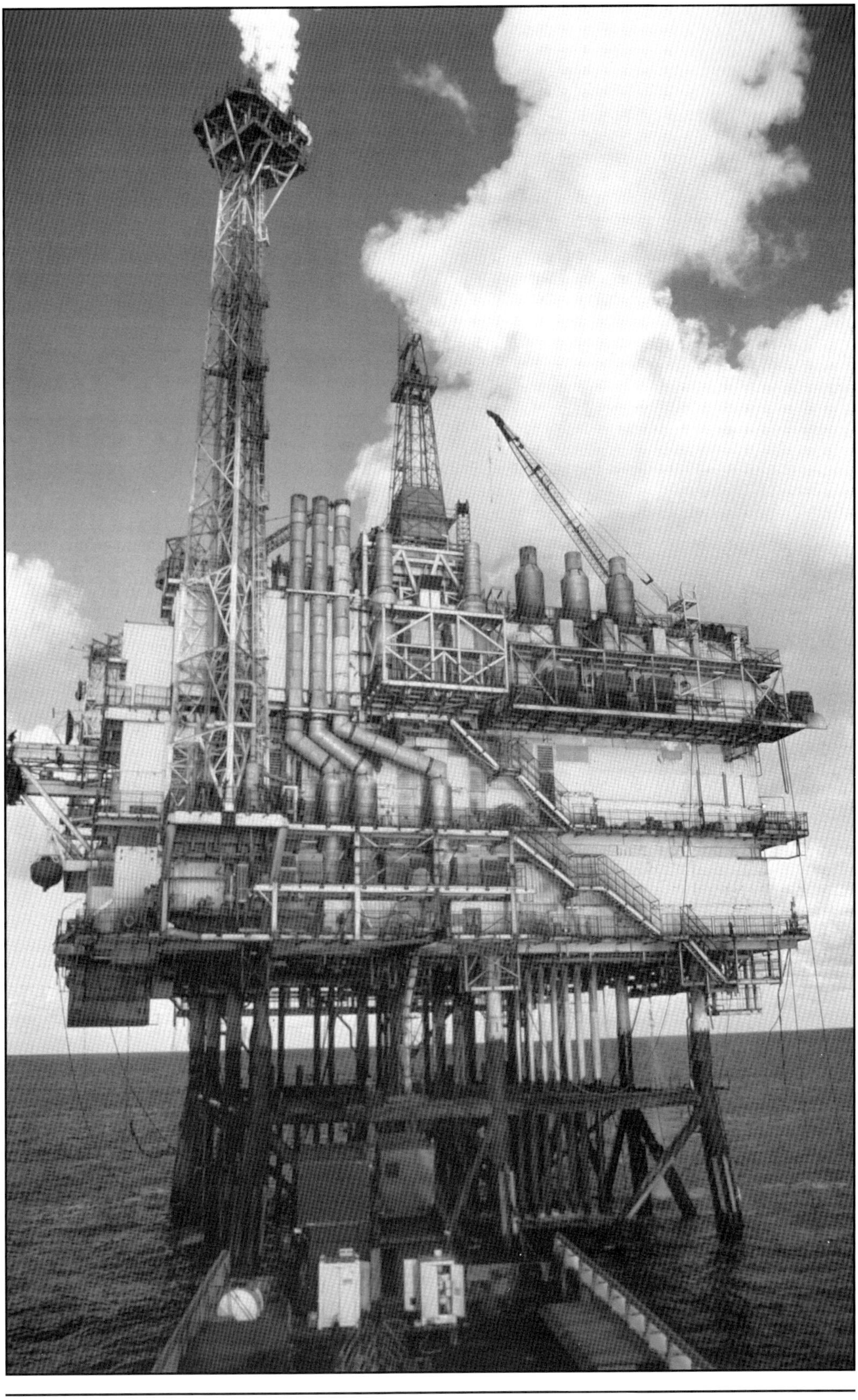

© Bev Morgan. All rights reserved.

Chapter 2
Training to Be a Commercial Diver

The more you know, the longer you live.

It takes many different skills to be a successful commercial diver, and generally speaking, the more skills you have, the more frequently you will probably work. Ideally, you want a good combination of both mechanical and technical skills.

One thing that you should understand up front is that any background you might have in recreational diving, such as being a scuba instructor or divemaster is not of great value in commercial diving. The only real advantage to having an extensive scuba background is that you will have a certain comfort level in the water, which is always important. Scuba gear is rarely if ever used in commercial diving, and being proficient as a scuba diver gives you no special advantage over a diver without this background.

Desirable Mechanical Skills

Some of the more desirable mechanical skills that a diver can have include rigging, welding (and cutting), pipefitting, and engine mechanics. You might wonder why we include engine mechanics in this group, but the reason is quite simple. Most of the machinery on any job is powered by diesel engines, and a person who can help keep a job going by coaxing a reluctant engine to work is a valuable addition to a commercial diving job.

Likewise, electrical skills are also considered quite valuable. A background in industrial electricity or electronics will serve you well in the diving industry. The talents you bring to the job and your willingness and ability to help keep the job running smoothly are what will help to advance your diving career.

Welding is just one of many skills you will need to be a successful commercial diver.

It's important to realize that even after you have completed your apprenticeship and become a diver, in most cases you will not dive every day, all day long. You will be needed to help set up the equipment whenever you go out on a new job, assist on deck and run dives for other divers. If all you can do is dive, you have limited value on a diving crew.

You can learn the basics of some of the skills we list here, like rigging or welding, by attending a good commercial diving school. Other skills, such as diesel mechanics, take much longer to master. If you don't possess a trade skill before you start diving school, it's unlikely you will be able to become proficient in these specialties during the short duration of most commercial diving courses.

Rigging

Every diver must be a good rigger, capable of working with wire and fiber rope, chain and chain binders, come-alongs, shackles, and other fittings. This is a fundamental set of skills that is essential.

Training to Be a Commercial Diver

Every diver must be familiar with rigging including the use of fiber and wire rope, slings, shackles, hooks, and other tools of the trade.

You must know how to tie knots and hitches, whip the end of a rope, and splice rope. You need to know when to use a fiber rope, such as manila, and which synthetic lines are best for particular applications.

You must be able to rig gear for lifting, direct crane movements, and be able to secure equipment aboard trucks and vessels for transport. You must have the ability to tie a knot without looking at it so that if you are working in black water, with zero visibility, you can do so with confidence.

Wire rope is used in many situations in industrial environments, particularly to lift heavy loads. It's also used for running anchor lines on large vessels and barges. As a diver you need to have the ability to perform basic wire rope splices and to properly attach wire rope clips.

We'll explore some of the fundamentals of rigging in a separate chapter later in this book.

Welding and Cutting

It would be unusual to go on a large commercial diving job where there was not welding and cutting equipment available for topside use. On an underwater construction or salvage job, welding and cutting will normally take up a significant part of the work.

Welding is used on most offshore commercial diving jobs to weld gear down to the deck of the ship and to fabricate special tools and fittings needed to complete the project. In most cases, the welding will be done with an electric arc machine.

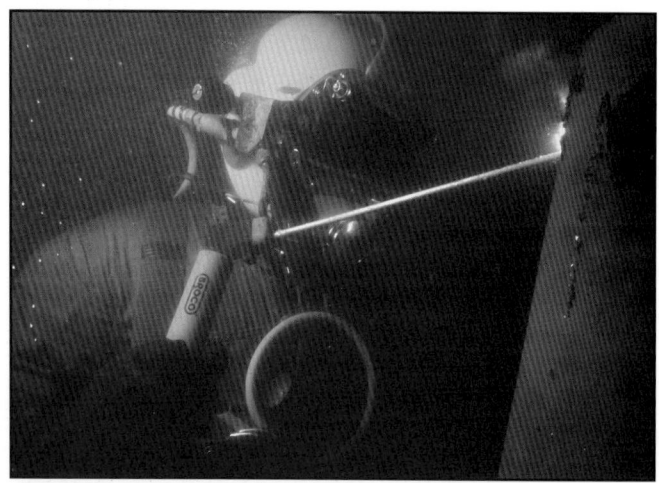

Welding underwater is a highly specialized skill that takes time to develop.

Cutting is also used in the fabrication of special items needed for the job as well as to "burn" or "scarf" off the welds that were used to attach equipment to the deck when the job ends. Most cutting done topside is performed using an oxy-acetylene torch.

Underwater, divers generally do more cutting or "burning" than they do welding. Welding underwater is difficult due to the "quenching" effect of the water, which causes a weld to cool rapidly. Welding underwater also will reduce visibility. In cases where high quality welds are needed underwater, divers install special welding "habitats" which can be pumped dry to provide a more favorable environment for serious repairs to platforms and pipelines.

Most commercial diving schools don't have the time to teach you to be a top-notch welder, so it's recommended that you take additional courses in this area to become as proficient as possible in your welding skills.

The use of underwater cutting torches will be covered in greater detail in the chapter on using tools underwater, later in the book.

Pipefitting/Plumbing

Divers use air-powered pneumatic tools, hydraulic tools, and breathing systems that all make use of pipe fittings and tubing to transport these liquids and gases properly. In many cases, there may not be an "off-the-shelf" system to meet the needs of the job, and divers frequently must build or plumb their own equipment.

Commercial diving companies frequently purchase "bare" decompression chambers, with no fittings installed, so they can plumb them to their exact specifications. This is a job that may be relegated to tenders.

Divers need to have talent in the basics of cutting, bending, and flaring copper and stainless steel tubing in order to assemble diving systems and make repairs. This equipment is found throughout the diving industry.

Engine Mechanics

Inevitably there is at least one, if not several, diesel and/or gasoline engines on every commercial diving job. Almost all air compressors in the diving industry are diesel powered and there will be at least one on each job. If the compressor stops, the job stops, so keeping it running smoothly is vital.

Other diesel-powered equipment that may be present on a typical diving job includes hydraulic pumps, generators, winches, and hot water systems. The diver who can fix these pieces of equipment is worth his weight in gold.

Even if you are not a diesel mechanic, you should understand the basics of how to start and stop the unit, engine maintenance including how to check the oil, change out

You must become familiar with the variety of fittings that are used in diving systems.

Training to Be a Commercial Diver

The ability to shoot photos, both topside and underwater, is a valuable asset.

filters, and other basic tasks to help keep the equipment on a job running smoothly.

Photography and Videography

The world of photography and video has changed rapidly during the past few years and for the commercial diver, this has made underwater photography much easier. Digital photography makes underwater inspection work more efficient and cost effective.

Despite the fact that digital photography has made it possible for almost anyone to produce a properly exposed photograph underwater, you still need to know how to set up the camera and housing, properly compose images, crop and manipulate the images using a computer, and print the images or transmit them electronically.

On a dive where underwater photographs or video are the end product of the dive, the client doesn't really care how skillful you are as a diver if the images don't contain the information that the customer needs. Although you may be able to digitally correct many problems in a photograph, if the basic information isn't there, you can't fake it, and this will be apparent to the client. You must photograph or video the subject the client has requested to see in a way that clearly illustrates its condition.

If you have no photographic or video background, take a basic digital photo or video course and follow it up with an underwater photography or video course. Learn how to retouch photographs on a computer and how to get the best possible prints from a digital image. If you have the time, learn how to perform basic video editing and grab still frames from video.

The more training and ability you have in each different skill used on the job, whether it is photography or basic tool wielding, the greater your value as a diver.

Technical Report Writing

On almost any diving job the customer will expect some type of written report at the end of the project. A well-written report, illustrated with photographs and drawings, will always convey a favorable impression to the client.

Most people find writing reports to be a tedious job, and if you have no writing experience, it can be an intimidating task. However, with today's computers and software, writing has become much easier. Most word processing software has built-in spelling and grammar checkers that will help you to produce a better report.

You can take classes in technical report writing at most community colleges and they will be well worth your time. What you will discover once you are working in the field, is that when you have the ability or willingness to do jobs that no one else on the project wants, like report writing, you can use these skills to negotiate for better pay or to go on the jobs on which you want to participate. The few hours you spend report writing, for which you will be paid, are well worth the time in helping to position yourself to go on the more desirable contracts.

On an inspection job, the report is what the client is paying for, so the report must be as polished and professional as possible. In addition to clear, concise writing, the report must contain elements such as a table of contents and an index, and be nicely bound so it makes a good presentation. Most clients won't pay the final bill until they receive the report they requested as the end product of the job.

Electronics and Computers

Electronics and computers have come to play an increasingly important role in our world and especially so in the diving industry. People who can diagnose and fix electronic equipment are always in demand, and especially offshore, where it may take days to get parts or a replacement unit.

Computer knowledge is also a valuable commodity in the diving industry. Aside from writing reports and editing photographs, today's computers can also be used to edit video inspections and produce polished presentations, prepare expense reports and time sheets, and keep job and diving logs. To truly be successful in today's workplace, you must be computer savvy.

Training in the use of computers and electronics is available through most adult education programs and community colleges.

Diving Skills

To be a good diver, you must be a good "waterman." We would define a waterman as someone who is completely comfortable and at home in the water, no matter whether they are on a calm tropical reef with 100 feet of underwater visibility, or in a rough stretch of the Pacific Ocean with heavy surge and three

As a tender you will be expected to have many practical skills, such as driving a forklift. If you aren't familiar with this type of machinery, you must take every opportunity at diving school to become comfortable handling this equipment.

Tenders are expected to load out the equipment for each job, so you must know how to run an electric hoist. Here, commercial diving students practice loading a decompression chamber aboard a flat bed truck.

Training to Be a Commercial Diver

To be a successful commercial diver you must learn to overcome your fears and have confidence in your abilities.

foot underwater visibility. Some people come by this naturally, and some people can learn to be comfortable in the water, but you must possess this level of comfort in the water to be a good diver.

You can't be thinking about whether your gear is working properly and still perform at your best underwater. You must learn to use the water to get your work done, and not try to fight the elements.

Most of the skills that you learned as a sport diver will not be applicable to commercial diving. However, in all probability, the more time you have spent underwater as a sport diver, the higher your comfort level will be as a beginning commercial diver. Your knowledge of the "science" of diving and your diving skills will help you to be a better commercial diver, but spearing fish or grabbing lobsters is not the same as bolting together a pipeline.

Don't expect anyone in the diving industry to be impressed with your sport diving accomplishments. These achievements are best kept to yourself unless you know that a fellow diver has an interest in this sort of activity, too. Most commercial divers don't have much interest in the recreational diving world and refer to scuba divers as "sporties."

Other Skills

Some of the other skills which are desirable include the following:

• Non-destructive testing (NDT):

Non-destructive testing is frequently used in the inspection of marine structures. This is an especially valuable skill for someone who works as a welder. It generally involves special equipment and techniques for inspecting the condition of underwater structures.

• Small boat handling experience:

It's not uncommon on a commercial diving job for divers to need to be able to handle an inflatable boat.

• Knowledge of oceanography:

A good understanding of the marine environment will help you in planning and conducting underwater work

• Machine shop experience:

The ability to fabricate simple tools and parts in a shipboard machine shop is highly valued on any commercial diving job.

• Organizational ability:

Although some diving jobs are simple, others have many elements and require good organization. Planning skills are key to conducting a smoothly running and productive job.

Confidence

To be a successful commercial diver you must be able to overcome your fears and develop the attitude that you can do anything that you make up your mind to do. This doesn't mean that you should take chances and perform dangerous dives. What it does mean is that you must learn to be confident in your talents and abilities, without being "cocky."

Everyone Has Different Talents

One of the things that you must understand about commercial diving is that there is a place for almost everyone in the industry, provided you have the proper work ethic. No matter what type of skills you have, if you are willing to work hard, you can be successful. The diver who is a good underwater photographer and technical report writer can be as much a success as the diver who is a top welder or construction hand.

The important thing to keep in mind is that you must capitalize on those areas where you are strong and improve the areas where you are weak. You should be at least familiar with each different specialty area within the diving business so that you can support any job that is going on even if you aren't the lead diver on the project.

Commercial Diving Schools

There are a number of commercial diving schools scattered around the world. While it may not be possible for you to visit all of the schools available, you should make the effort to visit at least the one that seems most appealing to you before you enroll.

There are two main categories of commercial diving schools, i.e., public colleges and private trade schools. Public college programs are usually longer, but more comprehensive. Private trade school programs may be completed in less time. If you already have a broad background in trade skills, this type of school may be the right choice for you.

Take the time to visit as many commercial diving schools as possible before you make a decision regarding which school you will attend.

Check out the equipment and facilities at each school you visit before you pick your school. Talk to the faculty as well as any students who are currently enrolled in the program.

Training to Be a Commercial Diver

If you don't have a strong mechanical background, you'll need to develop abilities in this area if you hope to be able to perform useful work underwater.

The first step in selecting a commercial diving school is to step back and make a critical appraisal of your own strengths and abilities. Of all the skills that we have previously listed in this chapter, which ones do you already possess talent in? What things do you need to learn?

If you come from a strong mechanical and technical background, then your focus should be solely upon gaining the knowledge of commercial diving equipment and techniques. However, if you have little or no mechanical ability, then you may want to attend a school that has courses to train you in some of the support skills you'll need to get ahead. As an alternative, you may want to take some courses at a trade school or community college before you enroll in commercial diving school. In any case, you'll want to compare the curriculum of the school to your own background and see how it supplements the areas where your knowledge is lacking.

Find out how long it takes to complete the school. Again, if you have a strong mechanical background and have lots of recreational diving experience, a short program may be entirely adequate. Conversely, if you have only a meager background in trade skills, attending a longer program with more emphasis on broadening your abilities will enhance your success. The shortest or least expensive school may not provide the comprehensive training you need to be a safe and effective diver.

Check to see where the training for the school is conducted. Find out how much of the training is conducted in a diving "tank" or swimming pool, compared to how much training is conducted in the open ocean or harbor environment. Training in an artificial environment is not as realistic as training in a harbor or other openwater situation.

Don't enroll in any commercial diving school without paying a visit to the school first. Look at the classrooms, the condition of the equipment, and where the in-water training takes place. Ask what their accreditation is and how long the school has been in operation.

Ask if you can sit in on a class or two during your visit (be sure to set this up in advance). Talk to the students who are currently enrolled in the program, and ask them how they feel about the training they are receiving.

See if you can obtain contact information for any past graduates of the school and talk to these people about how well the school prepared them for work in the industry. Ask them how effective the training was compared to what they have experienced in the real world.

You may also want to call several commercial diving companies to ask them how they feel about the graduates they have hired from the school. Ask to speak to the operations manager, as this is the person who will normally be responsible for hiring new tenders. Be sure to be polite and ask them if they have a minute or two to talk before launching into a string of questions. This may be the person who you will be asking for a job in the future! You don't want to offend them or make a nuisance of yourself.

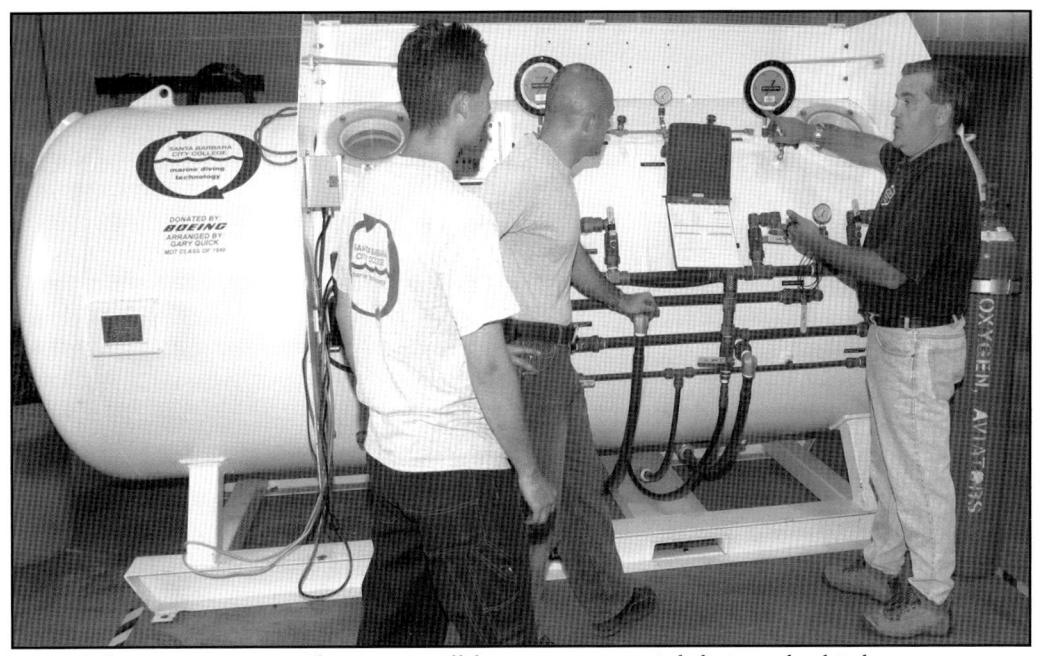

One of the most important things you will learn at commercial diving school is how to operate a decompression chamber.

Attending Commercial Diving School

Once you have selected a commercial diving school and start the program, you need to give the course your full attention. It's best if you can concentrate on the course without the distractions of a job or your social life, if you want to get the most out of the course.

First and foremost, your full attention should be given to the course because your life may literally depend on it. The things that you learn in commercial diving school may one day save your life, as well as the lives of those around you.

In addition, you want to be as knowledgeable as possible about your profession to make yourself as valuable an employee as possible. Another important reason to give yourself fully to your education is that the best students get the best recommendations for jobs when the commercial diving companies call the schools looking for employees.

Your personal pride in your own performance should also be an important factor in your motivation, because this is the type of attitude you must have to be a successful commercial diver. Although you will be compet-

When you graduate from commercial diving school you will be hired as a tender.

Training to Be a Commercial Diver

ing with other divers for work, at the end of the day you are also competing with yourself. You will know whether you have given the job your all every time you look in the mirror.

If you don't understand something while you are attending commercial diving school, don't be embarrassed to ask for the subject to be explained again. Chances are, if you didn't understand it, other people didn't understand it either.

Keep in mind that when you graduate from commercial diving school, in most cases, you will be hired as a "tender." This will generally be true unless you are exceptionally talented, or unless there is a shortage of divers when you graduate. Although this might seem to be unfair, the reality is that each commercial diving company has its own procedures and diving systems. Until you learn their way of doing things and gain experience under actual field conditions, you will not be ready to be a diver. This is the way it should be, so that you can learn in situations that are not as demanding as the deeper, more complex dives.

Bob Christensen prepares to dive with scuba on a commercial diving job in Alaska in 1965. Scuba is rarely used in the commercial diving industry today.

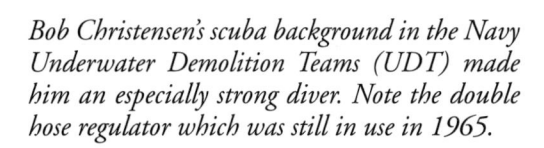

Bob Christensen's scuba background in the Navy Underwater Demolition Teams (UDT) made him an especially strong diver. Note the double hose regulator which was still in use in 1965.

True Tales of Commercial Diving from the Santa Barbara Channel

Although almost all commercial diving today is done with surface-supplied diving equipment, I got my start in the industry based on my scuba background in the Navy's Underwater Demolition Teams (UDT), the forerunners to the Navy Seal Teams.

The dive I discuss here is one of several foolish things that I have done using scuba gear. This is definitely not recommended…

A good many years ago, I got a call late at night from a diving contractor that I worked with. It seems that a floating drill ship drilling an exploratory well in the Santa Barbara Channel had lost 3 of the 4 guide wires that connected the ship to the blowout preventer stack (BOP) and the guideposts on the base plate. (The blowout preventer stack is a device that is used to control the pressures in a well while it is being drilled.) The drill ship had no diving gear on board.

The diving contractor, who was also a good friend, called myself and another diver who had very strong scuba backgrounds. He pleaded with us to go out to the rig with scuba gear and see if we could solve their problems. The drill ship was only in 130' of water and it would be a great selling point to get a rental diving spread on board if we could pull it off. The second diver, also a good friend and scuba diving buddy, agreed and off we went. We loaded our scuba gear on the crew boat and rode out to meet our fate on the drill ship.

My friend lost the toss so he made the first dive. He descended down the one good guide wire carrying a small messenger line for signaling. At the base plate he found the 3 broken guide wires piled all over the BOP stack and base plate. These he managed to clear away in his allowed bottom time and after the required decompression he surfaced to fill us all in on the situation on the bottom.

I was next and my job was to remove an old guide wire plug end from the socket on the guidepost. This was to be done by putting a chain stopper around the part to be removed and pulling it out with a winch on the ship. Here I am in the middle of the night sitting on top of the BOP stack in 130 FSW of cold black water while the surface crew jerked on the guidepost. The whole stack shook and I was having some serious thoughts, but the broken end eventually came out and I was able to attach 1 new guide wire.

With 2 wires now in place, the drilling rig could guide their tools down and complete repairs without further help.

At the time this was no big deal; I was happy, the drilling superintendent was happy and my employer was happy. In hindsight, however, this was not a smart thing to have done. By itself, diving at night on scuba to 130 FSW is not the brightest idea. If the chain snapped or anything else went wrong I could have been seriously injured.

Bob Christensen

© Bev Morgan. All rights reserved.

Chapter 3
The Physiology of Commercial Diving

You can always tell the divers by their Rolex watches and cowboy boots.

While all of the normal physiological issues that apply to recreational diving also apply to commercial diving, there are some unique issues that commercial divers must deal with that are quite different. In most instances, the physiological differences in commercial diving occur because the dives are either of extended duration or because the depths are much greater.

You should already be familiar with the basic physiology of diving from your recreational diver training. In this chapter we'll only address the physiological concerns that are unique to commercial diving.

Fitness to Dive

To be a successful commercial diver, you must be reasonably fit and in healthy physical condition. You don't need to have unusual strength, although certainly the more fit you are, the easier it will be for you to get the job done on your dives.

All reputable commercial diving companies require their divers to undergo a pre-employment physical exam as well as annual follow-up examinations to ensure that they are fit to dive. These exams are much more stringent than what you might submit to in order to participate in a recreational diving program and may include hearing tests, x-rays, and other specialized tests. Certain types of physical problems may exclude you from diving, such as back problems, heart defects, and breathing disorders, like asthma.

Diving tends to be as much a mental challenge as a physical one. We have found that it isn't always the most muscular diver who can get the job done, but the person who knows how to use their brain and figure out the best way to accomplish a particular task.

Part of the physical exam will also be a drug screen that you must pass. Commercial diving companies, and the firms for whom they work, are very serious about maintaining drug-free work places. If you have a drug or alcohol problem you won't be able to hide it for too long in this environment. Even some commercial diving schools now require drug screens prior to admission.

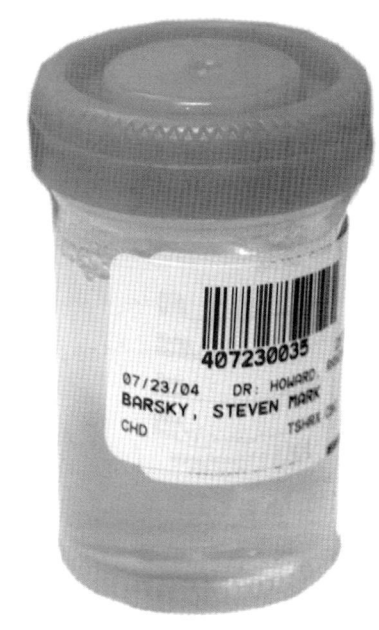

Pre-employment drug testing is common in the commercial diving industry. You may also be required to pass random drug screens while working for certain clients, particularly in the offshore environment.

The Physiology of Commercial Diving

Decompression Dives are Common in Commercial Diving

While every dive involves a compression phase and a decompression phase, in commercial diving many of the dives require "staged" decompression, i.e., a series of progressively shallower decompression stops for progressively longer times. On most commercial diving jobs, any time the water is deeper than 30 feet, decompression diving is standard operating procedure.

One of the common procedures used in commercial diving is a technique known as "surface decompression using oxygen," which is commonly abbreviated as "sur-d-O_2." This practice is designed to minimize the amount of time the diver must spend in the water undergoing decompression. It's commonly used any time a diver's decompression exceeds more than a few minutes, when the water is unusually cold, or conditions are such that it is dangerous for the diver to remain in the water.

The philosophy behind this procedure is that any decompression that can be completed in a warm, dry, and controlled environment is going to be better, i.e., more accurate, and usually safer, than decompression completed in the water. While the use of oxygen speeds up decompression, the risk of convulsions while breathing pure oxygen under pressure is always present. Performing as much of the decompression in a chamber as possible is a much more prudent approach. In addition, getting the diver out of the water frees up the work site so that the next diver can get down to the job at hand. Decompression times for deep surface-supplied dives may easily exceed an hour.

Various commercial diving companies

Surface decompression using oxygen ("sur-d-O_2") is a common procedure in the commercial diving industry.

This saturation technician is running decompression for several chambers at the same time.

may follow different schedules for surface decompression on oxygen, but the basic procedure is as follows:

• The diver ascends to his first water stop (he may have one or more water stops). The diver will frequently breathe an oxygen enriched air mixture in the water (nitrox), that may contain as much as 50% oxygen. (The exact mixture may vary at different diving companies.)

• Upon the completion of the water stop(s) the diver is brought to the surface and must be recompressed in the chamber to a depth of 40 feet of sea water in less than five minutes from his last water stop. Due to the short time span given to get the diver back down to depth, the diver usually ends up wearing his suit into the chamber and removing it inside.

• The diver breathes pure oxygen in the chamber (with breaks breathing ordinary compressed air) until his decompression is complete. The mask in the chamber normally has a special regulator attached to it that exhausts the excess oxygen out of the chamber.

Commercial divers also use a technique known as "saturation diving," where divers live under pressure for extended periods of time in a "saturation system." The theory behind saturation diving is that after 24 hours at any given depth, a diver is completely saturated with the inert gas in the breathing mixture (usually helium). Once the diver is saturated, decompression time is the same, whether the diver has been under pressure for 3 days or 30 days (or even longer).

Decompression following a saturation dive also varies according to the tables used by the diving company. The rough rule of thumb is that it takes approximately one day for each 100 feet of depth. For example, it takes between five and six days to decompress from a saturation dive to 500 FSW, depending on which set of decompression tables is used.

In the past, the incidence of decompression sickness was very high among commercial divers, but the annual number of cases has declined to an extremely low level. This improved safety is a result of more conservative dive profiles and improved decompression procedures.

The Physiology of Commercial Diving

Due to the risk of decompression sickness in commercial diving, government regulations in most parts of the world require the presence of an operational decompression chamber on any commercial diving job where the requirement for in-water stage decompression is possible. Provided the diver promptly reports any symptoms of decompression sickness to the diving supervisor, treatment can begin swiftly and it's possible to get complete recovery.

Diver Heating is a Major Issue

Most commercial diving companies recognize the fact that for a diver to work efficiently, he must be as comfortable as possible while he is underwater. For this reason, diving companies usually provide some form of appropriate thermal protection for their divers if the divers are not required to provide their own suits.

While wetsuits are adequate for relatively shallow dives in warmer waters, when the water is colder than 60-65 degrees F, the dive is for a prolonged length of time, or the diver is breathing a gas mixture containing helium, some other type of thermal protection is essential. Dry suits and hot water suits are the two most commonly used types of thermal protection.

Dry suits are known as "passive thermal protection," i.e., they do not use any active or external heat source. Dry suits are dependent on the amount and type of insulation worn under the suit and the amount of heat your body generates while working underwater. They are considered an effective form of insulation for cold water dives under some conditions, provided mixed-gas containing helium is <u>not</u> being used. Because helium breathing gas conducts heat away from the body very rapidly each time the diver exhales, it cools the diver from the inside out, countering the insulation properties of the suit.

A serious consideration with dry suits is the possibility of a suit puncture at depth, especially if the diver has a lengthy decompression commitment. Although modern dry suits are much more reliable than older models, the risk of a puncture always exists.

Hot water suits are the preferred solution

Hot water suits are often the preferred method for keeping divers warm in cold water.

for diver heating whenever possible because the systems usually provide a more reliable method of keeping the diver warm. Even if the work is relatively sedentary, such as inspection work or underwater photography, the hot water system will still keep the diver warm. A non-moving diver in a dry suit may chill if he is not wearing heavy insulation under the suit.

The typical hot water system includes the following:

• A topside source of heat

This can be a diesel-fired burner, a steam unit (popular on barges), or a system that "piggybacks" off a compressor and captures heat generated by the engine. The heating unit raises the temperature of the water and a pump circulates it to the diver.

• A mixing manifold

Mixing manifolds work much like the faucets on a bathtub to regulate the temperature of the water sent to the diver.

• Alarms for high and low (out of range) temperatures

• Insulated hot water hose

- Hot water suit

Hot water suits are like baggy, loose fitting wetsuits. The suits have a connection at the waist where the hot water hose connects to a series of perforated tubes inside of the suit. The perforated tubes run down the back of the suit and down each arm and leg, distributing the hot water throughout the suit.

In cold environments, or on saturation dives where the deck chambers are filled with helium-oxygen mixtures, the climate in the chamber must be carefully controlled for the comfort of the divers. Most chamber heating is done by circulating hot water through copper tubing located beneath the deck plates of the chambers.

Saturation Diving Poses Its Own Set of Challenges

Saturation diving presents a unique set of issues that every diver who engages in this type of work must understand. These physiological challenges include the High Pressure Nervous Syndrome (also known as "HPNS" or helium tremors), asceptic bone necrosis, and serious fungal infections.

The High Pressure Nervous Syndrome (also referred to as the High Pressure Neurologic Syndrome) is a condition that usually occurs during the rapid compression phase of a deep saturation or bell dive. The symptoms of HPNS can include nausea, drowsiness, loss of appetite, and difficulty performing mechanical tasks. Although the symptoms usually disappear after a short time at depth, if they occur during an emergency this could cause a dangerous situation. The exact mechanism of what causes these symptoms is not completely understood.

Another problem that can occur over the long term is a condition known as "asceptic bone necrosis" or "dysbaric osteonecrosis." In this situation, the heads of the long bones (such as the upper arm or upper leg), or the area between the shaft of the bone and the head of the bone, dies. This medical condition does not occur all at once, but is a progressive situation that may take years before the diver becomes aware of its effects, after multiple exposures on deep dives. In serious cases, this produces symptoms similar to arthritis in the sufferer.

Fungal infections are not unique to saturation diving, but the chances of contracting a fungal infection are greater in the warm, humid environment found in most saturation systems. This is particularly true during long saturation dives, especially when the degree of cleanliness inside the system may not be maintained at a high level.

Divers typically use ear drops such as Otic Domeboro as a prophylactic to prevent ear infections, but even if the drops are scrupulously used, infections may still occur, particularly in situations where the humidity rises above acceptable levels. These infections can become so severe that divers have had white pus running out of their ears.

Fungal infections of the hands and feet are also not uncommon. These types of fungus may cause sloughing off of the skin in large chunks. In many cases, these infections will disappear once the diver exits the cham-

Saturation diving poses unique physiological challenges for the diver.

The Physiology of Commercial Diving

ber environment, but this is not always the case, and sometimes the infections will persist for extended periods.

Divers must take care to keep the saturation system, which they are living in, and their equipment, clean to avoid the possibility of transmission of diseases such as hepatitis. In the close quarters of a saturation system, it's all too easy for infections to be passed from one person to another. This has happened in at least one case on record.

> **True Tales of Commercial Diving from the North Sea**
>
> My first night working as a tender many miles offshore in the North Sea was a sobering experience for someone who had never before worked in an industrial environment. We were working about 150 miles offshore, in an area known as the "Forties Field," the first producing offshore oilfield in Great Britain. I was on the midnight to noon shift and had just come out on deck. Our crew was inspecting the submerged portions of several oil platforms, performing underwater photography, video, and other non-destructive testing (NDT).
>
> We were engaged in surface-supplied diving down to 150 FSW, with the divers wearing full-face masks and hot water suits, where their air, hot water for the suits, and communications were all supplied by an "umbilical." The tenders' job was to help the divers get dressed and assist them into and out of the water.
>
> Although I knew how to tend the diver's hose and coil it properly, the more experienced tenders on deck told me to stand back and see how things were done. It was a blustery night, with the seas running between six and ten feet, and the 250 foot long supply ship we were working from was bucking up and down at anchor.
>
> As I watched the first diver surface at the end of his dive, I could see that he was having difficulty holding onto the ladder and removing his fins. Although there should have been a "stage" (mechanized hoist) to lift the diver out of the water, there was none. In desperation, the diver grabbed onto the ladder as it plunged below the surface and held on when it shot out of the water. Unable to completely remove his fins, he kicked them off so that he could climb quickly, letting the fins disappear beneath the waves.
>
> This was very sobering to me. As I watched an expensive pair of fins discarded without regard to cost, I realized that this was a serious occupation and one where quick thinking and good judgment are essential. If the diver had not been able to climb the ladder swiftly, he could have been injured, and he made the right decision in abandoning the fins.
>
> *Steve Barsky*

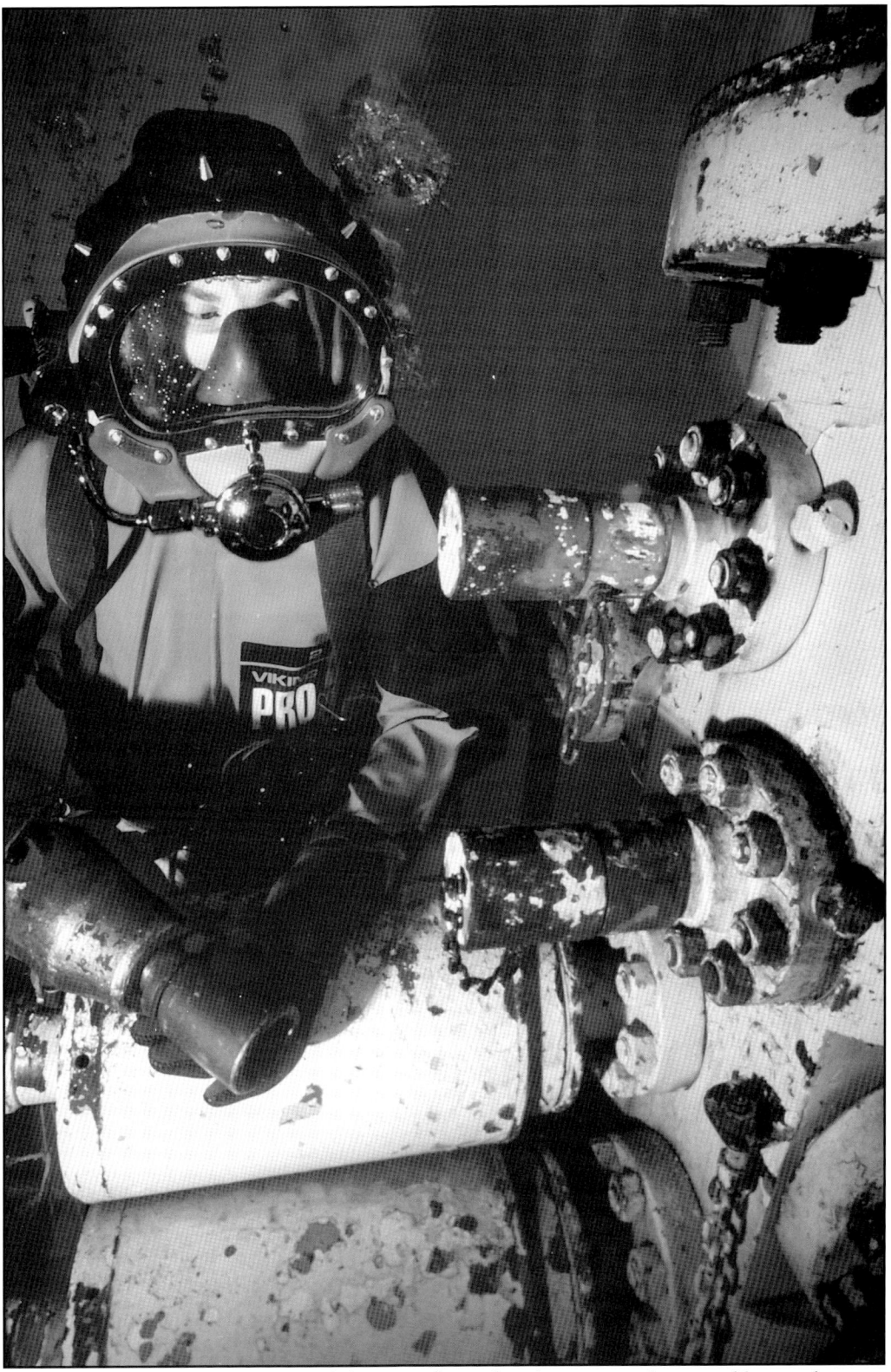

Commercial divers often put up with far more discomfort than a sport diver would ever tolerate.

© Bev Morgan. All rights reserved.

Chapter 4
Modes of Diving

A diver is only as good as his last dive.

For a commercial diver, diving equipment is the means of transportation that you use to go to work. Just as there are different types of automobiles to go different places, there are different types of diving gear to dive to different depths and perform various types of jobs. In some circumstances, you might want to use a 4X4 truck to get to a job site, while in other situations you might need a flat-bed truck.

In diving, we use many of the same components on different types of jobs, but they may be assembled in a variety of ways. In this chapter we'll look at the various types of equipment commonly used today.

Scuba Equipment

Scuba equipment is rarely used in commercial diving today, although there are a few situations where it is occasionally employed. Commercial divers tend to distrust scuba equipment for a variety of reasons including:

- Lack of communications
- Lack of a back-up air supply
- Lack of a safety line

As you will learn, there are many advantages to surface-supplied diving gear that make it much safer than using scuba gear.

Situations where scuba is sometimes utilized include inspection of the apparatus known as a "stinger" on a barge that is laying pipe. The stinger is the structure that supports the pipe as it goes over the side to the bottom. Scuba is also sometimes used for dives in the removal of line wrapped around the propeller

When pipe is laid in the water, scuba is sometimes used to inspect the "stinger" that feeds the pipe over the side of the barge.

of a work boat. However, even in these situations, most divers prefer to use surface-supplied gear if it is available.

The Association of Diving Contractors International (ADCI) which is the trade industry association for the commercial diving industry in the United States, has very strict guidelines regarding the use of scuba equipment for working dives. In Europe, the trade association is IMCA, the International Marine Contractors Association.

Government regulations also play a big

Modes of Diving

role in what type of diving gear may be used in certain situations. In the U.S., both the United States Coast Guard and the Occupational Safety and Health Administration oversee commercial diving operations and place limits on the use of scuba in the commercial industry. Generally speaking, OSHA tends to deal with jobs that take place inshore while the U.S. Coast Guard tends to deal with jobs that are offshore.

If you must use scuba gear for a commercial diving job, it is strongly recommended that you use a full-face mask, have some type of line so your surface support crew can pull you back to the vessel if there are strong currents, and use some type of communications system so you can talk with your support crew. Without these safety measures, you increase your risk substantially if you are using scuba in the commercial environment.

One of the biggest dangers in using scuba offshore is that you may be working out of sight of land. If you are swept away from the job, and sea conditions are rough, it may be difficult or impossible for your crew to find you on the surface. Scuba equipment should be avoided for most commercial diving tasks.

Surface-Supplied Air Diving Systems

Most commercial diving operations are conducted using surface-supplied diving equipment, although the breathing gas used may vary somewhat. A surface-supplied diving system is defined as a diving system where the diver's breathing gas is fed to the diver through a long hose, while the breathing gas supply remains on the surface. There are several ways systems like this can be configured.

The components of a surface-supplied diving system generally include the following items:

• Topside air supply

This may be either a low-pressure air compressor or high-pressure gas cylinders, or some combination of both. This will normally include some type of air filtration system.

• A back-up air supply

• Volume tank

Volume tanks are typically 30-gallon low-pressure gas cylinders that serve several purposes. First, they provide a small reserve of air in the event the low-pressure compressor fails. They also cool the compressed gas which causes moisture in the air to condense and in so doing, filters out some contaminants, so they are not pumped down to the diver.

• Breathing gas control manifold

The manifold is designed to selectively route air from a variety of sources to the diver.

• Pneumofathometer system

This is a simple system used to measure the diver's depth. It works by flowing air through a needle valve to a depth gauge located on the surface, and down an open ended hose that is part of the diver's umbilical. Once air flows out of the end of the hose, the diver notifies topside that air is flowing out of the end of the hose or that he has "bubbles." The person running the dive closes the needle valve and the air pressure trapped in the hose measures the diver's depth.

• Umbilical or hose

The umbilical usually consists of a minimum of three components: a breathing gas hose, a communications wire, and a depth sensing hose (also referred to as a pneumofathometer or "pneumo").

• Bail-out bottle and harness

Smart divers always wear an emergency breathing gas supply on a harness connected to their torso. This is an industry standard and government requirement in most parts of the world.

• Full-face mask or helmet

Unlike scuba masks, full-face masks cover the eyes, nose, and mouth, while diving helmets cover the entire head and keep it completely dry.

• Ladder or stage

The ladder or stage is used to assist the diver in getting into and out of the water.

Surface-supplied air diving systems may be used to support diving down to depths of up to 220 FSW, depending on company policy, industry standards, and government regulations in different parts of the world.

The Simple Guide to Commercial Diving

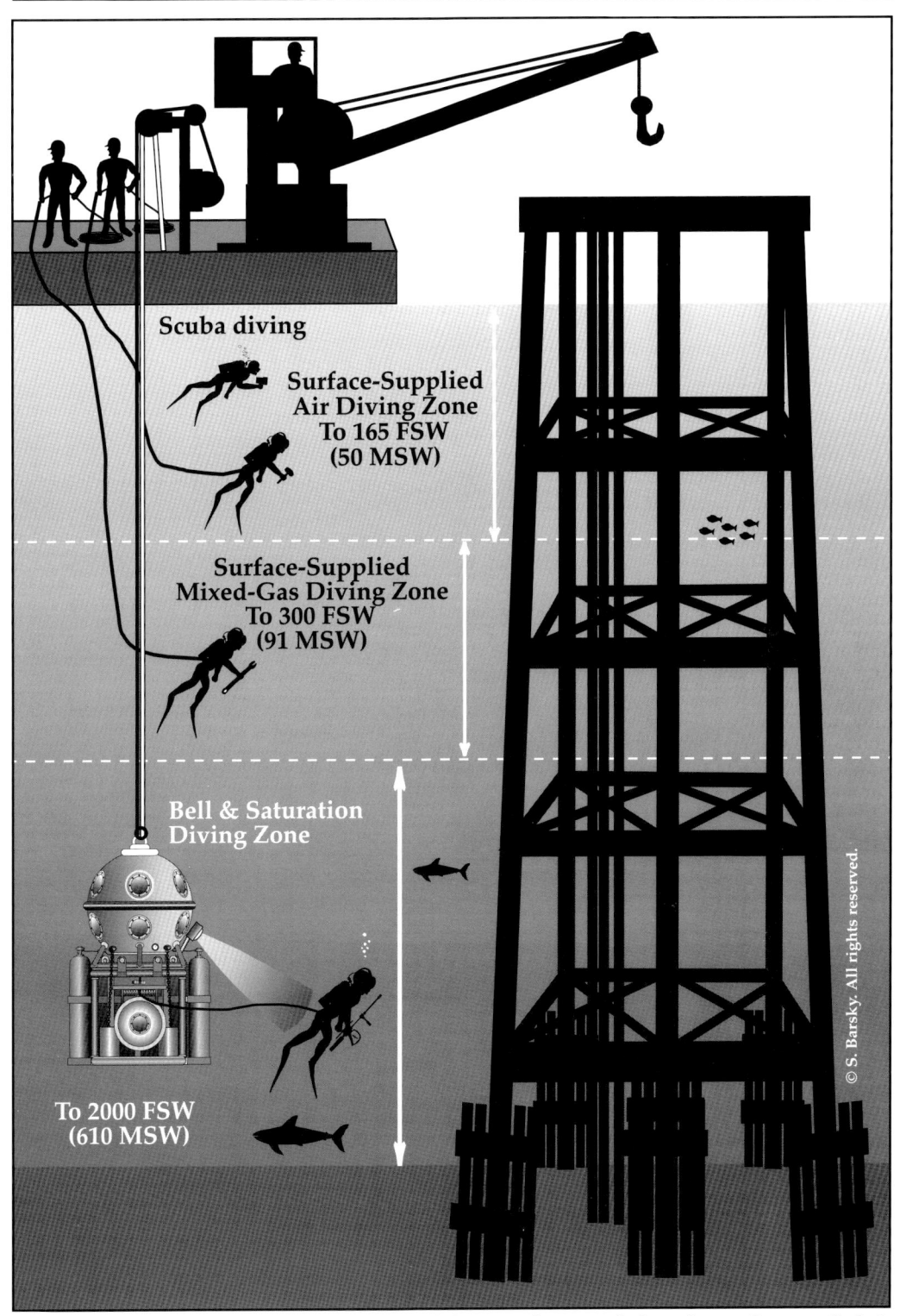

The normal modes of diving in the commercial diving industry include scuba, surface-supplied air diving, surface-supplied mixed-gas diving, and saturation diving. The mode of diving will generally be determined by both the depth of the water and the amount of work that must be done at that depth.

Modes of Diving

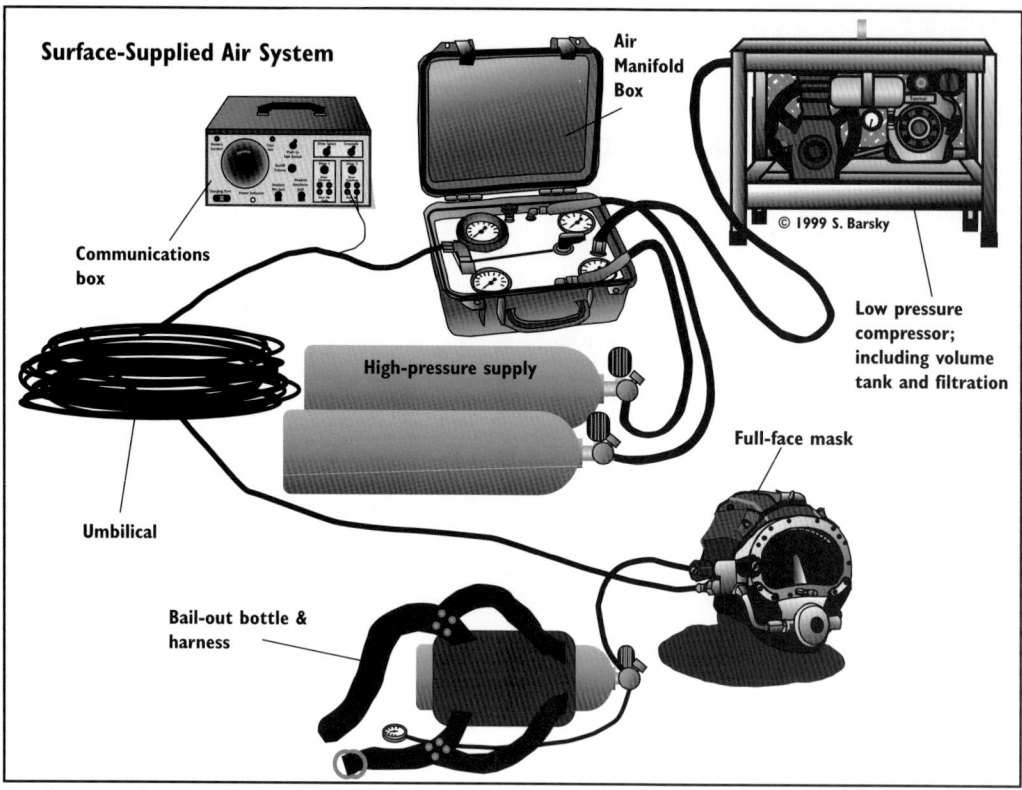

Surface-supplied air diving systems are relatively simple to set up and operate, once you understand how all the components go together.

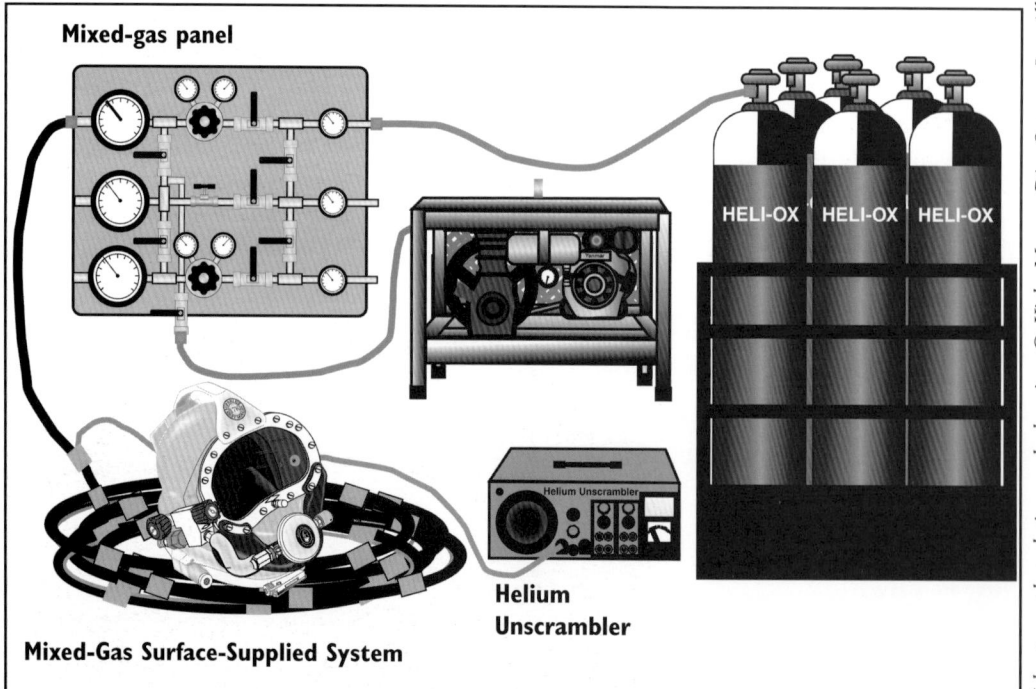

The surface-supplied mixed-gas system substitutes a mixed-gas panel for the air manifold and a helium unscrambler for the communications box.

Typically, the maximum depth for surface-supplied air diving doesn't exceed 165 FSW.

Surface-Supplied Mixed-gas

A surface-supplied mixed-gas diving system is very similar to a surface-supplied air diving system and has many of the same components with a few important exceptions. The mixed-gas system substitutes a mixed-gas manifold for the standard air manifold and includes multiple gas cylinders of pre-mixed helium and oxygen.

Instead of an open stage, mixed-gas diving systems normally include a covered stage or what may be referred to as an "open bottom bell." The strategy behind the use of this piece of equipment is that the diver has someplace to retreat to in the event of the loss of his breathing gas supply, rather than heading for the surface. It also provides a way to transport the diver to depth and better control of decompression.

The umbilicals used for mixed-gas diving are usually longer than those used for surface-supplied air diving, and may be as long as 600 feet, due to the deeper depths of these dives. Umbilicals for mixed-gas diving are also more likely to include a hose to supply the diver with hot water for use with a hot water suit.

Bell/Saturation Diving

Bell systems are normally used for dives that involve extended bottom times at depths beyond 200 FSW. In these situations, the decompression times are so long that it is safer and more comfortable for a diver to complete his decompression in a dry environment.

Saturation diving systems normally include all of the gear used for surface-supplied mixed-gas diving plus the following items:
• A "closed" diving bell, i.e., a bell with two hatches that is capable of withstanding exterior pressure and interior pressure
• A deck decompression chamber (or multiple chambers) with the capability to "mate" up to the bell to transfer the divers while they are still under pressure. The chamber will also usually be equipped with a medical lock for passing food and other items into the system and a pressure operated toilet.
• A mixed-gas panel capable of supplying a higher volume (flow) of gas to the diving bell. This panel is usually enclosed in a portable van. It will also usually support surface supplied diving.
• An environmental control system for maintaining a constant temperature and humidity in the deck decompression chamber

When you work as a diver in a saturation system you will be living in close physical proximity with the other divers in the team.

Annual Testing

All components of the diving system must be kept up-to-date with annual (or more frequent) maintenance as well as pressure and load tests, gauge calibration, air samples, and other measures. Before you start working on any new job, be sure to confirm that all of the equipment is up-to-date and operating within the proper parameters.

Author Steve Barsky stands in front of a saturation system in the North Sea, 200 miles south of the Arctic Circle.

Modes of Diving

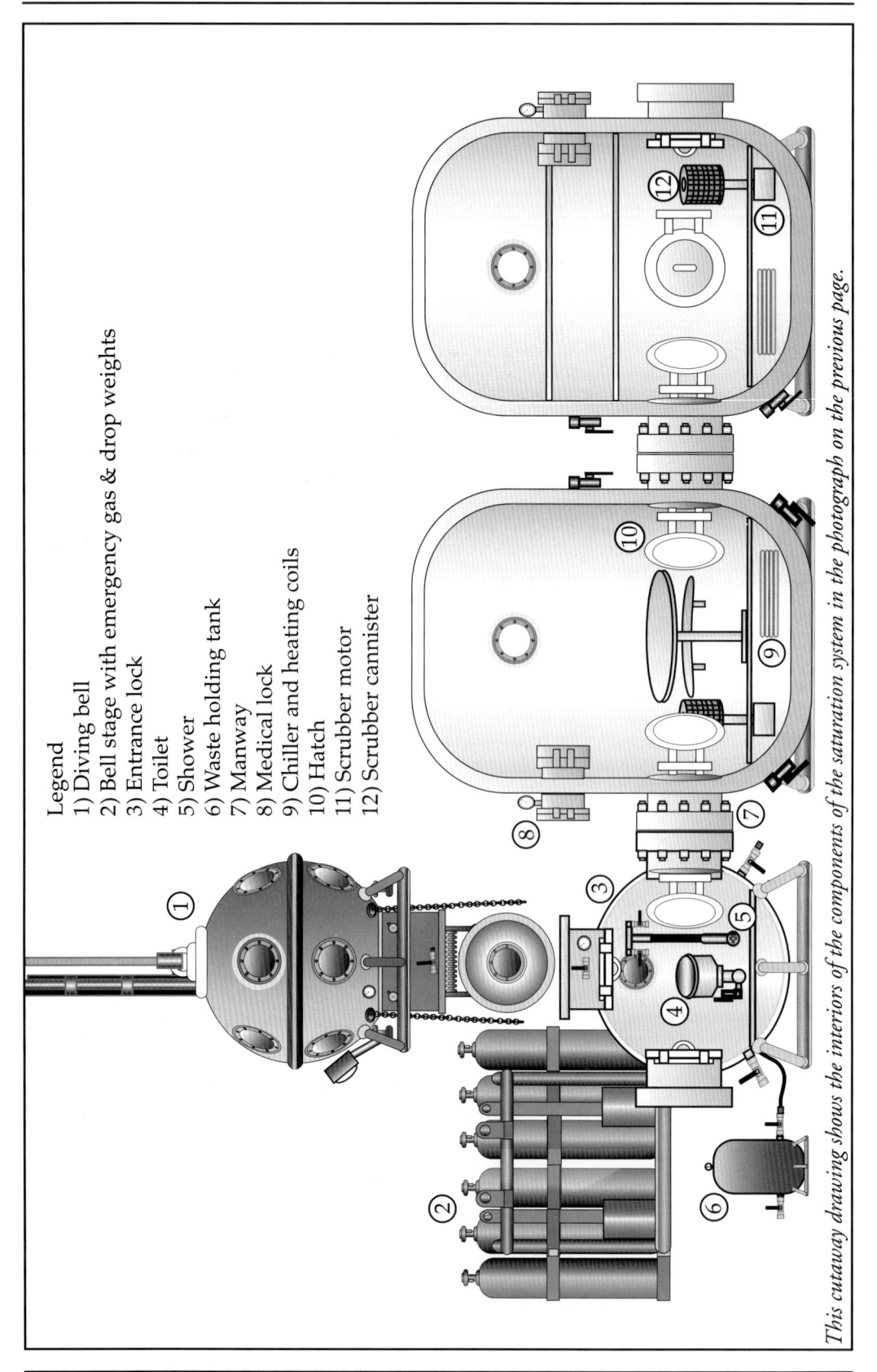

Legend
1) Diving bell
2) Bell stage with emergency gas & drop weights
3) Entrance lock
4) Toilet
5) Shower
6) Waste holding tank
7) Manway
8) Medical lock
9) Chiller and heating coils
10) Hatch
11) Scrubber motor
12) Scrubber cannister

This cutaway drawing shows the interiors of the components of the saturation system in the photograph on the previous page.

© Steve Barsky. All rights reserved.

34

True Tales of Commercial Diving from the Gulf of Mexico

As we closed the top hatch at the completion of a dive below 500 FSW in the Gulf of Mexico, I looked at my bell "mate" and smiled. We had just made a dive that would earn us several thousand dollars and everything had gone without a hitch.

We got a seal on the inner hatch and watched as the external depth gauge indicated our return to the surface. Looking up through the ports of the bell, we watched as the light changed from the jet black of the depths to aqua blue above 200 feet. A school of sharks swirled above us.

As we neared the surface, we braced ourselves for a bumpy ride as the bell crossed the air/water interface. On deck, the topside crew quickly disconnected the bell from the stage and mated the bell to the entrance lock. Once the trunk between the bell and entrance lock was pressurized, we climbed down into the entrance lock, removed our suits, and showered. The bell was lifted off the diving system so the topside team could clean it up and ready it for the next dive, whenever that might be.

It was mid-morning when we returned to the drill ship we were diving from and by the time I woke from my afternoon nap, I could see through the ports of the sat system that the seas were building quickly. By dinner, waves were breaking over the sat system, 15 feet above the sea surface, and the ship was heaving up and down. Although conditions were rough, I wasn't too concerned at that point.

I spent the evening reading and retired to my bunk at 10:00 P.M. In the middle of the night I was awakened by a sharp jolt to the chambers and a loud thump. I realized instantly that what was happening was that the surface crew was putting the bell back on the sat system. That was a bad sign, because I knew we weren't getting ready to dive in these conditions. The seas were still building and every third or fourth wave broke over the top of the saturation chamber where we were still decompressing.

Under the circumstances, reconnecting the bell to the system could only mean one thing, i.e., that the crew was preparing for the possibility we might have to be evacuated from the ship, because the vessel was in danger of sinking. If that happened, it would be an extremely hazardous situation.

The only way to evacuate divers from a sat system then was to put the divers back in the bell, and either put the bell on the deck of another ship (if there was time) or set it adrift in the water, if the ship sank quickly. When I asked the supervisor what was happening via the communications system, he gave an evasive reply.

If the bell was cast adrift with us inside, it would be a dangerous, rough ride. The bell would have been tossed about on the surface and we would have had to manage our own gas supply. We would be physically injured as the bell heaved about. If the bell was not quickly located, we would run out of electrical power and be forced to use the lung powered scrubbers. There would be no environmental control or light, no food or water, and no way to pass our own bodily wastes out of the bell. We could easily die.

If the crew could put the bell on the deck of another ship, which wouldn't have been easy under the sea conditions, we still would have had a difficult time, unless they could have gotten us to another sat system to which the bell could mate. During the ride to shore inside the bell, there would be no environmental control, although we might have power and communications. Whatever happened, we would face serious risks.

Fortunately, the weather subsided during the night and by morning the seas had decreased to less than ten feet. What could have been a dangerous situation passed without incident. We were lucky.

Steve Barsky

© Bev Morgan. All rights reserved.

Chapter 5
Risks in Commercial Diving

How can you tell if a diver is lying? Watch to see if his lips are moving.

Commercial diving is a profession that presents many potential hazards to divers and it is important to understand the risks involved. The pay that divers receive is partly due to the risk exposure they must face.

It's difficult to put an exact figure on the risks in diving because we don't have precise figures on the number of commercial divers, how many dives they make each year, and how many accidents occur. However, we know that divers work in industrial environments with heavy equipment aboard moving boats and in conditions where the underwater visibility may be zero. Frequently this work takes place at night, when the diver is tired, and in poor weather. Under these conditions, the risks of an accident may be quite high at times.

In the past ten years, the safety record of most of the responsible diving companies has improved tremendously and the number of accidents has decreased. Companies with poor safety records cannot profitably stay in business for too long.

As a diver, you are responsible for your own safety, more than anyone else. If the conditions are beyond those in which you feel comfortable, if you think the supervisor has

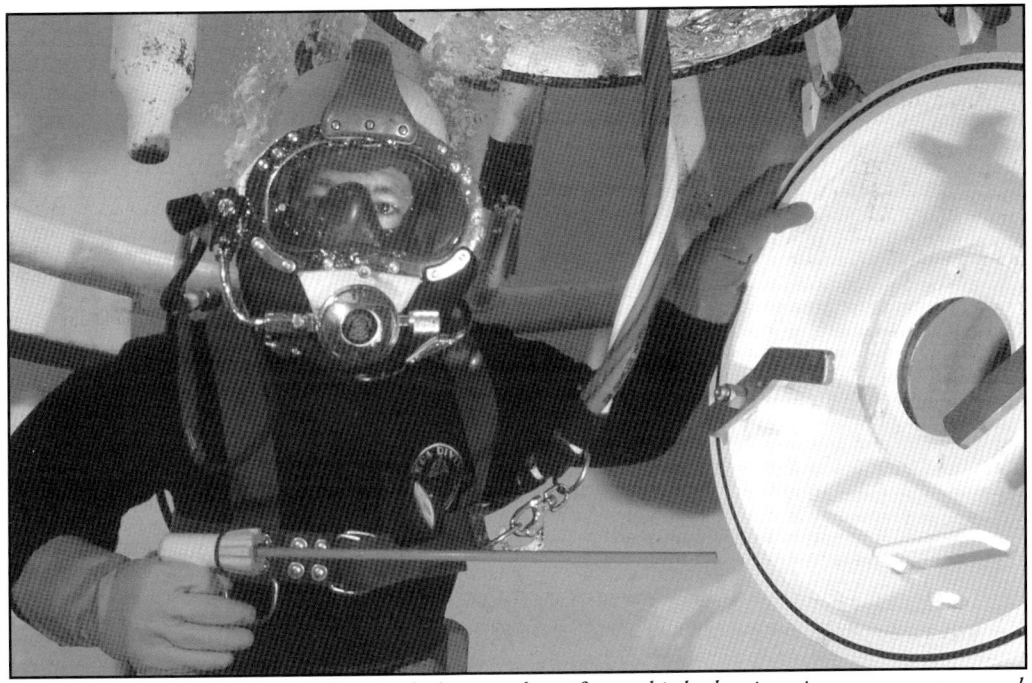

As a diver, it's your responsibility to decline to dive if you think the situation presents too much risk.

Risks in Commercial Diving

asked you to do something risky, or you are not feeling well for any reason, it is your responsibility to inform the supervisor that you are not up to making the dive. While you may feel that it is difficult to decline to dive, in most situations if you're reasonable and you speak up to voice your anxiety, you will probably find that there are other people who share your concerns about the circumstances. This is a common situation, so it's up to you to speak up.

There are numerous ways you can be killed or seriously injured when you are working underwater including drowning, pressure related injuries, marine life injuries, crane accidents, and explosions to name just a few. If you want to live a long life as a diver, it's your job to learn to recognize and minimize risks. There are many divers who have had long careers and have never been seriously injured while diving.

You should also understand that there are numerous ways that you can die or be seriously injured on a commercial diving job, even if you are not underwater. Ships sink, helicopters crash onto dive barges, people get washed over the side, drilling rigs catch on fire, cranes topple over, and numerous other accidents occur in the construction industry.

Drowning and Asphyxiation

Drowning is an accident that occurs when a person is submerged in water and is unable to maintain himself on the surface. Since human beings cannot extract oxygen from water, the person usually quickly stops breathing and death results.

Drowning is complicated when the person inhales water into the lungs. This can cause a situation where the heart beats erratically (ventricular fibrillation) and does not circulate blood. Death follows quickly under these conditions. Many drowning victims take relatively little water into their lungs.

Asphyxiation occurs when a person has nothing to breathe. In situations where the diver does not remove or lose his helmet or full-face mask underwater, but is rendered unconscious for some reason, death is usually by asphyxiation, rather than drowning.

Statistically speaking, drowning by itself is rarely a cause of death in commercial diving. There are usually other precipitating events that cause divers to become unconscious and drown or asphyxiate, such as squeezes, explosions, or differential pressure accidents.

Where drowning sometimes becomes an issue is in situations where the diver suffers a loss of his air supply, does not have a sufficient emergency breathing gas supply, and is unable to ascend before he passes out. For this reason, we strongly recommend that divers wear a bail-out bottle on every dive. Although there are situations where wearing a bail-out bottle may be awkward, the additional margin of safety is well worth the effort.

Pressure Related Injuries

Pressure related injuries, although infrequent, are probably the leading cause of commercial diving accidents and there are several ways they can occur. Pressure related injuries include squeezes, decompression sickness, and differential pressure injuries.

Squeezes

Squeezes occur when a diver has an air space in his body or attached to it (such as a helmet or diving suit), and the external water pressure is significantly greater than the pressure in the enclosed air space. Under some circumstances, squeezes can be fatal. Although this type of diving accident is rare, it can occur.

Today, all diving helmets and full-face masks are normally equipped with a device known as a "non-return valve" or "one-way valve." The purpose of this valve is to prevent the back-flow of air up the air supply hose in the event the topside supply is lost or the hose is severed near the surface. If this valve is not present, or if it malfunctions, the external pressure will attempt to force the diver's body into the helmet and up the hose. This can result in a painful if not fatal injury.

Just how bad this type of injury can be is demonstrated by an accident that took place in the Gulf of Mexico when a six man diving team was out on a relatively shallow water diving job. One of the divers wanted to check out the job site and jumped over the side without checking to see if the compres-

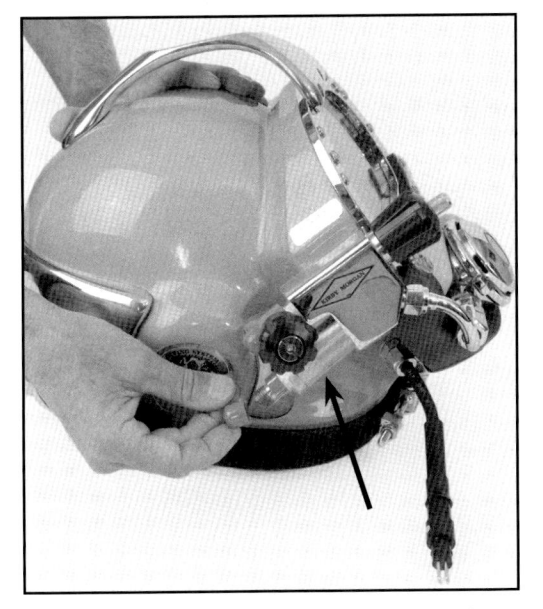

Every diving helmet or mask used for surface-supplied diving must be equipped with a non-return valve to help prevent a "squeeze" in the event the diver's hose is severed. The valve must be tested at the start of each diving day, and must be capped to prevent foreign matter from entering the helmet breathing system.

sor was on. He was also not wearing a bail-out bottle. The air to the helmet quickly ran out, the non-return valve was clogged with foreign matter, and diver passed out. When the tender hauled him to the surface, the diver was unconscious and bleeding from the nose and mouth.

Fortunately, the tender was well trained in cardio-pulmonary resuscitation and instantly began to work on the unconscious diver, who was revived in minutes. The blood vessels in the divers eyes ruptured as a result of the squeeze and the whites of his eyes were blood red, giving him the appearance of a vampire. This condition lasted for almost two months. If it hadn't been for the alert and responsive tender, the diver could easily have died.

Decompression Sickness

As we've already explained, the risk of decompression sickness for commercial divers is much lower today than it was in the past. In addition, since most commercial diving jobs have a chamber at the work site, divers who do suffer decompression sickness can be treated promptly.

Occasionally divers die as a result of decompression sickness, although this is extremely rare today. The most serious cases have involved divers who have made extended deep dives or saturation dives and fail to make their required decompression stops (omitted decompression). This is commonly referred to as "explosive decompression," where a rapid uncontrolled ascent is made to the surface following a prolonged, deep dive. Divers who experience this are often dead by the time they reach the surface.

Asceptic bone necrosis (dysbaric osteonecrosis) is thought to be one of the long term effects of decompression sickness because "silent" bubbles produce no immediate symptoms, but may cause problems years later. Due to the fact that the circulation in bones is poor, physicians believe that small bubbles that circulate freely elsewhere are trapped in the bones and cause long-term problems. Since there are no nerves in bones, there are no immediate symptoms when this occurs, and it is not until the bones begin to disintegrate that the problem becomes apparent.

Differential Pressure

Differential pressure, sometimes referred to as "delta-P" is one of the biggest causes of commercial diving accidents. Although differential pressure incidents don't always kill a diver directly, they frequently lead to drownings or loss of limbs.

In a differential pressure situation, there must be one area where there is relatively "high" pressure and one area where there is

Risks in Commercial Diving

Low pressure inside pipe

Whenever you work on any structure that has higher pressure on one side than the other, you must be extremely cautious. In this case, the inside of this pipeline is open to surface pressure at its upper end. If the diver opens the valve before the line is pressurized, anything close to the valve will be sucked into the pipeline.

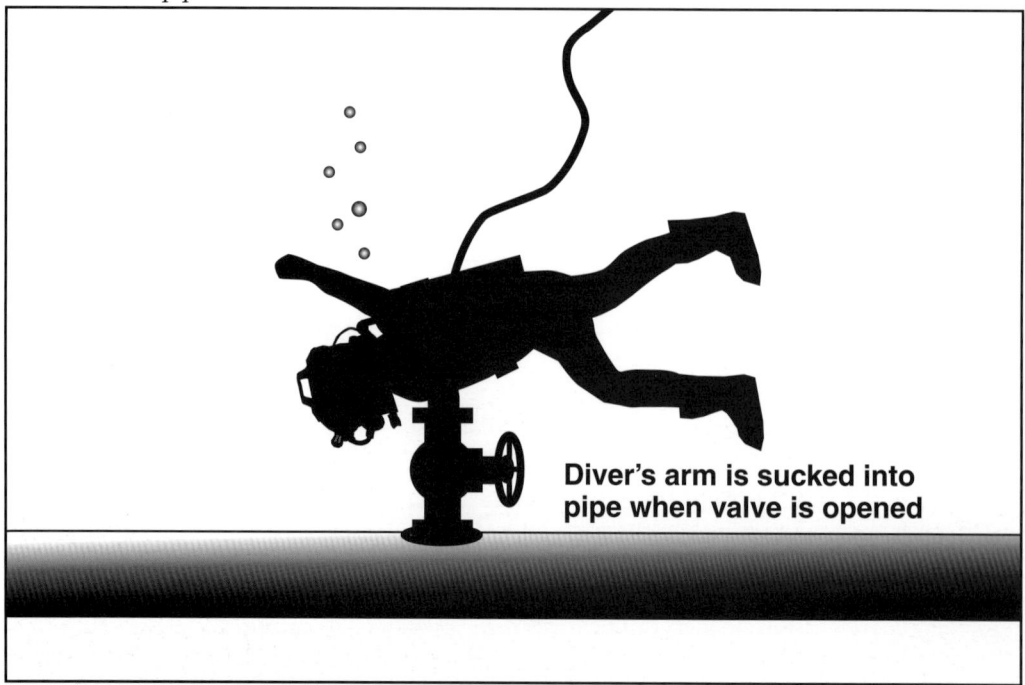

Diver's arm is sucked into pipe when valve is opened

This diver failed to make sure the pressure inside the pipeline was equal to the surrounding water pressure. When he opened the valve, his arm was sucked inside. This is known as a "differential pressure" accident and many divers have been killed in similar incidents.

low pressure. For example, a typical differential pressure incident might involve a diver working on a dam with a valve that when open, vents to topside pressure. If the valve is opened while the diver is working on or near it, the diver can be sucked up against the valve opening. If the valve is large enough, and the pressure differential is great enough, the diver could have an arm or leg sucked into the valve and even possibly ripped from his body.

Other pressure differential accidents have involved pipelines that vent to surface pressure or similar structures. In some cases, the diver has lost his helmet or full-face mask, which then leads to drowning.

Marine Life Injuries

It is extremely rare for a commercial diver to be attacked by a shark or other aggressive marine creature.

What is more common is for a diver to receive a minor injury such as a "nip" from a trigger fish. Although the bite from these small creatures can be quite painful, they rarely draw blood. If trigger fish grew to be as big as sharks, there would be no commercial diving in places like the Gulf of Mexico!

Underwater Explosions

In salvage, construction, and repair work, divers must frequently cut steel structures underwater. The fastest way to do this is with an electric arc-oxygen cutting torch, also known as "burning gear." An oxygen hose and an electric cable supply the necessary elements to burn the steel on the work surface. These devices use a tubular steel rod that flows oxygen to the tip of the torch.

As the metal is consumed, hydrogen and oxygen gas is liberated from the water by the electrical current and forms bubbles in the water, which will float up towards the surface. In addition, not all of the oxygen that flows through the torch is consumed.

Whenever you cut underwater using this type of equipment, you must take great care to ensure that the hydrogen and oxygen gas that escape from the torch do not accumulate in any structure above you. If they do, your torch can ignite an explosion that can knock you unconscious or kill you.

For example, if you are burning inside a wreck and hydrogen and oxygen become trapped in the compartment where you are working, it would be easy for an explosion to occur. All it takes is a spark from a cutting torch to ignite this explosive mixture. In order to avoid this type of accident, it is essential to cut vent holes in any enclosed structure to allow the gases to escape. Numerous divers have been killed due to this type of mistake.

Even a relatively small amount of gas build-up can be dangerous. In one incident, a diver was burning two and a half inch long monel bolts out of a flange when an explosion occurred. He didn't realize that he had created a pocket in the metal. When the explosion

Injuries from marine life are extremely rare in commercial diving.

Risks in Commercial Diving

Whenever you use a cutting torch underwater, you must be sure that any structure that you cut on is vented so that hydrogen and oxygen do not accumulate inside it. If you fail to do this, you could be subject to a powerful explosion which could be fatal.

occurred, it ruptured both of his ear drums, even though he had the physical protection of a diving helmet.

In the past, many different types of explosives were used underwater in salvage and construction work. However, the use of explosives in the offshore environment in U.S. waters is rare today, due to environmental regulations regarding their effect on marine mammals and turtles.

Divers who work with explosives must be sure to exit the water before any blast is detonated. If you are in the vicinity of an underwater explosion there is a strong possibility you will be injured or killed as the shock wave moves through the water.

Polluted Water

Diving in polluted water without the proper equipment can expose you to both short and long term health problems, depending on the type of pollutants to which you are exposed. If you primarily work offshore in the oilfields in the open ocean, your chances of being exposed to dangerous pollutants will usually be low. However, if you primarily work in harbors, lakes, rivers, or in coastal areas, your chances of coming in contact with toxic chemicals or biological hazards are quite high.

To properly equip yourself for diving in polluted water requires the use of a dry suit with mating dry gloves, and a helmet that is equipped with a special exhaust system to prevent the backflow of contaminants into the breathing system. The helmet must also connect directly to the dry suit via a special "yoke." Aside from the use of special equipment, diving in polluted water also requires specific training and procedures.

Biological hazards take numerous forms including viruses, bacteria, and toxic dinoflagellates. Each of these classes of organisms can cause serious illness and in some cases death. These organisms may be present in the water due to sewage spills or the presence of waterfowl or other animals near bodies of water.

It's also important to understand that there are thousands of different types of chemicals that also can cause serious injury, long term disability, or death. Chemicals are introduced into waterways through accidental means, or may be deliberately dumped there for disposal or even terrorist acts.

"Non-point source pollution" is the single biggest cause of water pollution in the United States, and probably in most civilized countries. This type of pollution occurs when any biological or chemical contamination is washed into the gutters or streams that feed into larger bodies of water. Common consumer items that contaminate waterways include:
- Lawn fertilizers and weed killers
- Fecal matter from household pets that defecate outdoors
- Tire dust and leaking oils from vehicles
- Leaking household septic systems

Divers who work underwater without the proper protection in polluted environments can absorb toxics through their skin. They may accidentally swallow or inhale droplets of pollutants that become aerosolized when they enter the breathing system of their helmet. Scientific studies of divers who have made repeated dives with inadequate protection in a polluted harbor over a series of years have shown that these divers contracted a variety of cancers at much higher rates than can be explained by other causes. Diving in polluted water is extremely hazardous.

Industrial Accidents

Commercial divers commonly work in construction or salvage environments that pose many hazards that may not involve diving at all, but can still lead to serious personal injury or death. These accidents are much more common than diving accidents, but the consequences can be just as serious.

Cranes on construction jobs are constantly moving equipment and materials around on the job site, and it's up to you to

Diving in polluted water requires special equipment, training, and preparations.

Risks in Commercial Diving

be aware of the movements of the crane at all times while you are in its vicinity. In addition, many workers have been injured riding the personnel baskets used to transfer crew members from a ship to a platform. Injuries have occurred when crew members riding these baskets have been slammed against the rail on a ship as the basket swings when it is lowered from a platform.

Entire crews of commercial diving companies have been killed when the ship they were working from sank in a storm. This has happened in various locations around the world.

In many cases, the divers are the most savvy workers aboard offshore vessels in terms of survival at sea, since many of the crew members are often people who don't even swim. For a terrifying account of a construction barge sinking in a hurricane read *All the Men in the Sea*.

There have also been incidents where lone crew members have been swept overboard from ships and barges when no one else was on deck and they were lost at sea. In cold waters, such as the North Sea, this type of accident can be fatal due to hypothermia, even if the victim is a good swimmer.

Personnel baskets like this are commonly used to transfer workers from a ship to a barge or other installation offshore. You can be injured if the basket accidentally crashes into the vessel when you're riding it.

Fires at sea are especially dangerous. This rig fire occurred in the Gulf of Mexico.

Fires aboard drill rigs and other structures are not unheard of and these situations can have deadly results. Author Steve Barsky was caught in a rig fire in the Gulf of Mexico where the entire crew had to abandon ship. Fortunately, only two crew members suffered any serious injuries in this incident, with one case of smoke inhalation and one apparent heart attack.

Emotional Stress

Commercial diving is very demanding on your personal life, as the job may frequently require you to spend long periods of time away from home on short notice. For the diver who is married or has a family, this can be extremely difficult.

Although we know of no scientific studies on the divorce rate among commercial divers, it certainly appears to be quite high, even among couples who seem to have solid relationships. If you are married, you should have a long talk with your spouse about the responsibilities involved in your work before entering the diving profession.

Most commercial diving companies are not sympathetic to anything but the most extreme of personal problems, such as a death in the family. They do not look kindly upon divers who want to leave a job in progress due to family problems. If you have a family and want to spend time watching your children grow up, offshore commercial diving is probably not a good choice as a career.

True Tales of Commercial Diving from Alaska

The following dive took place in the Cook Inlet of Alaska inside the leg of an oil drilling and production platform standing in about 100 feet of water. The legs of this platform were large cylinders approximately 14 feet in diameter. Equally spaced around the inside of this jacket were 30 inch diameter conductor piles through which the drilling operations took place and the oil was eventually produced. There were also several horizontal bulkheads equally spaced from the top to the bottom of the leg. A ladder descended down the leg and through openings in these bulkheads. The object of the dive was to cut (burn) a hole through the outer jacket at the lowest possible level for a reason that eludes me now, although the details of the dive itself are clearly etched into my mind.

I dressed into heavy gear, less the helmet and weights, and descended the vertical ladder to the bulkhead just above the water. My tender was there with the helmet and weights and I completed the dress-in. Climbing a vertical steel ladder in full heavy gear is a bit sticky, but I made my way to the ladder and climbed down until I entered the water. It was a great relief to descend below the waves and relieve the weight of the gear even though the water was very cold and totally black.

With the cutting torch in hand I descended by sliding down the ladder and slipping through the encountered bulkheads until I arrived at the bottom. Once on bottom the trick was to squeeze between two conductor piles to gain access to the wall of the outer jacket. (We had two sets of heavy gear on this job and the breastplate of one was too wide to get between the piles).

Having gained access to the jacket wall and situated myself as comfortably as possible, I proceeded to burn the prescribed hole through to the outside sea.

What joy success! I was more than happy to ease back through between the piles, find the ladder and carefully pick my way upward. I arrived at the dry bulkhead to the welcoming of my rather anxious tender and gladly shed helmet and weights.

There was reward in accomplishment, but this was one dive I did not care to repeat.

Bob Christensen

© Bev Morgan. All rights reserved.

Chapter 6
Commercial Diving Equipment

If you can't pound nails with it, it's no damn good…

Any gear used for commercial diving must be especially rugged to stand up to the demands of the industrial environment of underwater construction. Although some equipment that is used by sport divers, such as fins, find their way into the commercial world, items designed for commercial use must be built "like a cannon ball" (translate as indestructible) to withstand the abuse they will receive.

Most commercial divers approach their diving equipment as "tools" with the understanding that they need to select the right tool to get the job done under varying circumstances. On some dives, a dry suit might be the best way to get the job done, while on other occasions a hot water suit may be more appropriate. There is no diving equipment that will work on all dives or jobs.

Smart divers understand that their dive gear is "life-support equipment" and treat their gear with the respect it deserves. They make sure their gear is well maintained and carry the appropriate tools, manuals, and spares to keep their personal equipment in top condition.

Personal Diving Equipment

Depending on where you work in the world, you may need to supply certain items of equipment for your personal use, such as suits, fins, helmets, harnesses, gloves, and similar items. In other locations, the company may supply most, or all of your equipment, with the exception of small personal items, such as knives and gloves.

If the company supplies the equipment, it's up to you to satisfy yourself that the gear they provide is properly maintained and working correctly. Just as a skydiver packs his own parachute, it's your responsibility to make sure that any gear you plan to use is working satisfactorily. If you get to the bottom and your helmet is not functioning properly, there's really no one to blame but yourself.

Diving Helmets & Full-Face Masks

Diving Helmets

As a commercial diver, you'll probably end up using a diving helmet on some, if not all of your jobs. Although full-face masks are lighter weight and less expensive to purchase, nothing beats the protection provided by a full coverage diving helmet.

Helmets provide superior protection and communications, and should always be used in the following situations:
- Heavy construction jobs
- Ice diving
- Polluted water

There are two basic types of helmets on the market, free-flow helmets and demand helmets. In a free-flow helmet, there is no demand regulator. Air enters the helmet through a flow-control valve and exits the helmet through an exhaust valve. In a demand helmet, a demand regulator (nearly identical to a scuba regulator) is used to control the air supply for the diver.

Free-flow helmets may be less expensive

Commercial Diving Equipment

Free-flow helmets like this are popular for shallow water applications.

to purchase and maintain than demand helmets. Although demand helmets are more popular and more widely used, free-flow helmets are a good choice for certain situations.

Free-flow helmets are preferred for polluted water and for shallow water diving operations, although they can ice up in very cold water. They present less risk in contaminated water diving operations since there is no regulator diaphragm to leak, and the helmet always maintains positive internal pressure which helps to keep contaminants out. On the negative side, the communications with free-flow helmets are not usually as good as they are with a demand helmet and they require a compressor that will pump a large volume of air. In addition, it's not possible to wear a large enough bail-out bottle to supply the air flow required for a free-flow helmet.

Probably the most popular free-flow diving helmet on the market today is the Desco air hat. The helmet is made from a spun copper shell and readily withstands the rigors of the underwater environment. The design is very simple and it can be serviced with nothing more than a screwdriver and a wrench. Like most free-flow helmets, it tends to be positively buoyant in use and a jocking system must be worn to use the helmet properly.

Demand helmets are the most popular type of diving helmet in use today. Although they tend to be more expensive than free-flow helmets, they are popular for several reasons. First, they can be used with a smaller compressor than a free-flow "hat" or even with high-pressure cylinders. Communications are usually superior with a demand helmet, which is always important. Finally, free-flow helmets are not acceptable for mixed-gas diving because they would waste too much of the helium-oxygen mixture, which is very expensive.

The most popular demand diving helmets on the market are the SuperLite® or "KM" series of helmets manufactured by Kirby Morgan Dive Systems, Inc. (KMDSI) of California. These helmets have a rugged fiberglass shell and the hardware is brass, chromed brass, and stainless steel. Probably more dives have been made with helmets manufactured by KMDSI than any other diving gear.

The fit of your helmet can be individually customized by adjusting the amount of foam padding inside the head cushion that fits inside the helmet. This is important, especially if you will be making long dives. Lights and television cameras can also be added to your helmet handle.

You should always carry the manual, as

Demand helmets like this one are the most popular type used.

well as the required tools and spare parts for your helmet so that you are prepared to perform any maintenance on your helmet on the job, if necessary. Your helmet should be maintained in top working condition at all times because your life depends on it.

Full-Face Mask

Some divers prefer to use a full-face mask rather than a diving helmet. Full-face masks are lighter than diving helmets, have less drag, and are less expensive. For divers who aren't working heavy construction or in polluted water, a full-face mask may be an acceptable alternative.

The big drawbacks to full-face masks are that your head will get wet when you use one and the communications will not be as clear as with a helmet. In addition, a full-face mask will not give you the mechanical head protection provided by a helmet. Full-face masks are not considered acceptable for contaminated water diving if there is any possibility you will be killed or permanently disabled through exposure to the contaminants. There have also been cases where a full-face mask has accidentally come off of a diver's head, which is much less likely with a diving helmet. If you can live with these disadvantages, a full-face mask may be a good choice.

Although there are lightweight full-face masks on the market, such as the Divator MKII and the EXO-26®, these are generally not considered rugged enough for day-to-day use. For commercial diving, the Kirby Morgan Band Mask (KMB28) is considered the industry standard. It has the same front end as their SuperLite® helmet, but the rear portion is wet.

Some dive supervisors and commercial diving companies do not allow their divers to use full-face masks because they do not feel they are as safe as helmets.

Harness and Bail-Out System

When you are using surface-supplied diving gear, it's vital that you wear a harness to provide an attachment point for your hose and a means to wear your bail-out bottle. The

Full-face masks offer many of the same features as a helmet but without the same head protection.

harness also doubles as a lifting device to assist your topside crew in removing you from the water in the event you require assistance.

The harness should be equipped with D-rings to allow you to connect your dive hose, knife, lights, or other accessories. These D-rings are normally located on either side of

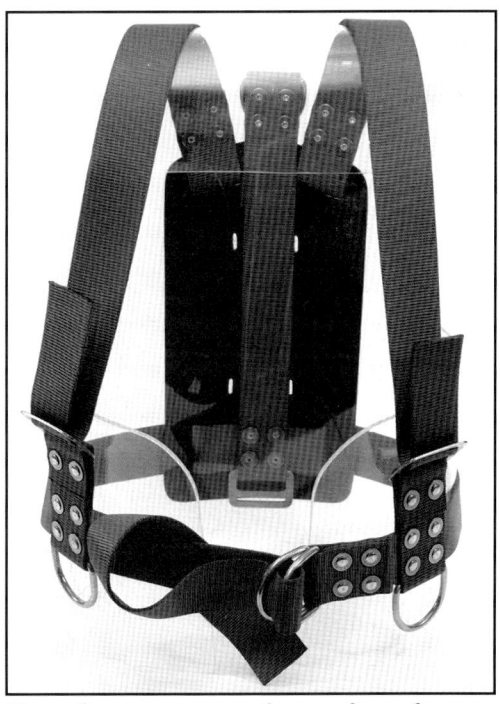

Every diver must wear a harness for surface-supplied diving.

Commercial Diving Equipment

It's a good idea to wear a bail-out bottle whenever possible.

Another technique to help prevent entanglement is to turn the bail-out bottle upside down, which also helps to shield the first-stage regulator from damage. This does require the use of a longer hose to connect the regulator to the emergency valve on the helmet or full-face mask. Some divers also put the entire bail-out bottle and regulator inside a bag, as an alternate method of helping to reduce the possibility of entanglement.

Commercial Diving Weight Belt

Commercial diving weight belts differ from the traditional sport diving weight belts you are used to wearing in that they do **not** have a quick release. The philosophy in the commercial diving industry is completely different from the sport diving industry. In commercial diving, because many dives are decompression dives, and because commercial divers almost always have communications, and usually some type of back-up breath-

your chest. Another D-ring located in the center of the back, just below your neck, will provide the lifting point for hoisting you out of the water in an emergency. Alternatively, there may be hoisting D-rings located on the chest.

We recommend that you wear a bail-out bottle on every dive you make, if you are wearing a demand helmet or full-face mask. Bail-out bottles don't work with free-flow helmets because the emergency gas supply would be used up almost instantly.

It's essential to select a bail-out bottle with sufficient capacity for the depth of water in which you are working. For diving down to 60 FSW, the minimum size cylinder which you should consider would be a 50 cubic foot cylinder. This will provide you with sufficient air for most situations. At deeper depths, you should consider a higher capacity cylinder.

Most divers use a couple of stainless steel hose clamps to attach their bail-out bottle to their harness. If you use this method of attachment be sure to trim the ends of the hose clamps so that there is a minimum of excess "tail" on the clamp which could snag any loose lines or wires resulting in entanglement underwater.

Commercial diving weight belts and harnesses are never equipped with a quick release.

ing system, the weight belt is almost never ditched in an emergency. The concern of the commercial industry is that if the weight belt comes off accidentally, the diver will make a rapid ascent and suffer from decompression sickness.

Divers who work in rivers or heavy currents sometimes wear a weight harness that will carry much more weight than a traditional weight belt. The shoulder straps on these harnesses transfer the load to the diver's shoulders to help reduce the possibility of lower back injury.

Divers who have successfully made the mental shift from recreational diving to commercial diving do not have a problem using a weight belt that does not have a quick release.

Thermal Protection
Wetsuits

Wetsuits provide reasonable thermal protection under the following circumstances:
- The water temperature is not significantly colder than 65 degrees F.
- You won't be spending more than an hour in the water.
- You will be performing work at a fairly high rate.
- You won't be diving in polluted water.

If your dive conditions are going to be outside those listed here, you need to consider either a dry suit or a hot water suit.

There are several problems with wetsuits that make them less than ideal for most commercial diving situations. Wetsuits are made from foam neoprene rubber, a material which contains thousands of tiny closed cells filled with nitrogen. When wetsuits are subjected to repeated compression underwater, the cells in the neoprene tend to collapse and the suit loses its insulation. If salt is allowed to dry in the nylon coating the suit, the salt crystals can also damage the cells, also destroying insulation capability.

Since water is allowed to enter the suit, and many commercial dives take place in polluted coastal waters, wetsuits should not be used in situations where there are chemical or biological pollutants in the water.

Dry suits are used by many commercial divers.

If you are doing a lot of diving, your wetsuit will probably need to be replaced at least every other year or whenever the material begins to get thin.

Some divers wear coveralls over their wetsuits to help protect them from abrasions. This is a good idea, provided the coveralls do not create too much drag. You may want to use some duct tape to close the ankles and wrists of coveralls if you use them.

Dry Suits

Dry suits are a good choice for diving in a wide variety of environments. They provide better thermal protection than wetsuits, and are the preferred type of suit for diving in polluted water. Although dry suits are more expensive to purchase initially, they have a longer useful life than most wetsuits and provide superior warmth for diving with compressed air.

For diving in polluted water, such as inside a harbor or on a sewer outfall job, a vulcanized rubber dry suit is the preferred choice. If you plan to dive in areas that have chemical pollutants, then you must take care to ensure that your suit, and all of your equipment, is compatible with the chemicals that are present. Keep in mind that even the best dry suits are not compatible with all chemicals, and that suits that would normally be compatible with a particular chemical may fail unexpectedly if they have been previously exposed to other compounds.

Dry suits are not normally used for diving with helium mixtures due to the high thermal conductivity of helium. In situations where hot water suits are not available, but helium mixtures must be used, divers have used argon as the gas inside their dry suits. One of the risks of this procedure is that argon can be absorbed through the skin and could possibly cause decompression sickness. Although there are no reported incidents of divers suffering from decompression sickness as a result of using argon inside their dry suits, you should use caution if you decide to use this procedure.

Hot Water Suits

Hot water suits are the preferred type of thermal protection for mixed-gas diving with helium-oxygen mixtures. They provide an active heating source that can be adjusted by the surface crew to meet the diver's needs at whatever level of work activity is demanded by the dive.

The typical hot water suit fits somewhat loosely and has valves at the waist where the hot water hose from topside connects to the suit. The valves control the flow of water down each arm and leg, and down the diver's chest and back. Hot water continuously flushes through the suit. Gauntlet gloves are normally worn to provide hot water circulation to the hands.

It's a good idea to wear a shorty wetsuit (short arms and legs) underneath your hot water suit. There are several reasons for this. First, if the topside crew is not careful, or the mixing system topside is defective, it's possible to be scalded by water that is too hot. Wearing a shorty suit will help to protect the more delicate parts of your anatomy from being burned.

Another reason to wear a shorty suit is that most divers do not own their own hot water suit, but wear suits that are provided by the diving company for whom they work. In

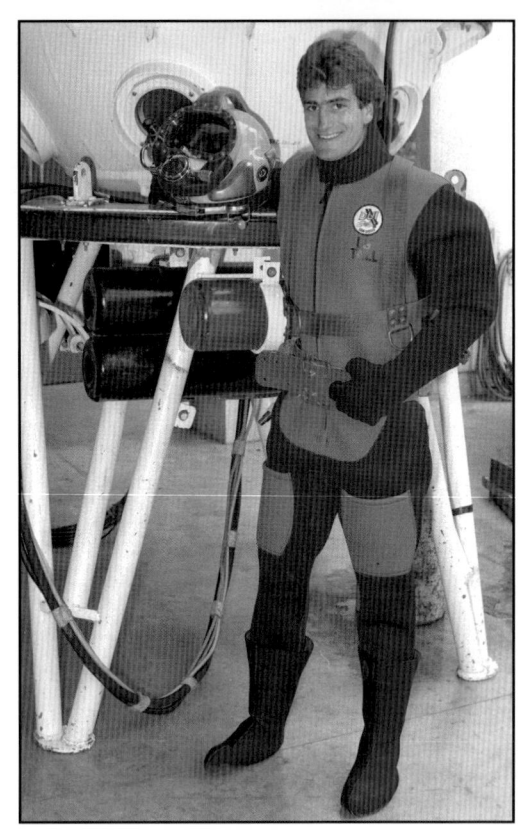

Hot water suits are considered essential for mixed-gas diving.

some situations, it's not uncommon for divers in saturation to suffer from fungal infections. Wearing a shorty suit may help to prevent you from experiencing this unpleasantness.

An additional reason to use a shorty suit is that a neoprene shorty can help to give you a little bit of buoyancy to help make you neutrally buoyant underwater. Since commercial divers don't wear buoyancy compensators, this can be a big help on some jobs. Just be sure to remember that a shorty that is locked in and out of a saturation system multiple times will eventually lose its buoyancy and will not be any help in maintaining any type of buoyancy control.

In most colder environments you'll also want to wear some type of thermal underwear between your body and the hot water suit while you're standing by awaiting your turn to dive. Thermal underwear is usually necessary to be comfortable in cold locations because the hot water suit by itself provides no real insulation when it is dry if you are stuck on the surface for any length of time waiting to dive. Running the hot water while you're waiting to dive is usually not an option, because the hot water is usually too warm to be comfortable at topside temperatures.

The worst case scenario is if you must stand by in a hot water suit that is already wet in a cold climate. Once the thermal underwear becomes wet you will get cold and the only way to maintain warmth, but not burn yourself, is to switch the hot water on and off while you are standing by. This is a miserable situation if you are trapped in these circumstances for any length of time. Unfortunately, it's not all that uncommon.

We've also heard a story about a jellyfish that was sucked up by a hot water suit machine pump. As the creature worked it's way through the system it broke up and was then sent down through the hot water hose to the diver. You can probably imagine the discomfort you might experience in this type of situation.

Knives

A knife is essential equipment for all dives for cutting rigging underwater or to help you release yourself from possible entanglement. For commercial diving, most divers prefer a knife with a folding blade and one that is equipped with a marlinespike for turning shackle pins.

Your dive knife should be attached to a lanyard and connected to your harness with a brass or stainless steel snap hook. The lanyard helps to prevent you from dropping the knife and attaching it to your harness means it will be at chest level where it is easy to find.

In situations where you know there is a possibility of encountering wires in the water, like diving from a drill rig or platform, it's wise to carry a pair of sidecutters with you so that you can cut away this type of nuisance.

Gloves

There are many different types of gloves that are useful for working as a diver, both topside and underwater. Since you'll be work-

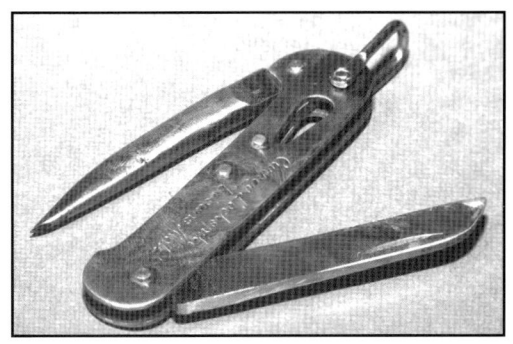

The diver's knife is used for cutting lines and opening shackles.

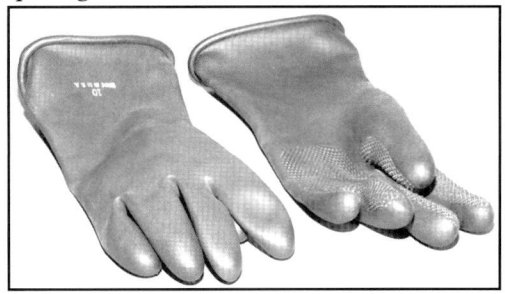

You will need different types of gloves for different jobs. For cutting and welding, or for contaminated water you will need heavy-duty rubber gloves.

ing with materials such as heavy metal objects, wire ropes, and a variety of tools, gloves are important to your safety and comfort.

For topside use, almost any type of leather work glove is acceptable, provided the gloves fit well and allow you good manual dexterity. While you may not want to wear gloves all of the time, any time you are handling items like wire rope, steel plate, or similar materials that have the potential to inflict cuts, a good pair of gloves will be invaluable.

In the water, you will always want to wear some type of gloves to keep your hands warm and protect from cuts. Some divers wear ordinary synthetic leather work gloves and these are perfectly acceptable, although they usually do not last for more than a few dives.

Wetsuit gloves are fine in temperate waters that are not polluted. They offer good protection in most situations.

In polluted water, the only type of gloves that are recommended are dry gloves, even if the water is "only" biologically polluted. The danger in using ordinary gloves in biologically polluted water is that if your hands get cut,

Commercial Diving Equipment

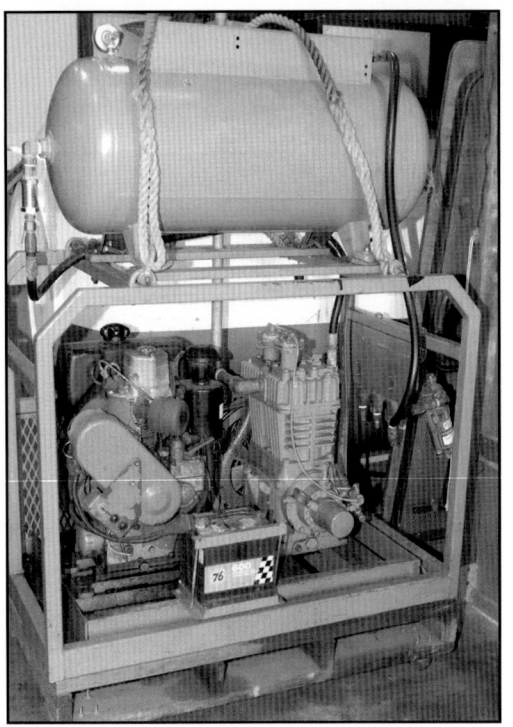

Most compressors used for commercial diving are powered by diesel engines.

you can be badly infected. Even if you are not cut during a dive, an open cut on your hand is subject to infection in polluted water. Some infections in polluted water are so serious they may require surgery.

There are several different types of dry gloves that are available and your choice will usually depend on the type of work in which you are engaged. If you are doing inspection work, then gloves made from nitrile or similar materials are probably adequate. However, if you are engaged in any heavy work or are using tools, you will probably do best to use gloves that are made from the same material as the suit itself. They have the greatest abrasion resistance and are the most impervious to punctures.

Heavy Hardware
Air Compressors

Most of the compressors used on commercial diving jobs are heavy-duty systems with diesel engines to provide the power. The most popular compressors used in the diving industry are made by Quincy and the models most commonly used are the 325, 370, and 5120. These are all large, noisy units that are designed to run for many hours and deliver sufficient air for multiple divers.

While a 325 or 370 compressor is generally used for shallow diving down to 60 FSW, the 5120 can easily support a diver down to 165 FSW and beyond. If the job requires a decompression chamber, then a 5120 is considered a necessity, and on a big job there will usually be at least two compressors this size.

Every diver needs to know how to check the oil in the compressor and the engine, how to start the compressor manually, how to change the air filters, and how to drain the volume tank of condensate. This is a basic piece of gear that is essential to all commercial diving operations.

Every compressor system will also be equipped with a filtration system to remove particles, oils, and other contaminants from the breathing air after it has been compressed.

Manifold

Once the compressor pressurizes the air for the diver, it is fed through a hose to a volume tank and then to a manifold to ensure that the diver receives the correct amount of breathing gas. The manifold has several purposes. First, it allows the diving supervisor to monitor the air pressure the diver is receiving, at a distance remote from the noisy compressor. In addition, other alternate air supplies can be connected to the manifold so that in the event the main air supply is lost (i.e., the compressor fails) the supervisor can instantly switch the diver to another source of air. In many cases, the alternate air supply will be from high-pressure cylinders.

Most commercially available air diving manifolds today will include a low-pressure connection, a high-pressure connection, a high-pressure regulator, and a pneumofathometer system. The pneumofathometer is designed to accurately measure the diver's depth. The system uses a small amount of air that is used to pressurize a small diameter hose that is part of the diver's umbilical. The hose, which is open at its bottom end is connect-

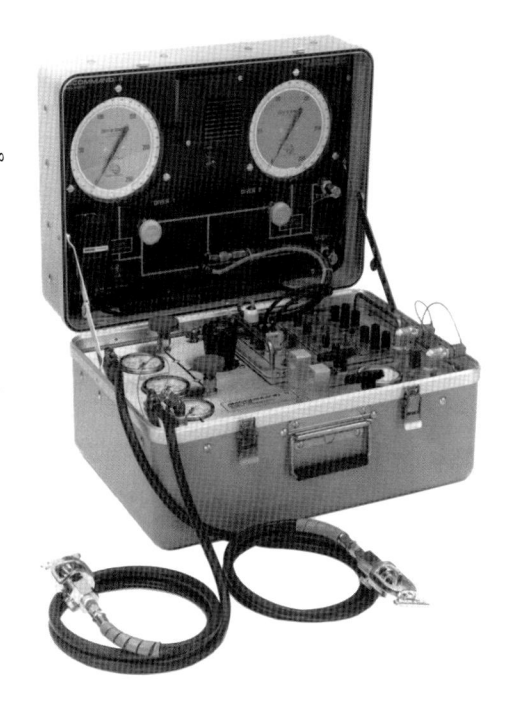

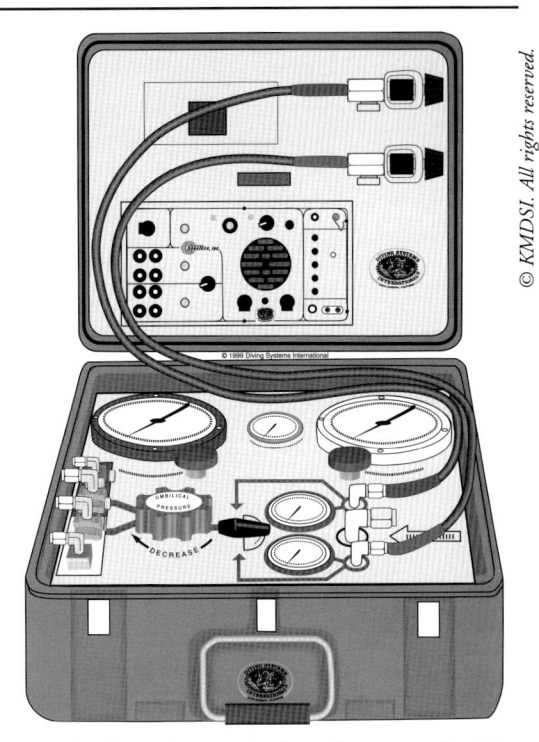

Diver's manifolds are designed to monitor and control the flow of air to the diver from topside. Most will accept both high-pressure and low-pressure breathing gas sources.

ed to a large and very precise depth gauge. A valve controls the flow of air through the gauge and down to the end of the hose.

To take a reading, the manifold operator opens the valve and keeps it open until the diver tells him that air is flowing out the end of the hose, or that he "has bubbles." At that point, the valve is closed and the air pressure trapped in the hose provides a reading of the diver's depth. The reading should always be taken at the diver's chest.

Air diving manifolds are simple to operate and every diver is expected to know how to use them properly. When you are operating the manifold you are directly responsible for the safety of the diver in the water. This is a huge responsibility and must not be taken lightly.

Communications Box

Communications are considered required equipment for commercial diving so that the diver can maintain a running conversation with his support team topside. It's not considered safe to dive without communications.

In the commercial diving field, hard-wired communications systems are the industry standard. These systems can be wired with either two or four wires, however, two-wire systems are by far the most common.

Two-wire communications systems are commonly referred to as "push-to-talk" systems. In a push-to-talk system, communications can only go one way at a time, either surface-to-diver, or diver-to-surface. For topside to talk to the diver, they must push a toggle switch down to transmit, much like you would with a walkie-talkie or other two-way radio. The advantages of this system is that it is simple to wire and repair and relatively inexpensive. The disadvantage is that whenever the toggle switch is depressed, topside cannot hear the diver. Users of these systems must learn to keep their communications brief so that they do not put the diver in a situation where he cannot call for help if he needs it.

Four-wire communications systems are commonly referred to as "round-robin" systems. This arrangement is like talking on a telephone; everyone can talk and be heard at the same time. Despite the obvious advan-

Commercial Diving Equipment

tage to this type of system, four-wire communications are not as popular as two-wire arrangements. Four-wire systems are a bit more difficult to set up and repair, and they are definitely more expensive to purchase and maintain.

Most communications boxes are battery powered, although they may have a 110-volt charging system for the batteries. If you are using a "com" box with a 110-volt charger and you want to use the charger while the diver is in the water, you must use a ground fault interrupter (GFI) between the com box and the power source. Without this type of protection, the diver could receive a serious electrical shock in the event of a short.

Umbilical

The diver's umbilical or hose is his lifeline to the surface. Umbilicals can be almost any length, but the "typical" umbilical is usually not less than 300 feet in length. Very long umbilicals have been made to penetrate far back inside pipelines and other structures.

The basic components of all umbilicals are a hose for supplying the diver's breathing gas, a communications wire, and a pneumofathometer hose. Other items that may be added to the umbilical include a strength member (safety line), a power wire, a television cable, and a hot water hose.

These components are normally taped together using duct tape, although there are also twisted umbilicals available on the market today. Twisted umbilicals are preferred for diving in polluted water since chemical pollutants may damage the duct tape and the tape may absorb some pollutants and be difficult to decontaminate.

Most umbilicals used in the commercial diving field are designed to sink, which means that you will need to learn to work with the hose underwater so it does not become entangled in items on the bottom. The advantage to a sinking umbilical is that it does not float on the surface where it could be entangled

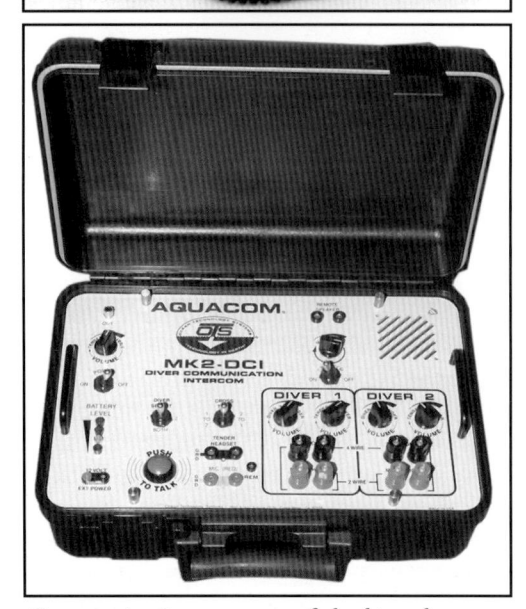

Communications are one of the big advantages of surface-supplied diving. These "com" boxes make communicating with the diver easy.

The typical umbilical includes a breathing gas hose, a communications wire, and a pneumofathometer hose.

56

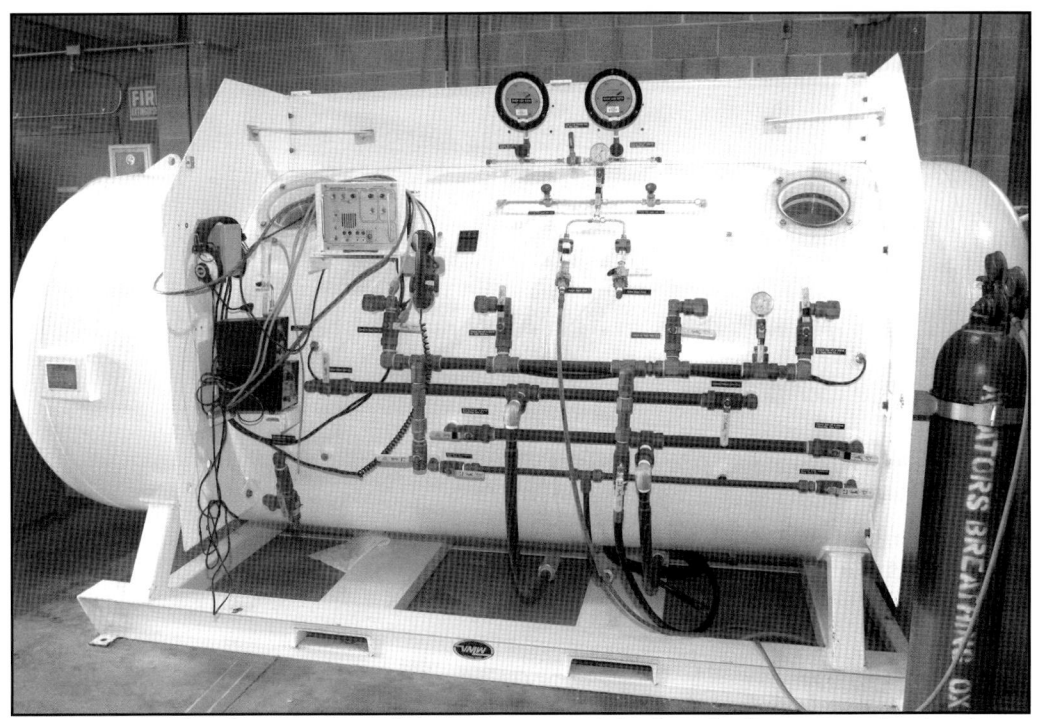

Decompression chambers are required equipment on any job where the divers are performing decompression dives or working below 80 FSW in the U.S.A.

in the propeller of any vessel that happens to pass through the dive site.

The umbilical must be treated with respect at all time, and you must not stand on it, or allow other people who are not part of the diving crew to abuse it. Although they are relatively rugged, umbilicals can be damaged.

The umbilical is normally coiled up for use. There are two methods of coiling the hose; either over and under (clockwise), or in a figure eight, if space allows. Either method is acceptable. As a tender, you will spend a great deal of time coiling hoses, and it's important to learn how to do this properly.

Decompression Chamber

Hyperbaric chambers are common in the commercial diving field. They are required on any job where the divers are performing decompression dives or are working below 80 FSW. Chambers are routinely used for a procedure known as "surface-decompression on oxygen" as well as for the treatment of decompression sickness. Every person on a commercial diving job should know how to operate the chamber.

Surface decompression on oxygen, or "sur-d-O_2," as it's commonly called, is a procedure where the diver completes a portion of his decompression in the water, surfaces, and is rushed into a decompression chamber on the surface. Decompression in the chamber is performed using oxygen, which speeds up the decompression process. This is a common technique used in the commercial diving industry for deeper dives.

Most decompression chambers used for surface-supplied diving are known as "double-lock chambers" that have a 54 or 60 inch diameter. A double-lock chamber has two compartments, an inner compartment or "lock" where the diver undergoes decompression, and an outer lock which allows other people or equipment to enter or exit the chamber while the inner lock remains under pressure.

Chamber operation is very simple, and although the plumbing and valves may look complicated at first glance, they are easy to understand. Each lock has valves to put air into the chamber and to vent air (exhaust) out of the chamber.

In addition, there are controls for oxygen

Commercial Diving Equipment

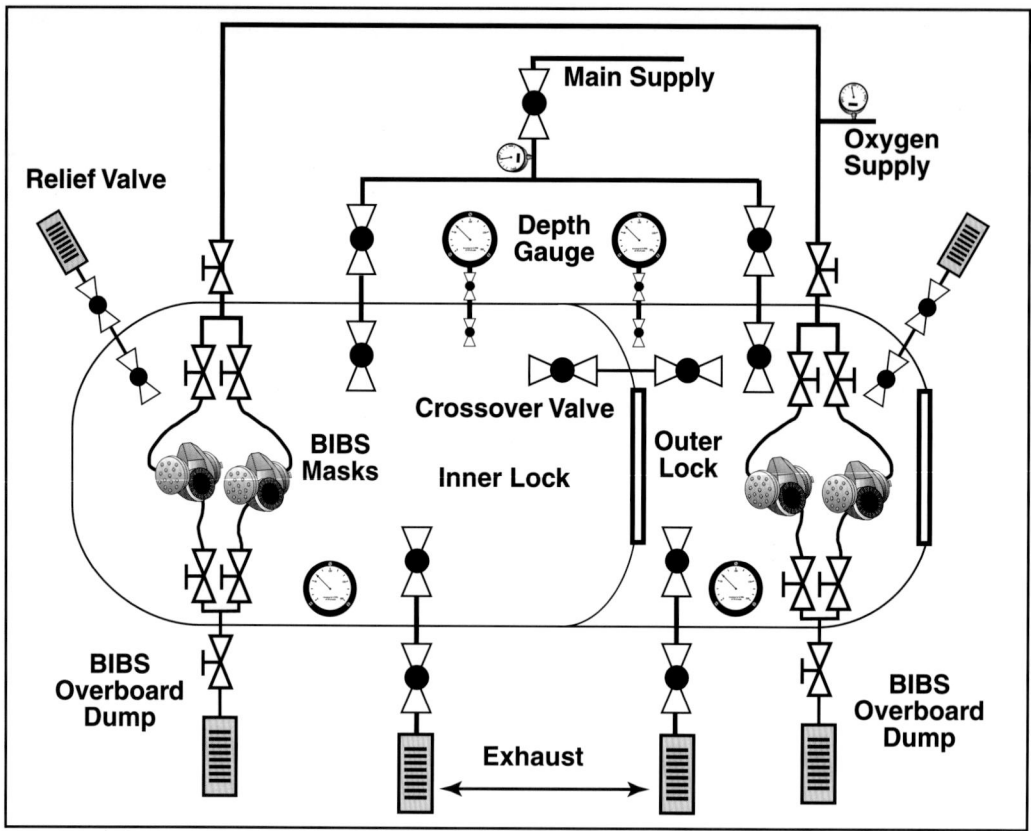

You must understand the plumbing on any decompression chamber you operate. Since not all chambers are plumbed identically, it's important for you to take the time to understand each chamber before you run it.

flow to the half-masks (also known as "BIBS" for Built in Breathing System) used for breathing pure oxygen, "penetrators" for communications, and over-pressure relief valves. Most commercial chambers are plumbed so that there is a redundancy to all controls inside and out, although there will frequently be a topside over-ride to all valves.

Chambers are built to a strict engineering code known as "PVHO" or Pressure Vessel for Human Occupancy. This code was developed by the ASME (American Society of Mechanical Engineers). Diving bells and chambers for saturation diving must also meet the same code.

Stage

Although a ladder can be used to climb out of the water, this is often an impractical if not dangerous method for divers to exit the water at the end of their dives. In heavy seas, a diver could be seriously injured trying to use a ladder. A much more efficient and (usually) safer method of getting out of the water is to use a "stage." The stage can usually be lowered to a sufficient depth that will be reasonably safe for the diver to use it.

Most diving stages are made from steel and are open on at least one side for the diver to enter and exit. Hand-holds are located inside the stage for the diver to grip and steady himself as the stage is moved. It's important to keep your body inside the stage at all times whenever it is being hoisted.

The stage is lowered into the water, well below the surface, by a davit or hoist. When the diver is inside the stage, he informs topside and the stage is lifted out of the water.

There are some specific techniques for using stages that we'll explore in the chapter on working as a diver.

Mixed-Gas Diving Equipment

Mixed-gas surface-supplied diving is much less common today than it was in the past, but there are still some jobs where it is used. Most large companies that have a deep diving job to do have a tendency to perform the work using a saturation system, which provides a much safer way to dive.

Mixed-Gas Diving Manifold

In mixed-gas diving, the air diving manifold is replaced by a more sophisticated manifold that allows up to three different gas mixtures to be put on line if needed. The well designed mixed-gas manifold will allow the operator to have multiple choices in how to route the gas to the diver's hose.

Most mixed-gas manifolds have at least two high-pressure regulators for controlling the gas pressure to the diver and will have a low-pressure air supply connected to the panel as well. Better manifolds will also usually include a metering valve that can control the pressure in the rare event that both regulators fail. If the manifold is used for saturation diving, too, it may also include an additional supply of reclaimed helium and oxygen.

A stage is the preferred method for getting a diver in and out of the water.

Mixed-gas diving manifolds will usually support all types of surface-supplied diving.

Commercial Diving Equipment

Helium unscramblers help to make divers' helium speech more intelligible for personnel topside.

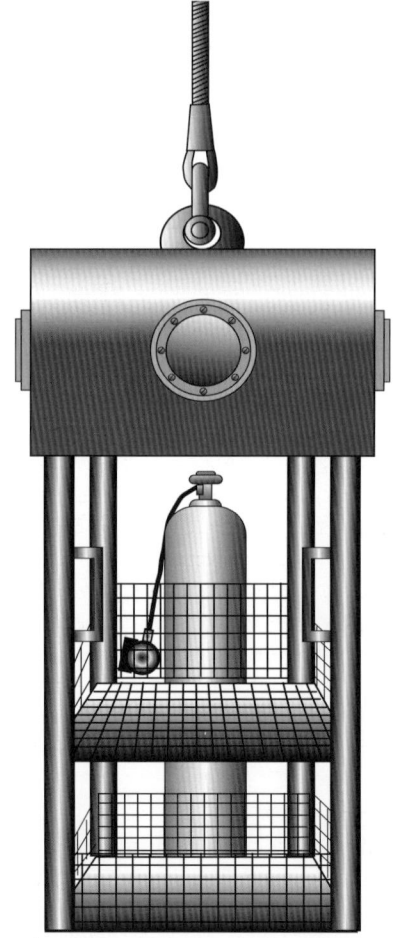

On a deep dive, an open-bottom bell is required equipment.

Helium Unscrambler

When you breathe a helium-oxygen mixture during a deep dive, your voice will be distorted due to the different density of this mixture compared to air. In order to make "helium speech" more intelligible, several diving equipment manufacturers have developed special communications boxes specifically for this purpose.

Even with the best helium unscrambler it can be difficult to understand all divers, particularly at deeper depths. Most diving supervisors and life support technicians will turn off the unscrambler from time-to-time to help them develop a "helium ear" so that they will be able to better understand a diver in case no helium unscrambler is available.

Open Bottom Bell

An open bottom bell is basically a diving stage with a compartment on the top of it that is open at the bottom and allows the diver to stick his head up inside an air (breathing gas) environment. The idea behind the open bottom bell is that the diver has someplace to go close by where he can breathe in the event of an emergency on a deep dive. Unlike a diving stage, an open bottom bell is normally lowered to the depth where the diver is actually working.

Open bottom bells are typically equipped with either a gas supply hose or a couple of large "K" size gas cylinders. They are required equipment for all deep dives.

One-Atmosphere Suits

One alternative to ambient pressure diving is the "one-atmosphere suit," which is like wearing a personal submarine. The operator inside is kept at normal surface pressure and can make extended "dives" with no decompression.

There have been a number of variations on this type of suit during the past 40 years including the JIM and WASP suits, both of which have been used by Oceaneering International, one of the world's largest diving companies. Although these suits provide superior environmental protection for the op-

The Simple Guide to Commercial Diving

The Wasp one-atmosphere diving suit allows deep dives without the need for decompression.

erator, it is more difficult to perform useful work from inside of them. The conventional commercial diver, exposed to the surrounding water pressure and temperature has better manual dexterity and can usually work faster and more efficiently.

Even though one-atmosphere suits eliminate the need for decompression, other risks remain, and there are several ways in which a person can be injured or killed while using these systems. If the suit springs a leak or the operator is trapped on the bottom, this could be fatal.

Bell/Saturation Systems

There are numerous configurations for bell/saturation systems, but every system will include at a minimum a diving bell, an entrance lock, a saturation chamber, a control van, and an environmental control system.

Diving Bell

There have been many different designs for diving bells, but almost all are either spherical or cylindrical in shape. All diving bells will also have a bottom hatch where the diver enters and exits the water. Some may also have a side hatch for connecting up to an entrance lock on a saturation system.

Like a decompression chamber, the plumbing on the inside of the bell will usually mirror the outside of the bell, and there will also be controls topside in the control van. The plumbing must provide a way to put breathing gas into the bell, vent gas out of the bell, and deliver hot water. There will also be penetrators for electrical lighting and communications, and there may be a television cable penetrator, too.

Inside the bell there will be a scrubber for removing carbon dioxide from the bell environment, and a heater that circulates hot water to help keep the divers warm. A manifold mounted in the bell allows the diver inside the bell to monitor the gas supply for the diver in the water.

The bell will always have an emergency gas supply connected to it so there is something for the divers to breathe in the event the topside supply hose is severed. An emergency power module is also considered essential. Most bells are also equipped with a block and tackle to assist the diver inside the

Commercial Diving Equipment

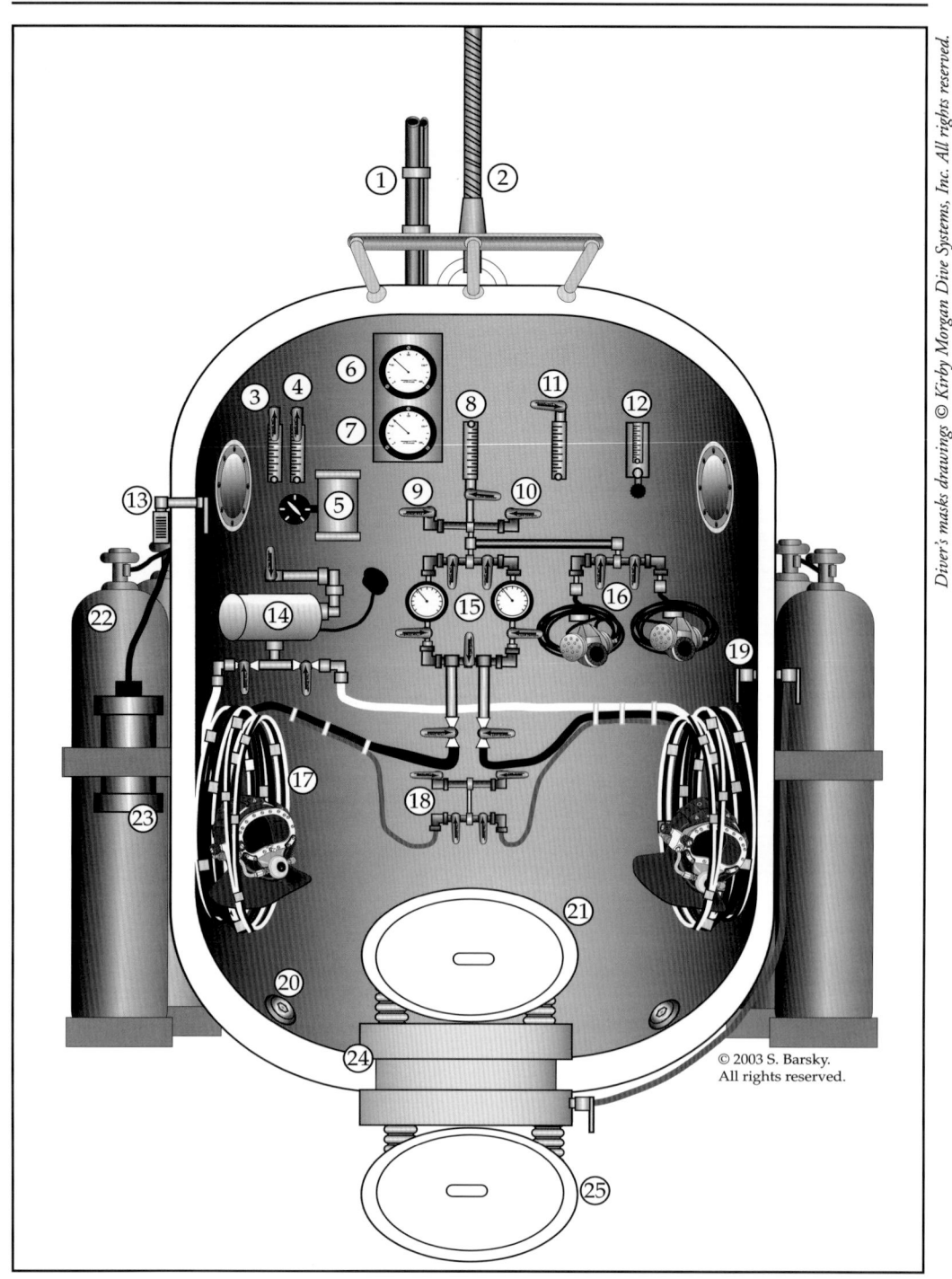

Components of a "typical" diving bell: 1) umbilical 2) main lift wire 3) topside controlled exhaust 4) topside controlled (gas) supply 5) carbon dioxide scrubber 6) external depth gauge 7) internal depth gauge 8) bell blow down 9) main gas supply control 10) emergency gas supply 11) bell controlled exhaust 12) oxygen make-up flowmeter 13) relief valve 14) bell heater 15) divers supply manifold 16) BIBs manifold 17) diver's umbilical and mask 18) pneumo supply 19) trunk equalization 20) drop weight control mechanism 21) upper hatch 22) emergency gas bottle 23) emergency power supply 24) trunk (manway) 25) bottom hatch.

bell in hauling in an unconscious partner. An electronic locating pinger should be mounted on every bell so that it can be found in the event the umbilical and lift wire are accidentally severed.

Although the "typical" diving bell is about the size of a compact car, the space inside it is usually extremely cramped by the time you add in a couple of diving hoses, two divers wearing hot water suits, and two diving helmets or masks.

In rare situations, the bell is considered the only way to evacuate divers from a ship that is about to sink. Since the bell is usually the lightest and most portable hyperbaric chamber that will connect to the sat system, it can be used for evacuating saturation divers (who still require decompression) in an emergency. Today, most diving operations are equipped with some type of "hyperbaric lifeboat" which allows the crew to quickly transfer divers out of harm's way. This is a much better option for evacuating divers in decompression from saturation.

Entrance Lock

An entrance lock may be an independent hyperbaric chamber that connects to a series of chambers, or may be part of a larger chamber in a saturation system. The purpose of the entrance lock is to provide a place for the divers to transfer back into the system following a dive while remaining under pressure.

In many situations, the entrance lock will also contain the shower and toilet for the saturation system, since this is where the divers will re-enter the chamber complex following a dive. Most entrance locks are rather small and cramped compared to the rest of the saturation system.

Saturation Chamber(s)

The chambers used in most saturation systems are much larger than those used for air diving decompression. Since divers who are in saturation may remain under pressure for a month or more at a time, there must be space for the divers to stand up, sit down to eat, and bunks for sleeping.

Most saturation diving systems have been designed to be modular, so that additional chambers can be added to the system, according to the number of divers needed to do the job. Modular designs also permit the chambers to be configured according to the available deck space on the ship or barge.

Each chamber is fitted with interior and exterior plumbing to control the atmosphere inside the system. Carbon dioxide, oxygen levels, temperature, and humidity all must be kept within acceptable limits to keep the divers comfortable and safe. A "medical lock" is also fitted on each chamber to allow items such as food and clean clothes to be passed in, and dirty dishes and soiled linen to be sent out.

Environmental Control System

Without an environmental control system, saturation diving as we know it would not be possible. The purpose of the environmental control system or unit (also referred to as an "ECU") is to control the temperature and humidity inside the chambers for the comfort and safety of the divers who are housed inside.

The temperature inside the chamber(s) must be controlled so that it is neither too hot nor too cold, and the humidity must be kept at a level that will help to reduce the possibility of fungal infections.

One of the most effective methods of controlling both the temperature and humidity is to circulate cooling and heating fluids through copper tubing underneath the floorboards in the chambers through a chamber mounted environmental control unit. By circulating the chamber atmosphere over these coils, any moisture will condense on the cold coils and the atmosphere will be warmed.

Sodasorb® is a chemical absorbent (sodium hydroxide) in granular form that is typically used to remove or "scrub" the carbon dioxide from the chamber environment. The chamber gas is passed through the scrubber and the carbon dioxide chemically reacts with the absorbent. The by-products of the reaction are heat and moisture.

Sodasorb® is an alkaline material that is

Commercial Diving Equipment

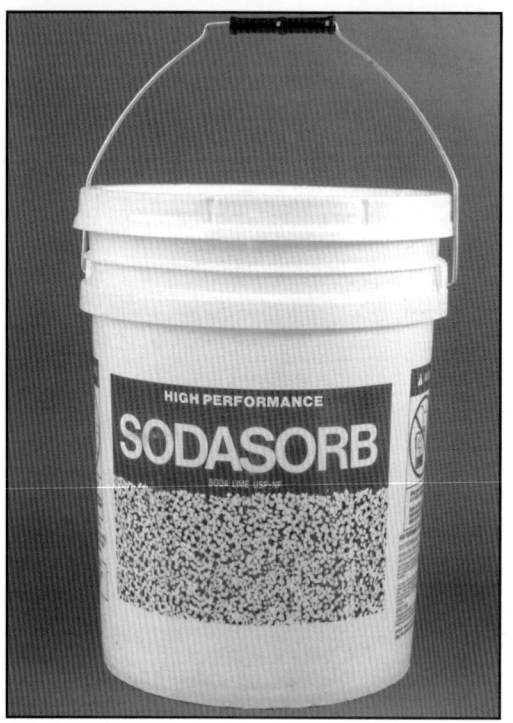

Sodasorb® is the most commonly used chemical absorbent used to remove carbon dioxide from saturation systems.

somewhat caustic in nature. You should always wear gloves, a particle mask, and eye protection whenever you handle Sodasorb®. This is the same material that is used in semi-closed and fully-closed circuit rebreathers used in recreational, scientific, and military diving.

Control Van

Every saturation system will have at least one control van where the bell and topside chamber(s) can be monitored. However, unless the installation is very small, it is much more common for there to be a separate van for running the dives and one for maintaining life support for the divers in the chamber(s) topside.

In the dive control van, there will normally be a panel or wall mounted mixed-gas manifold, as well as controls for hot water for the bell, communications, and television monitoring.

In the life support van, there will be systems for monitoring all of the chambers, including carbon dioxide and oxygen levels,

On a saturation diving job, it is the responsibility of the life support technician (or "sat tech") to take care of the divers who are living in the chambers.

and valves for controlling the depth. There will also be communications so that the life support technician can talk to the divers in the chamber(s).

Oxygen levels are normally checked using an electronic oxygen analyzer. Carbon dioxide levels are also regularly checked using an electronic analyzer, or with a hand pump and a calibrated, disposable, glass Drager gas detection tube as a back-up.

Drager tubes are filled with a chemical that changes color in response to the presence of carbon dioxide. A small quantity of the chamber gas is pumped through the tube and the degree of color change provides a measure of how much carbon dioxide is in the system and whether it is time to change out the Sodasorb® in the scrubber.

As a tender, you might be assigned to take the hourly readings for the life support system on a saturation diving job.

Bell Launch Systems

Every diving bell must have some type of handling and launch system to put the bell into the water, lower it to the proper depth, and recover it without damaging the bell or injuring the divers inside. There are many different systems in use, but all are powered by hydraulics that are usually run off a diesel engine or an electric motor.

It takes skill and teamwork to properly launch a bell and recover it. The deck crew must work together carefully because it's also possible to injure the tenders handling the bell if people aren't paying attention to what's happening.

In the early days of saturation diving, when the seas were rough, the bell became a wrecking ball and took out other deck equipment and crew members if people were careless.

On older sat systems, the umbilical for the bell was attached to the lift wire by "chain stoppers" as the bell was lowered to the bottom. Chain stoppers are short loops of chain with pelican hooks on them. The chain is wrapped around the lift wire and the pelican hooks connect to D-rings that are connected to the umbilical. The D-rings are located at

Launching and recovering a diving bell is always a team effort.

regular intervals along the length of the umbilical. Chain stoppers are connected to the lift wire and umbilical as the bell is lowered to the bottom. They are removed as the bell is brought back to the surface. Although these systems may still be in use they are much less common today.

Today, umbilicals are normally mounted on special reels that make launching and recovering the bell much safer. The bell launch system will usually have some type of motion compensation system that automatically corrects for any movement of the ship.

Dive Support Vessels

There are many purpose-built diving support vessels (ships) that are scattered throughout the world today. These are ships that have been built from the hull up specifically for diving, and have a saturation system and other surface-supplied diving gear mounted permanently on the vessel.

These vessels typically offer extended dive support for long periods of time (up to a

Commercial Diving Equipment

© Oceaneering International

month or more) on location. They will carry not only the ship's crew, but the diving crew as well.

Vessels like this are used for diving support.

True Tales of Commercial Diving from the North Sea

The Ekofisk Field was one of the first producing oilfields in the Norwegian sector of the North Sea. It featured distinctive circular concrete platforms, with holes through the walls to allow seawater to circulate through the structure. The accommodations and machinery were mounted on multiple levels high above the water.

We were diving inside the walls of the platform to inspect the "conductors," i.e., pipes that carry the oil from below the sea floor up to the platform where it can be connected to a wellhead and routed through a pipeline to shore. The water depth inside the walls was 150 FSW.

The air diving system we were using was mounted on a track inside the walls of the structure and could be pulled around to the position needed using an air tugger (air powered winch). It was a primitive system with an electrically heated decompression chamber which we would heat up between dives and then disconnect the power to reduce the danger of fire before each diver entered it.

On the second day of work, we ran out of oxygen at the diving station, but there was a rack of oxygen cylinders three flights up. Getting it down to the dive station would mean getting the assistance of the crane driver, opening hatches and maneuvering the dive platform. To me, it looked like it would take several hours to get the additional oxygen down to our level, but the dive supervisor insisted it could be done in minutes and that we could work just as safely doing air decompression. He maintained that we needed to keep the work going.

I took the position that if it would only take minutes to get the oxygen down to the dive station, then we should do it. I explained that I didn't want to compromise my safety by decompressing on air and that if someone got bent or had an accident we would need oxygen immediately. When the supervisor persisted with his position that we continue working without oxygen on hand, I refused to dive until the oxygen was brought down to the work site.

Begrudgingly, the supervisor stopped the diving and we proceeded to locate and move the oxygen. It took a lot more time than anyone thought because other equipment had to be moved to maneuver the cylinders to where they were needed and all of the hatches on the platform were not perfectly aligned. Ultimately, it took almost four hours to get the oxygen down to the dive station, which would have been way too long if we had experienced an emergency.

Steve Barsky

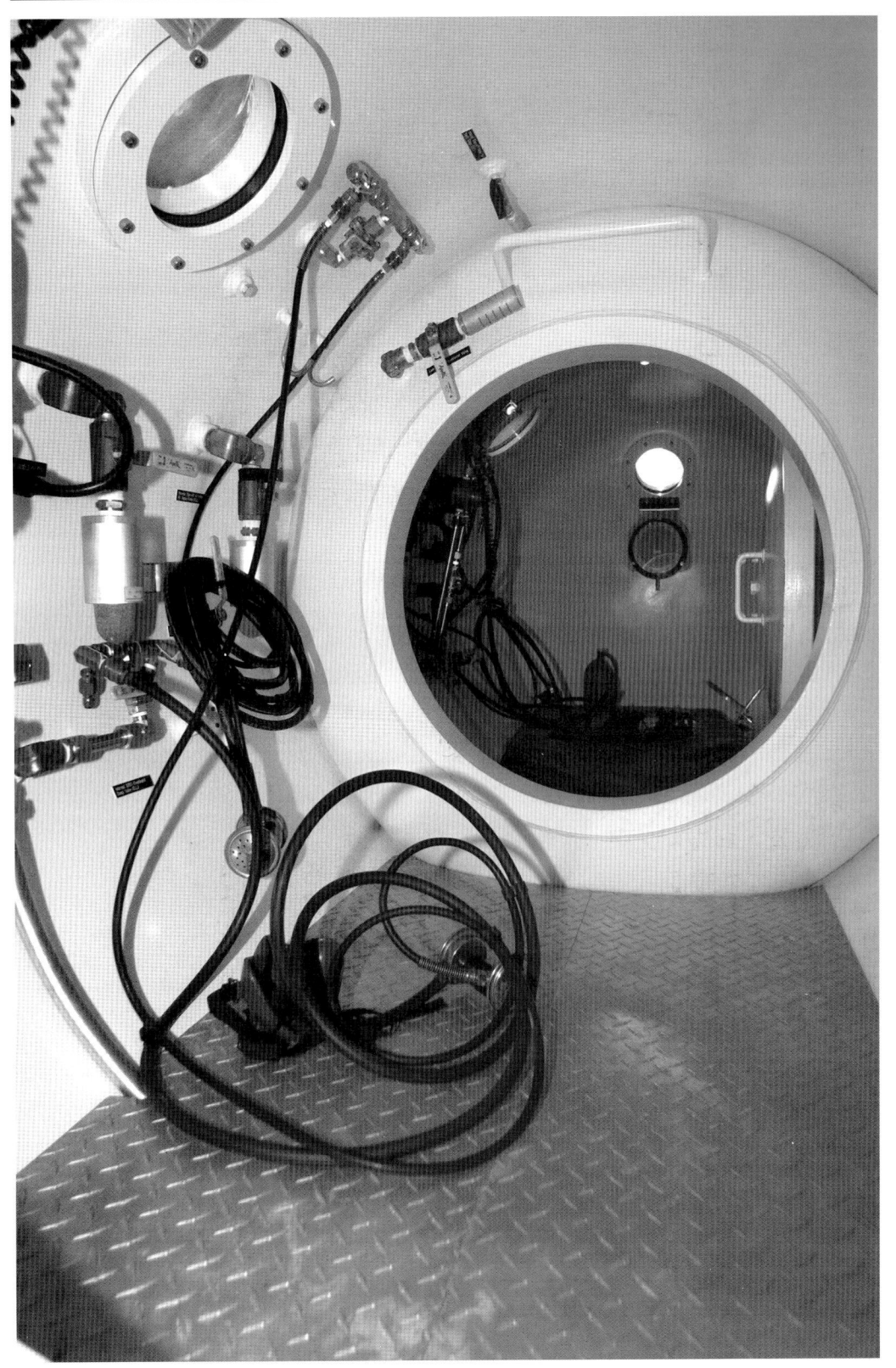

The interior of a double-lock decompression chamber does not provide many creature comforts.

© Bev Morgan. All rights reserved.

Chapter 7
Employment as a Tender

Open up another pack of tenders!

Before you complete commercial diving school, you need to consider where you want to work. Do you want to work as an "inshore diver," tackling jobs in harbors, at dams, and along coastal piers? Or, would you prefer to work as an offshore diver, working in the oil patch, hundreds of miles offshore? These are very different job environments and not everyone is suited to these distinctly different locations.

Sometimes there may not be a choice in where you work, particularly in a tight job market. In those situations, you must be willing to go where the work is located. For example, the job market in California is almost always very limited, particularly when it comes to work in the oil patch, but there is almost always work for oilfield divers in the Gulf of Mexico.

Who Do You Want to Work For?

There are advantages and disadvantages to working for both large and small diving companies, and it's important to put these in perspective when deciding where you want to work and for whom. There's no such thing as the "perfect" job and even the best companies have their problems.

Large diving companies usually have more work and the jobs they have tend to be larger and more complex. In many cases, they will take place in deeper water and require more equipment, manpower, and time. If you want to gain experience in mixed-gas diving and saturation diving, your best opportunity to do so will be with a large dive company.

As a tender, you must decide whether you want to work for a large offshore diving company or a small inland firm.

Larger commercial diving companies will also usually have regular training opportunities, good benefits packages (such as health care), stock programs, and retirement packages. Divers who work for large companies and participate in mixed-gas and saturation diving usually can make more money than divers who work for smaller dive companies who only work in shallow water.

Employment as a Tender

International travel is occasionally possible, and domestic travel is very common, when you are working for a large diving company. If you have the desire to venture beyond your home town, this may make working for a large company quite attractive.

Before you make your decision, there are a number of disadvantages of working for a large dive company that you should consider. First, in a large company, unless you are talented and have something special to offer, you may become lost in the shuffle as just another employee. These companies can be rather impersonal and often demand that people work through vacations, forgo honeymoons, and ignore personal family crises. You may find this difficult to believe, but we've seen all of these situations occur. The better the diver you are, the more demands there will be on your time, and sometimes the only way to escape is to turn your phone off. Of course, you don't want to do this too often, but there may be times when this is the only way to get some time to yourself.

Small companies may also be quite busy, depending on their location, the capabilities of their crew, and how aggressively they market themselves. However, most small dive companies are not capable of undertaking the deeper, more complex jobs, and are usually limited to relatively shallow water work. If you have no desire in becoming involved in mixed-gas or saturation diving, then a small diving company may be the right choice for you.

In a small dive company, everyone usually is expected to be capable of fulfilling any role on a particular job, and there may be more opportunities to dive. Another advantage of working for a small diving company is that on many of their jobs you may be able to go home at the end of the day, or at least for the weekend. It's also much easier to be a "star" in a small company than it is in a large one.

Probably the biggest disadvantage to working for a small diving company is that there will probably be more periods where there is little or no work, although this can occur with any diving company. Smaller companies also tend to have fewer benefit packages for their employees.

Preparing Your Resume

Your resume should start out by listing any jobs you have had during your life, with special emphasis on any jobs that used the skills that are valued by the diving industry. If you have been a welder, pipe fitter, electrician, diesel mechanic, mechanical engineer, or have other similar talents, these are the abilities that you should emphasize. A diver with a solid background in engineering can go almost anywhere he wants to work, once he has some experience under his belt.

If your jobs have only been in positions that do not directly relate to the diving industry, you should list these, with emphasis on any areas that could potentially relate to working for a diving company. For example, if you have experience in writing reports, processing digital photographs, or an extensive computer background, these are skills that are useful in almost any business.

If you have little or no work experience, and your only training beyond high school is commercial diving school, be sure to emphasize any other specialized courses you may have taken at diving school, such as Emergency Medical Technician (EMT) or non-destructive testing. Most companies value field experience over school training, but if you have gone to the trouble to take additional training this shows that you are motivated. Be sure to also list any military training you may have such as explosives, machine shop, or similar courses.

In addition to your education and work experience, your resume should list your local address and cell phone number or beeper number. Do not list your sport diving experience or recreational training on your resume.

If you have any letters of recommendation from former employers or instructors from your diving school, be sure to attach these to your resume. These can be a big help in securing a position.

Finding a Job

Unless the diving industry is going through one of its big "boom" periods, where everyone who graduates from commercial diving school gets hired, you may find it takes

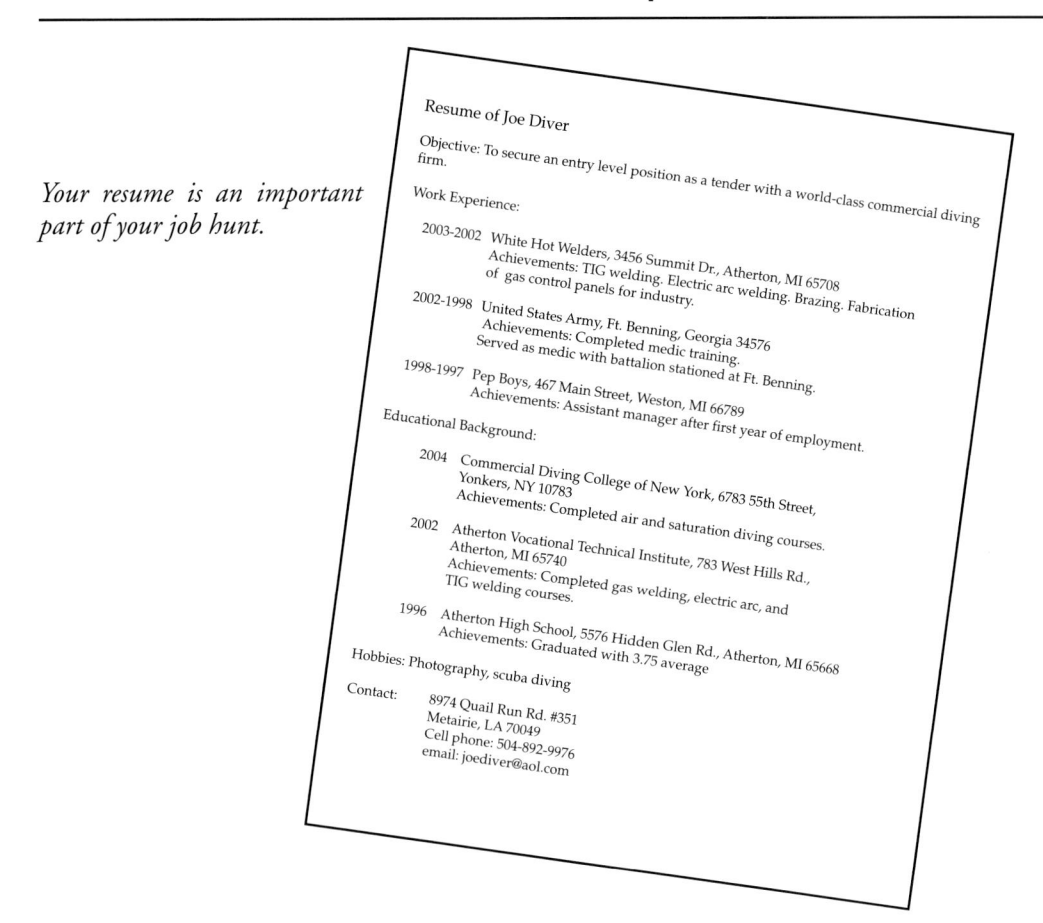

Your resume is an important part of your job hunt.

> **Resume of Joe Diver**
>
> Objective: To secure an entry level position as a tender with a world-class commercial diving firm.
>
> Work Experience:
>
> 2003-2002 White Hot Welders, 3456 Summit Dr., Atherton, MI 65708
> Achievements: TIG welding. Electric arc welding. Brazing. Fabrication of gas control panels for industry.
>
> 2002-1998 United States Army, Ft. Benning, Georgia 34576
> Achievements: Completed medic training.
> Served as medic with battalion stationed at Ft. Benning.
>
> 1998-1997 Pep Boys, 467 Main Street, Weston, MI 66789
> Achievements: Assistant manager after first year of employment.
>
> Educational Background:
>
> 2004 Commercial Diving College of New York, 6783 55th Street, Yonkers, NY 10783
> Achievements: Completed air and saturation diving courses.
>
> 2002 Atherton Vocational Technical Institute, 783 West Hills Rd., Atherton, MI 65740
> Achievements: Completed gas welding, electric arc, and TIG welding courses.
>
> 1996 Atherton High School, 5576 Hidden Glen Rd., Atherton, MI 65668
> Achievements: Graduated with 3.75 average
>
> Hobbies: Photography, scuba diving
>
> Contact:
> 8974 Quail Run Rd. #351
> Metairie, LA 70049
> Cell phone: 504-892-9976
> email: joediver@aol.com

some time to get hired as a tender. Sometimes, the larger diving companies will visit the commercial diving schools or call them to recruit new tenders, but this doesn't always happen.

When you graduate from commercial diving school you will need a couple of things to get hired. First, and foremost, you will need a sufficient bankroll to see you through your job hunt, and/or be willing to take whatever work you can get to support yourself while you hunt for a job in the diving industry. You should plan on being able to support yourself for a minimum of six months until you get hired. You will also need a reliable car to get around for your interviews and for getting to and from diving jobs once you're hired.

Another critical item that you will need during your job hunt and once you are employed is a cellular phone or a beeper. You must have a way for people to contact you because you may get hired on short notice.

You also will need to be available on a round-the-clock basis once you are hired so that you can be reached when the jobs come in, which can be any time of the day or night, and any day of the week. If you can't be reached, you won't get the work.

If there are no companies that are hiring in the area where you would like to work, you need to be prepared to go where there are jobs. In the United States, the most consistent work for divers is in the Gulf of Mexico, where there are over 3,000 offshore structures located primarily off Louisiana and Texas. The most likely cities where a new tender can find a job include New Iberia, Louisiana and Houston, Texas.

Unless they are desperate for personnel, commercial diving firms will not hire people over the phone. You must be living in the local area, with a local address, if you hope to get a job. The best time to get hired on is the spring, although diving companies will hire

Employment as a Tender

You will need a reliable vehicle while job hunting and once you are employed.

year-round, depending on their job needs.

Take the time to do a bit of research about each diving company with whom you plan to apply for a job. Almost all companies have a web site today, and you should spend some time becoming familiar with the type of work the company does, who their clients have been, and where they work.

The approach you should take is to visit every diving company for whom you hope to work to see if you can get an interview, or at least drop off your resume. When you visit the company's office, you should arrive neatly dressed in clean, casual clothes. By casual clothes we mean a nice pair of slacks (not blue jeans), a polo shirt or similar attire (no T-shirts), and a pair of well-polished shoes.

Be sure to be polite, friendly, and patient with the receptionist because this is the person who can help get you in the door. Ask the receptionist if you can make an appointment to see the operations manager, or whoever is responsible for hiring tenders, or if they have specific times that they interview new tenders. Sometimes, you will get to meet the operations manager on the spot, and you should be prepared for this possibility.

If you can't get in to see the operations manager, ask the receptionist if you can leave a resume. If you are unable to leave a resume, don't give up. You may have to go back to see a company several times before they are at a point in time where they are hiring.

Interviews

If you're persistent, you will get the chance to interview with the company for whom you would prefer to work. It's important to take the interview seriously. Don't try to be funny or entertaining.

Stress whatever skills you have beyond diving throughout the interview. Diving companies need people who can help them solve problems and can keep the job running.

A cell phone is usually the best way for employers to contact you when they need you, which may be on short notice.

You should project a confident, but not cocky, attitude. You want to convey that you are the type of person who can get the job done, that you are a team player, and that you can think creatively.

Be sure to be prepared to ask intelligent questions that show that you already know something about the company. Ask about past jobs that the company has done, and where the company wants to go in the future.

At the conclusion of the interview, if you have not been offered a job, ask for the chance to show what you can do. Explain why you want to work for this particular company and what you feel you can contribute. Thank the person who conducted the interview and follow up with a formal note that simply thanks the person for taking the time to talk to you.

Pay Rates and Work Schedules

Pay rates for people working in the diving industry vary widely according to what part of the country (or world) you're working in, the type of job you're on, and the company for whom you work. Your pay will also be contingent on the skills you bring to the job.

As a beginning tender, your wages will usually be low, certainly much better than minimum wage, but by no means will you be making a high income. Most companies pay one rate for working in the shop and a much higher rate for working offshore. When you are working offshore you are usually guaranteed a 12-hour minimum day, plus your meals and housing are provided. In the U.S. if you work more than 12 hours offshore in a single day, you will normally be paid overtime.

When you dive as a tender, you will usually be paid as a diver for that day. If you work overseas, in many cases you will be paid by the day, rather than by the hour. A good tender might make between $24,000 and $30,000 per year.

Most big jobs are divided up into two twelve-hour shifts, with a day crew and a night crew. However, on some jobs, the schedule may be very erratic, with the diving taking place when the construction crew needs it, at any hour of the day or night.

If you're working on a big job, you will normally be working seven days a week, twelve hours a day, until the job is complete. If the job has been scheduled to go on for many months, there will usually be a crew rotation, with most people working 30 days offshore with 10 days of leave. During busy periods, you may have the opportunity, or be expected to work more than 30 days at a stretch. It's not uncommon for divers working in remote locations to work 90 consecutive days offshore before taking a break.

Once you become a diver, your pay will normally increase substantially, although to make a lot of money, you have to spend a good deal of time offshore and make a lot of dives. Most companies pay divers depth pay when they dive, in addition to their daily rate. Depth pay is normally paid by the foot of depth, although some companies do not start depth pay until the diver descends below 50 feet.

Depth pay usually works on a sliding scale, and the deeper you dive the more money you make. For example, depth footage might be calculated as follows:

0-50 FSW	$0.00
50-100 FSW	$1.00/foot
100-150 FSW	$2.00/foot
150-200 FSW	$3.00/foot

For a 165-foot dive, you would earn $195.00 for the dive, plus your day rate, plus any overtime, in this example.

Some companies pay what is known as "pressure pay" for each hour a diver is in saturation, in addition to their hourly rate or day rate. In addition, this pressure pay may vary according to the depth of the dive; i.e., below 500 FSW the company pays a higher rate than for dives shallower than 500 FSW.

Divers with more skills, or supervisors who are in demand, can usually negotiate pay rates that are outside of the company's normal pay policies. Once you are at this level you will have more of a choice about which jobs you go on.

When you're hired be sure to ask for a copy of the company's written pay policy.

Employment as a Tender

On the Job

Once you've been hired by a diving company, your initial work will probably involve spending some time in their shop helping to prepare gear for upcoming jobs and cleaning and repairing gear that has been returned from jobs. There are several important things that you can do that will help to get you out in the field quickly.

Always arrive early for work and be prepared to stay late. You don't want to be the type of person who shows up at the last minute for work and leaves the minute the clock strikes five. You want to have the reputation as a person who does whatever it takes to ensure that the job gets done. This is appreciated on all jobs, but it's a trait that is especially appreciated in the diving industry.

Diving companies typically get two types of jobs, i.e., those that are scheduled projects, such as construction or inspection, and those that involve emergency repairs or inspection of some type of underwater structure. However, no matter what type of job is about to get underway, all of these projects will be mobilized with equipment out of the company shop or storage yard.

In larger diving companies, there is almost always some work going on at the shop, whether it is fabrication of new equipment, repairing an umbilical, or repainting a compressor. Tenders are expected to put in their time in the shop, although typically this work pays less than time spent offshore. Since all of the jobs are mobilized out of the shop, the more time you spend in the shop, the more likely you are to be selected to go out on the jobs that come in unexpectedly. Ultimately, your promotion from tender to diver is usually at least partly dependent on the amount of time you have spent offshore, so it's important to get as much time as you can in the offshore environment.

Probably the most important skill you must develop is to learn how to get along with everyone on the job. There may be people in the company who you personally dislike and would not socialize with voluntarily, but you must find a way to overlook any annoying traits they may have and figure out something to like about them. The better you get along with other people, and the more of a team

Your ability to get along well with other people will play a major factor in your success in the diving industry, and throughout your life.

player you are, the more successful you will be as a diver. Go out of your way to help other people and you will find yourself being recruited to go on every available job.

People who don't fit in and aren't accepted by the rest of the crew will quickly be run off by the supervisor. There have been plenty of people who were probably perfectly competent divers, who have been booted off jobs because they just weren't "one of the gang."

Hand-in-hand with getting along with the other divers in your company goes the old adage your mother told you that if you don't have anything nice to say, don't say anything at all. Be sure to avoid making negative comments about other divers, even if they have been uncooperative on the job. Treat everyone on the job with respect, just the way you would like to be treated. Everyone in the company must like you and trust you for you to be as successful as possible.

Don't Gripe

It's common for tenders, and even divers, to gripe about the poor pay they are receiving for the work they are doing. The best way to earn more money is to demonstrate a willingness to do more work than anyone else on the job, no matter what you are being paid. This is usually the best way to advance in any company, but is especially appreciated in the diving field.

Always try to keep busy, even if there is no "work" at the moment. In some parts of the world, where divers are stationed on construction barges, there may be extended periods of downtime, while the crew is offshore, but there is no diving going on. During these intervals, you must look for things to do to demonstrate that you want to contribute to the company. Paint things, fix things, build things, and look around for what needs to be done and do it without being asked.

Look for the dirtiest, nastiest tasks that need to be done, that nobody else wants to do, and jump in and do them before anyone else gets to them. For example, on a saturation diving system, one of the most disgusting jobs to be done is to clean out the entrance lock after a long saturation dive. Since the en-

Always look for the dirtiest jobs and do them with a smile on your face.

trance lock is where the divers shower and use the toilet, the bilge under the floorboards is usually covered with a foul smelling slime that nobody wants to clean. Do this job a couple of times, without complaining about it, and you will soon have the reputation as the type of person who everyone wants along on their crew, because you can be counted on as a dependable, agreeable person.

Nobody wants to be trapped on a barge for 60 or 90 days with someone who is disagreeable and always complaining. It's bad enough to be offshore when you're missing a holiday, your significant other, or spouse. How well you get along with others will be a major part of your success as a commercial diver.

Always Be Available for Work

If you are a good diver, the more available you make yourself, the more you will work. Diving company management gets very upset with divers who don't make themselves accessible. Don't turn off your cell phone or screen your calls unless you've just gotten back from

75

Employment as a Tender

90 days offshore and need a couple of days to take care of personal business. You never know, you might miss the biggest job of the year if you don't answer the phone.

Developing Your Confidence and Attitude

As a tender, you must begin to develop the confidence and attitude that you can accomplish *anything* underwater. This is another important key to success as a diver. This doesn't mean that you must do stupid things or take chances that you know are foolish. You must be confident enough in your own abilities that you will succeed in any job you undertake. The words "I can't" are not something that is normally part of the vocabulary of a successful commercial diver.

It is this attitude that you must develop and maintain, starting when you are a tender, that will help to define your abilities as a diver. Part of this attitude is that you must learn to think "outside of the box," to find new and creative ways to succeed where others fail. If you doubt that you can do the job, you probably won't be able to do it.

Crew Sizes and Assignments

Depending on the size and location of the company you work for, you may be sent out on jobs that have no more than a three-man crew working from a tug or supply ship, to a 24-man crew working aboard a 400-foot long barge. The three-man crew is the smallest team size recommended by the Association of Diving Contractors International (ADCI).

Shallow water air diving jobs (down to 60 FSW) are usually where you will find yourself working as part of a three-man crew, provided the job is not too extensive. In this situation you will be running the diver's air control panel, operating the communications box, and tending the hose. If the diver has confidence in you, and he has used up all of his bottom time, you may even get to dive.

On a deep air diving job (60-200 FSW) there is less chance of getting in the water as a tender, but it does happen. On this type of job, you will usually find yourself spending more time tending and running the decompression chamber. The same thing is true on a mixed-gas diving job, although there may be some opportunities to make some of the shallower dives that don't pay as well.

On a saturation diving job, unless there is surface-supplied air diving going on simultaneously, there may not be much opportunity to dive. Your chores as a tender will be to support the saturation divers in every way possible. In addition to launching the bell, lowering tools, and maintaining the machinery, you may find yourself assigned to assist the life support technician.

Sometimes there will be a break in the saturation diving in the middle of a job and the team will shift to air diving for a few hours or even days. In these circumstances, if there are not many divers on the job, you may find yourself a part of the regular diving rotation.

No matter what tasks you are assigned, even if they are not the ones you enjoy the most, you must look at them as an opportunity to learn, even if it involves skills with which you are unfamiliar.

Tender's Responsibilities at the Start of a Job

Tenders have many responsibilities on commercial diving jobs, ranging from keeping machinery fueled and operating to preparing gear and tools to be used by divers. If you want to spend the least amount of time being a tender, you must learn to think like a diver. The sooner you begin to act like a diver and develop the right attitude and work habits, the sooner you will find yourself promoted to being a diver.

At the start of any job, the tenders will be involved in:
- Loading the equipment for the job onto the trucks that will transport the gear out to the work site.
- Loading gear aboard the ship or barge.
- Fastening equipment down to the deck of the ship.
- Running the hoses to connect the compressor to the dive station and decompression chamber.
- Testing the equipment once it is installed to make sure everything is functioning properly.

The Simple Guide to Commercial Diving

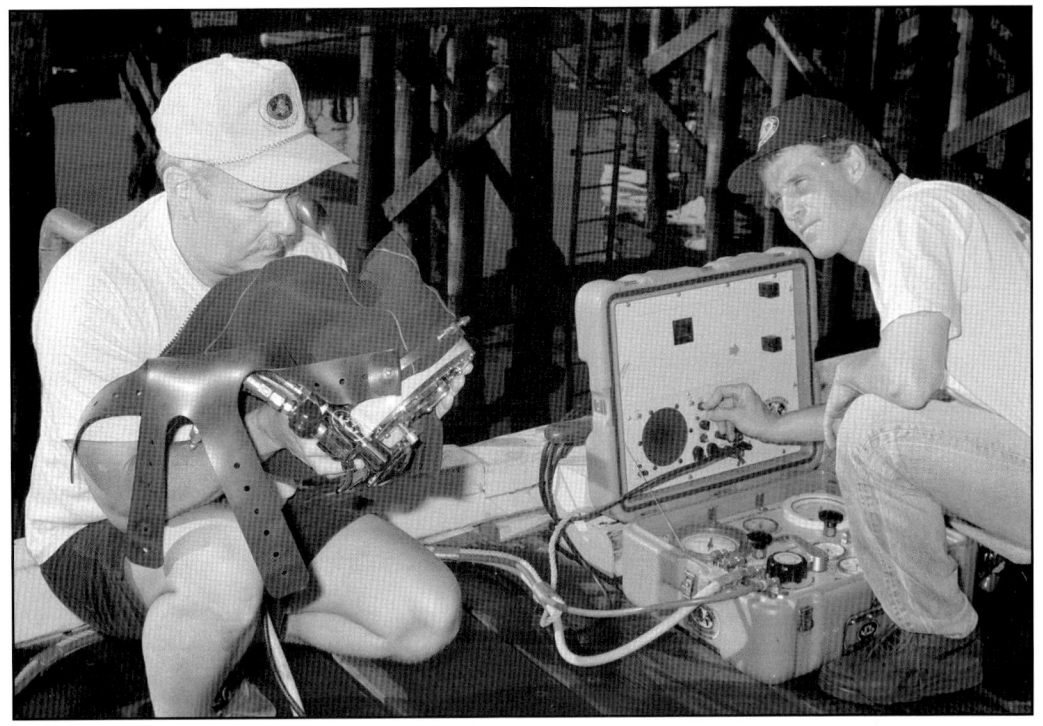

As a tender, it's your job to help set up the diving equipment and make sure everything is working properly.

You may be asked to perform other duties as well, and you should look for things that need to be done without waiting for instructions.

Dressing and Tending the Diver

As a tender, you need to find out the preferences of each diver on the job, and how to prepare the gear they will be using to satisfy their needs. If a particular diver wants some extra manila line attached to his hose for use in rigging underwater, you should see that the line is prepared and ready so that the diver does not need to ask for this each time he enters the water.

Each diver will want his gear set up in a particular way and may want more or less assistance in getting dressed in. Almost everyone will want you to connect their helmet to the hose, to connect the bail-out to the helmet, and to apply dishwashing soap to the inside of the lens on the mask or helmet. Find out what each diver wants and be sure their gear is prepped when it is their turn to dive.

Most divers will want you to hold their bail-out bottle and harness while they slip into it, and they will hold their mask or helmet while you connect the snap shackle on the hose to the D-ring on their harness. You'll also find the majority of divers will don their helmet or mask by themselves, although if they are wearing a band mask they may need you to fasten the spider (head harness that holds the mask on their head).

Some divers may want their gloves taped on with a bit of duct tape and you should have a roll at the dive station for this purpose. Be sure to leave a tail of tape sticking up and fasten the sticky side back against at least an inch of the sticky side so there is something to grab onto when it's time to remove the tape. Without this tail it will be difficult to remove the tape quickly when the diver surfaces at the end of his dive.

While the divers are in the water, tenders are expected to keep a firm grip on their diver's hose and pay out slack or pull the hose in as the diver requests. Never leave the diver's hose unattended for even a moment! The tender must be constantly vigilant for anything on the surface that might pose a threat to the

Employment as a Tender

Tenders must be alert to everything that is going on in the area where the work is taking place. They must keep watch for anything that could pose a hazard to the diver.

diver, such as a ship passing through the dive site, or a heavy load being lifted overhead by a crane. Notify the diving supervisor immediately if you see anything that you think might be a threat to the diver's safety.

You will also need to lower tools to the diver and recover them. However, you can't just throw these items over the side. Think about how you would want them rigged if you were making the dive and set them up that way.

Tools will normally be lowered using a messenger line connected to the down line with a running shackle. When you lower tools to the diver, turn the shackle so the pin does not rub against the down line and unscrew itself. Feed the messenger line out at an angle at least six to ten feet away from the down line so that the messenger line can't spiral around the down line and wrap itself up, preventing you from lowering the tools.

If the diver is working at a relatively shallow depth, you may need to pull the down line up and down to get any items you are sending to the diver to slide down to him. Sometimes it's just not possible to get items all the way to the bottom, especially if the boat is a long way from the dive site, and the diver may need to come part way up the down line to get the tools.

A really good tender can sometimes tell exactly what the diver is doing just by the feel of the hose. Periodically, you should come up on the diver's hose until you can just feel him and then slack off the hose a few feet. Never put any hose in the water unless the diver asks for it.

Other Tasks for Tenders

During the quiet hours on a job, tenders are expected to keep themselves busy without asking what needs to be done. This may include such jobs as painting the equipment on deck (if the system has been installed on a barge that may remain at sea for months or years), changing oil and filters in the running machinery, fabricating tools and other equipment that will make the job run smoother or more efficiently. For example, on some decompression chambers there might be no bracket to hold an oxygen analyzer for monitoring the chamber environment. A thoughtful tender would recognize this and build a bracket (from scrap steel aboard the ship) to hold the analyzer to prevent it from flying off the top of the chamber and being damaged when conditions are rough at sea.

On a saturation system, the tenders will be responsible for securing the diver's meals from the galley of the ship, launching and recovering the bell, and assisting in any way that is needed to help keep the job moving forward.

Setting Up and Running an Underwater Cutting System

Most underwater cutting is done with a special torch fitted with a tubular steel electrode through which oxygen flows to make the cut. The complete set-up includes the following:
- A topside DC welding machine
- A "knife-switch"
- Oxygen cylinders
- A cable for the torch with an oxygen

The Simple Guide to Commercial Diving

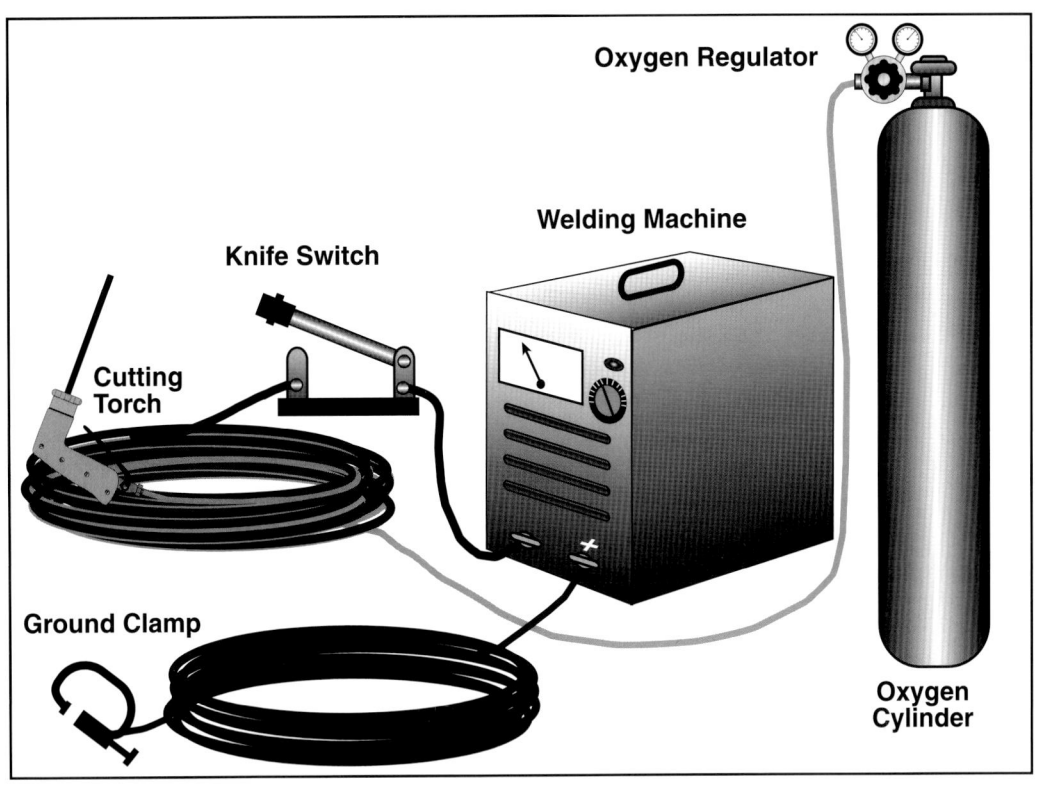

A typical system for underwater cutting includes the components shown here.

hose connected to it
- A cable with a ground clamp on the end
- Cutting torch with flash arrestor, rubber washer, and collet
- A supply of cutting rods

A schematic of the proper set-up for underwater burning is shown above. The ground clamp, which is attached to the work, is attached to the positive terminal on the welding machine, while the torch is connected to the negative terminal. This arrangement is known as straight polarity, electrode negative.

The most popular rods for cutting underwater have a hollow tubular design filled with a combination of thin mild steel rods and special alloy rods. The special alloy will burn once ignited whether electricity is supplied or not, providing there is sufficient oxygen. These types of rods will not only burn steel, but also will cut through non-ferrous materials such as brass or even rocks.

Personal equipment the diver will need to take with him includes the following:

- Insulated rubber gloves
- A quiver to hold the rods

You want a quiver that can be closed and opened with one hand, and that drains water when you bring it to the surface.

- A scraper and wire brush to clean the site for the ground and where you will cut.
- A welding lens for your mask or helmet to protect your eyes. A lens that can be flipped up and down works best.
- Insulated rubber gloves without seams (not wetsuit gloves!) Nitrile gloves or any dry glove used with a dry suit work well.
- A four-pound hammer
- A set of pliers to remove rods that are stuck in the torch
- Extra collet and washer
- "Hanger" checker to make sure you've cut completely through (a hacksaw blade on a lanyard or a thin bladed knife work well).

Before the diver enters the water, you should always double check the polarity of the welding set-up to ensure that everything

Employment as a Tender

Be sure to respond to the diver each time he calls for you to "Make it hot!" or "Make it cold!"

is working properly. Before you perform this test, be sure to don a pair of rubber insulated gloves.

With the welding machine on, and the knife switch open, take the ground clamp and the tip of a rod in the torch and submerge them in a bucket of water so they are an inch or two apart, but NOT touching. Close the knife switch and bubbles should form on the surface of the rod indicating the correct polarity.

If you are running the dive on a three man operation, you will need to operate the knife switch for the diver. Be sure that you are working in a dry location and that you are wearing your steel-toed boots which should also have an insulated sole.

Take special care whenever you are operating the knife switch. It's always a good idea to wear gloves when you are operating this device to help protect you from electrical shock.

It's not uncommon for a knife switch to arc whenever the connection is made or broken. The flash of light from the switch is just as damaging to your vision as a welder's arc. Never stare at the switch when you make or break the connection.

Whenever the diver needs to make a cut, you will need to close the switch, at which time he will tell you to, "Make it hot!" Whenever the diver requests this, close the switch firmly and tell the diver, "It's hot." When the diver has finished his cut or used up the rod in the torch he will tell you to, "Make it cold." Once you have opened the switch, tell the diver, "It's cold."

You will also be controlling the regulator for the oxygen supply to the torch. Make sure that the supply pressure is correct for the water depth you are working in, according to the manufacturer's recommendations for their torch and rods. Generally speaking, most burning rods today require lots of oxygen to burn effectively, so keep an eye on the regulator and be sure to maintain the correct pressure to the torch as the pressure in the gas cylinder drops.

Running the Decompression Chamber

Running the decompression chamber is another important responsibility that normally will fall to the tenders. If you are not familiar with the decompression chamber being used on the job, get someone to show you its peculiarities or spend some time operating it before you have to run it with anyone inside so you understand its operation. Most chambers are quite simple and if you've spent any time running one of them, you should be able to adapt quickly to a different chamber.

Before the diver gets in the water, check to

make sure that the chamber is set up properly and everything is working correctly. Check to be sure that the compressor that is connected to the chamber is not the same one that will supply the diver in the water, otherwise you will "starve" the diver in the water for air when you open the supply valve on the chamber. Check the operation of the chamber itself, be sure that there is enough oxygen on hand, and test the communications. Be sure that there is a jug of cold water in the chamber for the diver to drink, as well as a bottle for the diver to urinate in, and that both are clearly marked.

If the divers are performing surface decompression on oxygen (sur-d-O_2), it will be up to you to get the divers into the chamber quickly and back down to depth to complete their decompression. The procedure for sur-d-O_2 is very straightforward.

At the end of his bottom time, the diver ascends to the first decompression stop, which may be deeper than 40 FSW. He completes all of his water stops up to and including a 30 foot stop. In most cases, the water stops will be performed with the diver breathing an oxygen enriched air mixture (nitrox).

The diver then surfaces and within five minutes from leaving his last water stop, must re-enter the chamber and return to 40 FSW on oxygen, where he continues to breathe pure oxygen (with "breaks" breathing chamber air) and completes the balance of his decompression.

When the diver hits the deck, he will remove his mask or helmet, and bail-out bottle and harness. The tender will then accompany him to the chamber.

Normally, with a double lock chamber, the inner lock will be pressurized to a depth of about 70 FSW and the outer lock will be open. The diver will enter the outer lock and close the door. The diver will then open the cross-over valve and equalize the pressure between the inner and outer locks. While the chamber is blowing down to depth, the diver will remove any remaining equipment.

Once the inner hatch is open, the diver closes the cross-over valve and climbs into the inner lock, leaving any remaining wet gear in the outer lock as the tender brings the outer lock back to the surface. As soon as the diver enters the inner lock he puts on an oral-nasal mask, known as a BIBS (Built-In Breathing System) mask and starts breathing pure oxygen.

In the early days of diving, many divers would take a lit cigarette with them into the chamber and smoke it in the outer lock while they were removing their suits. This is an extremely dangerous practice and has lead to fires and serious injuries. If the diver you are working with wants to do this, you must tactfully but forcefully find a way to prevent this.

Surface decompression on oxygen is a commonly used procedure in the commercial field, and greatly reduces the amount of time the diver must spend in the water decompressing while increasing safety. It's much better to decompress in a chamber on oxygen where the environment is comfortable and secure, and the depth can be controlled precisely, rather than in the water.

When you are running the chamber, you

Every tender must be proficient in operating decompression chambers.

must pay careful attention to what you are doing. You should have a clipboard with the diver's decompression schedule, as supplied by the diving supervisor. You must also have a pen and a stopwatch for keeping track of the time. Your watch should be synchronized with the dive supervisor's watch.

Have another tender double check your time schedule if the supervisor will permit this. The diver doesn't get a second chance to get a correct decompression schedule if you make a mistake. Most companies today will automatically treat a diver for decompression sickness if the schedule has been compromised, even if no symptoms are present. This is a very expensive mistake.

Your main chores while the diver is in the chamber will be to keep track of the time and notify the diver when he is supposed to take air breaks. You will also need to vent the chamber regularly, normally two out of every five minutes, to keep the oxygen level in the chamber low. There should be an oxygen analyzer connected to the chamber, if possible, to monitor the oxygen level inside to be sure it does not get too high.

When you vent the chamber, you will be opening the exhaust and supply valves simultaneously. Watch the depth carefully and strive to maintain the depth within one foot of where it is supposed to be at any given time. You want to keep the depths and times as accurately as possible.

Make sure that the diver does not go to sleep while he is in the chamber. Although he may become annoyed with you for bothering him, it is important that he remain awake throughout his decompression. A sleeping diver can partially dislodge his mask, which would prevent him from getting pure oxygen and raise the oxygen level in the chamber to unacceptable levels. If the diver sleeps on his arm or in an unusual position, he may cut off his circulation, which would increase his chances of suffering from decompression sickness. Sleep may also hide symptoms of decompression sickness, such as a loss of vision, when the diver is not awake to experience them.

Be sure to keep the diver informed of what you are doing so that he isn't unduly startled when you vent the chamber or begin an ascent. Tell the diver at least 15 seconds before you initiate any action that affects the chamber environment.

Never leave the chamber unattended. If you need to go to the bathroom, you're hungry, or have some other personal needs, get another crew member to cover for you while you take care of these issues. If you turn the chamber over to another crew member, be sure your watches are synchronized so that the clock times accurately reflect what took place. The run time for each stop should be regulated with a stop watch.

When you bring the chamber up to the surface, be sure to add a little air from time to time to help reduce the condensation inside the chamber so you can see the diver and to maintain a comfortable temperature. If you find the chamber is coming up too quickly, stop the ascent until the chamber is at the proper depth for the elapsed time. If the chamber is ascending too slowly, do not speed up the ascent to make up the time; just adjust the rate so the balance of the ascent is at the correct rate.

On some jobs there may be only one compressor used to supply both the decompression chamber and the diver in the water. This is not a good situation and should be avoided whenever possible. When there is only one chamber, it's not a good idea to put another diver in the water until the previous diver has completed his decompression in the chamber, or at least is on his final ascent. It's better to wait for the diver to clear the chamber and blow it back down to depth before starting the next dive.

Divers should undergo a rapid field-neurological exam at the completion of decompression to check to see if they have any symptoms of decompression sickness. You should know how to administer this exam and record your findings along with the decompression or dive log. See the appendix at the end of the book for directions on how to perform this exam.

Treating a Diver with Decompression Sickness

Even when everything has been done properly, divers still occasionally get decompression sickness, and it may be your responsibility as a tender to handle the treatment. Running the chamber for a diver experiencing decompression sickness is not much different than running the chamber for regular decompression, but it takes considerably more time.

As a tender, the decision to treat a diver for decompression sickness and which treatment table to use should not fall to you, but in certain circumstances this may be unavoidable. Whenever possible, you should attempt to get direction from company management as to how they want the case handled. Treatment decisions are basically medical decisions and unless you are a doctor, this will usually be outside your area of expertise.

In some cases, however, you will be in locations where it may be difficult to establish communications with management on shore, or the diver's symptoms may be so serious that treatment cannot be delayed. In these circumstances, the old saying, "When in doubt, recompress," applies. If the diver gets relief at depth, there will be little doubt that he is suffering from decompression sickness.

If you are on a job where a diver is suffering from decompression sickness, someone should accompany the diver into the chamber. This is important, in case the diver is suffering from, or develops, serious symptoms. As a tender, you may be the person assigned to accompany the diver during the treatment.

During the treatment, be sure to note any changes in the diver's symptoms and write them down, as well as the time when they occurred. Follow the treatment schedule exactly and do not alter it unless given specific directions from someone in a position of authority to do so. In most cases, if the treatment tables are altered, they are extended to deal with a diver who is not responding to the treatment.

Since most treatments are long, you must take particular care to ensure that the diver does not fall asleep during the treatment.

Diving as a Tender

While you are a tender you will undoubtedly be given the opportunity to make some dives, most of which will be dives in shallow water or dives that the other divers on the job have no desire to make. For example, author Steve Barsky's first commercial dive was inside the harbor in Peterhead, Scotland, to set up and test some equipment designed to strip paint off a pipe underwater. Steve got the dive because the water was shallow and the dive had to be made in a wetsuit rather than a hot water suit, conditions which made the dive unattractive to the divers on the job to which he was assigned.

When you are a tender, each dive you make will be carefully evaluated by the divers and supervisors on the job. Although most people make mistakes and rarely do well on their first one or two dives, you must be able to start producing on your early dives if you hope to be promoted to diver.

Packing Up the Job

At the conclusion of a diving job, the tenders will usually be expected to assist with the demobilization of the job, including inventorying the spares and hardware, disassembling the system, packing the gear up for shipment, and assisting with unpacking the gear when it returns to the shop. Don't run off at the first opportunity. Stay on the job until the supervisor departs or you are instructed to leave. Demonstrate that you are a motivated and eager employee.

Tools for Tenders

As a tender, you will need a certain number of tools and personal items to assist you in doing your job. Although you can get by without all of these items, having them available will make it easier for you to do your job. These items are as follows:

• Car or truck

Just as you need a car to go on your job hunt, you will need some form of personal transportation for getting to and from the dock or airport where you depart for your jobs. Your car must be reliable, but you may not want to leave a shiny, new car at some of the docks from which many dive jobs de-

Employment as a Tender

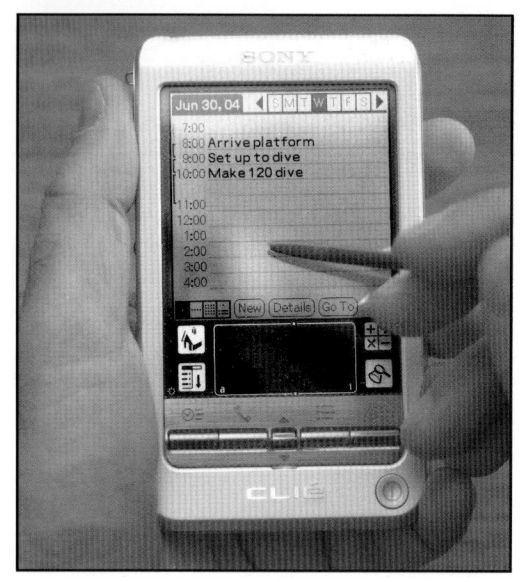

You need some method of keeping track of your time offshore, making notes, and recording addresses and contacts. A Personal Digital Assistant is a good way to do this.

part. A motorcycle is usually not the greatest form of transportation, especially if you have to carry any significant amount of gear, or if you're based in a location like Louisiana where it frequently rains heavily.

• Cell phone or beeper

Every diving company will expect its divers to be available at a moment's notice and to maintain either a cell phone or beeper. Of the two, a cell phone is probably the better choice.

• PDA or daily planner

You will need a personal digital assistant (PDA) or a printed daily planner. This item has multiple purposes, but the two most important will be to allow you to keep a record of the hours you have worked and dives you have made for pay purposes, and to provide a reminder for tasks and contacts that you may want to follow up with on the job. For example, you might use a PDA to remind you when the oil needs to be changed on a compressor, to keep notes about the people you've met so you remember their personal details, or for other similar tasks.

• Steel-toed boots

A pair of steel-toed boots is one of the most important safety items you can own when working on a commercial diving job. You want to prevent injuries to your feet and good steel-toed boots are invaluable for this purpose.

Steel-toed boots used for working topside should be a slip-on design, so that you can kick your boots off easily in the event you fall in the water, and so they are easy to remove when you are entering the accommodations of a ship or barge (so you don't track grease inside). The soles should be non-skid, provide excellent traction and be chemically resistant. An elevated heel is recommended for safety and comfort.

• Hard hat

Most companies will require you to wear a hard hat to avoid head injury on the job. This is especially important when you are working on a ship or barge underneath an offshore oil platform or in similar environments.

• Knife

A good knife is absolutely essential for working with fiber and synthetic lines. You will be constantly cutting lines and you need to be able to do this quickly and easily.

You need a knife that's large enough to cut through heavy lines, so a small pocket knife is

Steel-toed boots will help to protect your feet in the industrial environment of commercial diving.

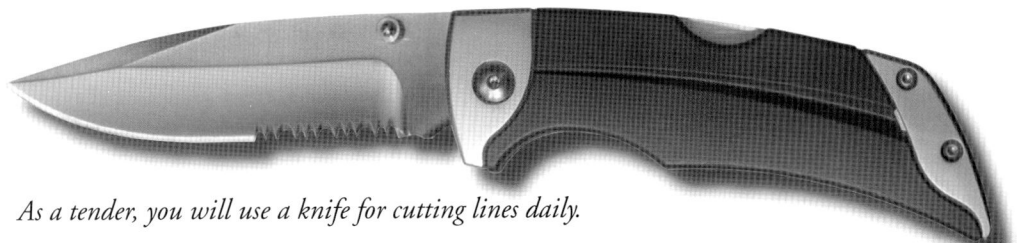

As a tender, you will use a knife for cutting lines daily.

Courtesy of Gerber Knives

not usually adequate. For most applications, a good size folding knife with a 3-5 inch blade works well. Combination tools like a Leatherman® that combine a knife blade, pliers, and screwdriver also work well.

Hard as it may be to believe, some companies today do not allow their personnel to carry knives. The company for whom you work will spell out their policy for you when you are hired.

• Watch

You need a highly accurate and rugged wrist watch with alarms.

• Electrical tape

Always carry a roll of waterproof electrical tape. It's handy for many things, but especially for "whipping" the end of a line so it does not come unlaid.

• Crescent (Adjustable) Wrench

Although adjustable wrenches are not the best tools for working on brass fittings, there's no substitute to having an adjustable wrench in your back pocket so that you can instantly tighten a fitting without having to go search for the proper size wrench. Certainly, if you are going to perform serious repairs you'll need to go hunt down the right tools, but on a commercial job a small crescent wrench is usually invaluable. Savvy tenders weld a gas-bottle key to their wrenches, and attach a braided lanyard to the wrench with a brass snap hook to fasten the wrench to a belt loop. They keep the wrench in their back pocket so that it's always available.

• Gas Bottle Wrench

Most tenders will carry a small cylinder wrench with them that is used for opening large high-pressure cylinders, i.e., "K" bottles.

• Foul Weather Gear

No matter where you work in the world, you will almost invariably need a set of foul weather gear for working in the rain. Look for a rugged set that doesn't cost too much. This type of apparel can usually be found in a store that supplies commercial fishermen.

• Work Vest

Most clients will require everyone working on the deck to wear a marine "work vest" (life jacket). These vests are usually compact enough not to get in your way and will help to protect your safety anytime you are working around the water.

• Gloves

As a tender, you'll always want to keep a set of work gloves in your back pocket, if you're not already wearing them.

• Wetsuit or Dry Suit

If you get the opportunity to dive while you are a tender, you can probably borrow a helmet from one of the divers, if your company does not provide them, but you will definitely need your own suit for a proper fit.

• Credit card

As a tender you will undoubtedly find yourself traveling from your local area, at least out of state, and if you work for a large company, possibly internationally. Under these circumstances, you will need a credit card for booking hotel rooms, meals, flights, and other necessities of travel.

Even if your company books your hotel rooms and flights, you will still need a credit card for those times when you are stranded between flights, your clothes are lost, or you have other emergencies. There may even be times when you will need to buy parts or supplies (for which the company will reimburse you) to help keep the job going.

• Duffle bag

As a diver traveling across the U.S., you'll need a heavy duty, soft-sided duffle bag for transporting your clothes. Hard suitcases do not work well aboard ships or when travel-

Employment as a Tender

As a tender, you will get the opportunity to make dives in shallow water.

ing by helicopter. Look for a bag that is made from waterproof material.

• Small Tool Box

In most cases, the company you work for will provide the hand tools you will need for the job. However, it doesn't hurt to carry a few tools with you for those times when something is missing. Besides the already mentioned adjustable wrench, screwdrivers, pliers (or sidecutters), and similar tools are always useful to have on hand.

• Briefcase/Laptop Case

You'll probably want a briefcase or laptop computer case for carrying your paperwork, plane tickets, passport, PDA or laptop computer, reading materials, and other essential documents.

You will need all of the previously mentioned items and more to travel comfortably and work properly as a tender, especially if you work offshore and travel out-of-state or overseas.

Breaking Out

Once you begin to get the opportunity to dive, if you do well, the chances will increase in their frequency. When this happens, you will know you are doing well and are on your way towards becoming a diver.

It's crucial to keep in mind that your safety is of the utmost importance at all times and you must never compromise on this principle. In some circumstances, people will ask you to make dives that are dangerous and you must use your best judgment to know when it's appropriate to turn down a dive. If you think the situation is bad, talk it over with some of the other people on the job whom you respect and get their opinions. In most cases, when one person speaks up and says they think a situation is not good for diving, chances are that other people will then feel comfortable in voicing the same feelings, but it takes a courageous person to speak up first.

Fear is a natural thing in diving, and it's the person who does not admit to fear who is usually the most dangerous person on the job. We've never seen anyone laugh when somebody said they were afraid or thought a particular dive was too dangerous.

Once you gain some diving experience, many companies have an intermediate position they call "diver-tender," that pays more than being a tender, but not quite as much as being a diver. It usually takes at least six months to a year to get promoted to this level.

Your goal when you dive is to do each job underwater as quickly as you can, without making any mistakes. Your reputation as a diver will be based upon your ability to get the job done quickly and accurately. The faster you are and the greater the number of dives you complete successfully, the better your reputation will be.

It takes most people anywhere from a year to several years to "break out" or be promoted to the status of being a diver. If you're not prepared to put in this amount of time to become a diver, then this may not be the right profession for you. If you stick around and have any talent at all, you will become a diver, but if you leave you've wasted a lot of time and money without achieving your goal.

Promotion to diver status means several things, but chief among them is that you will be making more money than you did as a tender. As a diver, you will not be expected to perform some of the more menial tasks on a job, but if you are smart, you'll help out wherever you can do so.

Once you become a diver, it's important to keep things in perspective and remember that just a little while ago, you were still a tender. Treat the tenders on the job with the respect you would like to receive and help teach them how to do their job. You'll have their loyalty and support as you are promoted through the ranks.

True Tales of Commercial Diving from the California Coast

My first working gas (HeO_2) dive occurred from a drill ship anchored off Central California. This dive took place in the middle of a weekend night, which was not unusual.

At the time, I was working on an air diving job off Morro Bay, California during the week. The Morro Bay job was started using scuba from the beach out and continued, once in deeper water, by introducing an old set of heavy gear and self-training the four divers on the crew in its use. We all felt pretty smug by getting the heavy gear on the job and training ourselves so we would have heavy gear qualification. Also, after diving the air heavy gear for quite a few dives I was given the opportunity to make a gas training dive from a barge in 240 feet of water off Santa Barbara on an off weekend. This gas dive was made in a heavy gear air hat that had been fitted with a second stage scuba regulator fitted between the bottom of the face port and the top of the neck ring. Air was delivered through the usual air control valve, but when on gas the diver closed the air control valve, leaned forward and breathed off of the regulator.

The telephone rang late one evening and I was told to meet the rest of the crew for transportation to a drilling rig. I was the third diver on a gas dive crew and had no expectation of getting wet. (The gas helmets on this job were all fitted with the scuba second stage regulator).

The ship was anchored in over 500 feet of water. Fortunately, the problem was a broken hydraulic pipe at the 360-foot level. The job entailed squaring up the end of the break in the pipe, cutting a thread on the clean end and screwing on a quick connect fitting. The broken pipe ran vertically up along the conductor pile and to gain a purchase to make it possible to work the diver locked a pipe wrench on the pipe and used it to sit on while working on the break.

The first diver successfully squared up the broken end and started to cut a thread before his time was up. The second diver managed to cut a bit more thread on his dive, but could not complete the job. Also, somehow the pipe die was lost.

"OK! Get him suited up."

"Who me? Yes you!"

I will have to admit to having great trepidation about the situation, but proceeded to load on the tools, enter the water and descend to the work site. Having had very little experience with gas, I was awed with the mental clarity caused by the lack of nitrogen.

I started the die on the previously cut thread and proceeded to attempt to turn it with a pipe wrench, as the die handle had been lost. Turning the die was more than difficult and I was able to make only about one turn. Since I could not cut any more thread, I removed the die and screwed the quick connect fitting onto the very minimal thread. When the fitting was snug, I snapped on a mating fitting attached to a temporary hydraulic hose. Pressure was applied, the fitting held and I was euphoric.

Bob Christensen

© Bev Morgan. All rights reserved.

Chapter 8
Working as a Commercial Diver

A diver is only as good as his last dive.

Just as the pressure is strong on a tender to prove himself, there is also pressure on the new or "break-out" diver to prove his worth. It's always important in this type of situation to keep your head and not let yourself get talked into situations that are not safe.

Your most important tool as a diver is your brain and your ability to think through potential problems before they occur. Take the time to analyze each dive before you get in the water so you will have a plan for how to do the dive and how you will handle different situations should they occur. Make sure you have all of the tools and equipment you need ready to go and that they are in good working order.

The ADCI (Association of Diving Contractors International) requires that a Job Hazard Analysis (JHA) be completed before each dive. This is a formal procedure for identifying the sequence of the dive, evaluating the potential hazards you might encounter, determining safe procedures and protection, and assigning responsibility. The JHA is a very important part of helping to ensure your safety and must not be omitted. The JHA may also be referred to as a "JSA" or "Job Safety Analysis," or as a "JHR" or "Job Hazard Review."

Safety Gear

Whenever you dive, it's vital to be sure that you have the right safety equipment and that it's operating correctly. Just because you have a bail-out bottle doesn't mean the bottle is full or that the regulator is working properly. Always check your gear for proper operation prior to diving.

As a diver, you must constantly be thinking about your safety.

You may need additional safety equipment for dives with certain specialized tools. For example, if you are using a high-pressure water blaster, you should wear a pair of foot guards, also sometimes referred to as a "metatarsal guards," to help protect you from accidentally shooting yourself in the foot with the blaster. Although this may sound funny, these blasters produce 10,000 p.s.i. or higher of water pressure and more than one diver has been seriously injured using this equipment.

Working as a Commercial Diver

Job Hazard Analysis (JHA)

#1 - Before the dive starts break the job into individual, observable steps.

#2 - Identify potential hazards with each job step. Consider environmental and health hazards.

#3 - Recommend safe procedures and personal protection equipment.

#4 - Assign a specific person responsibility for implementing safety procedures or protection.

#5 - Distribute the JHA to all personnel involved in the job or task.

#6 - Modify the JHA as the job situation changes....

A Job Hazard Analysis (or Job Safety Analysis) should be performed before every working dive.

If you will be welding or cutting underwater, you'll want to equip your helmet with a welding lens to help protect your eyes from the light of the arc. This equipment is vital to protecting your vision.

Just Say No – Sometimes...

Sometimes you have to know when it is time to turn down a dive. If you feel the circumstances surrounding the dive are too dangerous, you are under no obligation to dive. You always have the right to refuse to dive and you should not suffer any consequences for doing so. Again, we've always found that if we turned down the dive, nobody else stepped forward to make it in our place.

If you do get hassled by a supervisor or company management for refusing to dive, don't back down. Do what you think is right, even if it means looking for a new job. It's better to be alive and uninjured than the alternative.

Standing by to Dive

On most jobs, the diving will go on continuously until the work is completed. The supervisor will normally set up a "diving rotation," that is the order in which people will make the dives. While the first diver is in the water, the diver who will make the second dive is standing by to make his dive, as well as acting as a safety diver for the person who is already working in the water.

When you are the standby diver it is important for you to be ready at all times to go to the immediate aid of the diver who is in the water. This means that you need to be dressed in to everything except your mask or helmet. Your suit needs to be on, you need to be wearing your harness and bail-out bottle, and your fins should be on your feet. The only thing you should need to do is to don your mask or helmet and get into the water, and that should take less than a minute to do.

As the standby diver, you should be able to hear the communications between the person who is running the dive and the diver. Most dive stations will be set up so that this is possible, either with a separate speaker, or you may be able to hear at least the supervisor through the speakers in your mask or helmet. If you can hear that there is a problem, you should be starting to don your head gear before the supervisor even says anything.

Pay attention to what's going on while you are standing by so you are ready to act

Standby divers have the responsibility to be prepared to enter the water at a moment's notice.

Working as a Commercial Diver

If you must enter the water by jumping, turn on the free-flow on your mask or helmet first.

instantly if you are needed. You would want whoever stands by for you to be equally prepared.

Communicating with Topside

During your dive, you must communicate with topside frequently to keep them informed as to your progress and location in the water. Just as airplane pilots and police officers have certain terms and phrases they regularly use to keep their communications brief and understandable, divers have their own language. We will explain these terms as we discuss different tasks that divers perform.

When you speak to topside during your dive, the supervisor or life support technician will confirm they heard your transmission by responding with a "Roger" or by repeating what you said. When you are spoken to by topside you must also respond with a "Roger" or by repeating their instructions.

Keep your communications as brief as possible so that you are prepared to listen to directions from topside.

Entering the Water

You may be expected to enter the water as soon as the previous diver exits the water and the next standby diver is ready to go. However, there may be a slight delay if the job you're on has been set up to use only one particular hose for diving and the second hose for standing by, and your mask or helmet needs to be transferred to that hose. There may also be a delay if the supervisor needs to brief you on the progress of the job or the dive plan has changed.

If you can enter the water by using a stage this is preferable to jumping. If you have to jump, be sure to turn the free-flow valve in your mask or helmet on slightly before you enter, to help prevent the exhaust valve from inverting and flooding your mask.

Sometimes if the visibility is poor, or there is a strong current, the stage may be connected to the down line by a running shackle. This can make it much easier to get to the job site.

Depending on the conditions and the depth of your dive, it may be appropriate for you to exit the stage so that your hose leads through the side of the stage. This makes it easy for you to find the stage at the end of your dive, especially if the visibility is poor. The tenders can still feed you hose and haul it back in when they need to do so.

As soon as you enter the water, tell topside, "Diver in the water." When you leave the surface, tell them, "Diver on the down line, leaving the surface," so they know when to start the clock for your descent.

As you descend through the water column, it's essential for you to provide instructions for the tenders in regards to your hose. A good tender will not provide you with any slack in your hose unless you request it. If you are making a descent in deep water you can tell topside, "Slack the diver as he goes." Once you reach the bottom, if you are not moving away from the down line, simply say, "All stop on the diver's slack."

Using the Down Line

Commercial divers always work with a down line, which is a stout nylon or polypropylene line strung from the surface down to the work site. The purpose of the down line is to provide a direct link to the job site so that you do not waste any time locating the site and to provide a way to lower tools to the diver efficiently.

The down line will normally have a weak link on its lower end made from manila, so it can be broken if need be, without the need to send a diver to the bottom to disconnect it. The manila line is spliced to the nylon or poly. An "eye" is spliced into manila to connect the down line to the structure you are working on at the bottom. The line is taken around the structure and a shackle is used to fasten the eye back on the line. The pin on the shackle should be positioned through the eye in the manila so that the pin does not rub on the down line itself and unscrew it.

The first diver in the water is responsible for establishing the down line at the work site. When you are taking the down line to the bottom you will need to tell topside to, "Slack the downline and slack the diver." If this task falls to you, try to pick a place to attach the line where it will not chafe against the structure. When the down line is connected to the structure, be sure to tell the com box operator that you have it established and where it is located on the structure.

Once you've connected the line to the work site, be sure that you don't take a turn around it yourself so that you are prevented from making a direct ascent to the surface. Have the topside crew take the slack out of the line so that it is taut, by telling them to, "Come up on the down line and make it "fast" (i.e., tie it off)." It's also important to ensure that you do not spiral around the line as you are making your ascent to the surface at the end of your dive.

If you need additional tools during the dive, the tenders will lower them to you using the down line. They will connect another heavy shackle to the line with a light weight line connected to the shackle. Any items to be lowered to you will also be connected to the shackle. The shackle and tools are then dropped down to you using this second "messenger" line. You can also send items you don't need back to the surface when the tenders retrieve the messenger line and shackle.

If the down line has already been established on the bottom when it is your turn to dive, just be sure that you make your descent to the bottom and your ascent to the surface on the same side of the line. If you don't, your hose will be wrapped around the down line and you will not be able to make a direct ascent to the surface in an emergency.

Managing Your Diving Hose

As a diver, one of the most important skills that you can learn is how to manage your diving hose underwater. Commercial diving hoses are heavy and awkward, especially if there is a hot water hose as part of the bundle. You need to be aware of where your hose is at all times.

Most hoses used by commercial diving firms are sinking hoses, although in recent years some of the "twisted" umbilicals on the market have been designed to float. There are advantages and disadvantages to both types of hose.

If you are working with a sinking umbili-

Commercial divers always work with a downline.

© *Kirby Morgan Dive Systems, Inc. Photo by S. Barsky*

cal on an oil platform and you are in mid-water, between the bottom and the surface, there will be a "belly" in the umbilical where it dips down from the surface to your position. This belly will be subject to drag from any currents running through the site.

Umbilicals that sink will lie on the bottom when you are working there, and they snag easily on any obstructions. If you have any sort of visibility it's important to watch for this as you work your way along.

When you are using a sinking umbilical and you must move away from where the down line is fastened, you'll want to pull some slack to you and coil up some hose to pay out as you move across the bottom. You'll need to tell topside how much slack to give you before you start to move.

Floating umbilicals pose a different set of difficulties. Floating hoses will float to a point near where you are located and then arc down through the water column to you. This means that they are less likely to snag on obstructions underwater, but they could be caught in the propellers of any boats that might pass through the dive site.

Divers working in strong currents have sometimes tied their hoses off to parts of underwater platforms to help reduce the drag on their hose and make it easier for them to stay in position. We don't recommend this procedure because you must untie the hose before you can surface. In an emergency, you could be trapped underwater.

In some cases, it is considered acceptable to use a welding rod bent in a single loop to secure your hose to a structure when there is a strong current. This will help to relieve the strain on the hose but can still be pulled free if needed. Check with your supervisor to see if this is acceptable to him before you use this technique.

ROVs

It's not uncommon today for a diver to be accompanied on his dives by an ROV (Remotely Operated Vehicle). These swimming "robots" are controlled by an operator on the surface who can see where the vehicle is going. Most ROVs have multiple thrusters that allow them to maneuver in any direction, at least one (and possibly several) video cameras, and perhaps a manipulator (robotic arm) to allow the ROV to perform mechanical work.

ROVs range in size from the very small units, that are basically nothing more than a "swimming eyeball," to large "work class" ROVs that may have as many as three cameras and two mechanical arms that allow sophisticated movement and manipulation. The ROV is powered by a tether connected to a topside generator and controls. The ROV operator may work side-by-side with the diving supervisor during the course of a dive.

Some divers are uncomfortable having an ROV at their side because the diving supervisor (and potentially the client) gets to watch everything that the diver does underwater during the dive. The positive side of this is that the supervisor can usually suggest ways to help you get the job done more quickly and with improved safety. In addition, the ROV can provide lighting and be used to carry tools.

ROVs have taken over some of the work that was traditionally done by divers, such as inspecting pipelines and platforms, replacing anodes, pipeline "tie-ins," and other tasks. It usually costs less to operate an ROV than to put a diver on the bottom, particularly in deep water. ROVs today operate at depths that far exceed a diver's capabilities. If an ROV is damaged or destroyed, the consequences are not nearly as serious as when a diver is injured or killed. Although some divers worry about ROVs completely replacing them, there will probably always be work for divers underwater.

Working in Black Water

While sport divers don't normally dive in conditions where the underwater visibility is zero, commercial divers must frequently dive in situations of this type. This lack of visibility increases the risk factor for all types of dives, but especially on any dives where you must rig lines or cables or where heavy objects are lifted underwater.

It's especially important that you do not trap any of your equipment or parts of your body inside any bights of line or cable that

The Simple Guide to Commercial Diving

Remotely Operated Vehicles commonly accompany divers on many jobs today. The ROV can provide lighting and carry heavy tools for the diver.

Working as a Commercial Diver

will be lifted underwater. If you are careless, it's possible to pinch off your hose or cut off a limb in this type of environment, when the line or cable tightens.

If you must rig in black water, be sure to take the time to double check that your hose and body are clear of all lines and fittings before any lift is made. The safest place to be during a lift will usually be on top of the load until it is clear of the work site.

Bell and Saturation Diving

Working out of a diving bell is one of the most exciting types of dives that you can do. It's a real rush to see the depth gauge indicating a depth of 300 feet or more, and being able to look out of the port and see your bell partner working outside, while you are sitting dry inside the bell and listening to the diving supervisor talking on the communications system. Of course, the fact that you are making a lot of money while doing this helps make it exciting, too!

There's a good chance that your first bell dive will start out with you entering the bell at atmospheric pressure on the deck of a barge or ship, rather than from within the pressurized chamber of a saturation system. You'll don your hot water suit and harness before you enter the bell. Your helmet may have already been connected for you by one of the tenders.

It's crucial that you know where every valve and gauge is inside the bell and that you can locate them by feel if all power is cut to the bell and there is no internal lighting. Prior to ever making a bell dive you should take every opportunity possible to hoist yourself up inside the bell and memorize the location of every piece of equipment.

Just as a pilot walks around his airplane, to be sure that everything is in working condition before he takes off, it's a good idea to take a walk around the bell and satisfy yourself that everything is working properly, both inside and outside of the bell. This is especially important if your dive is the first dive at the start of the job and the diving system has just been installed offshore. If there is anything that you don't feel is working properly, you'll want to see that it gets fixed before you make your dive. You'll want to pay particular attention to the emergency gas supply, emergency power supply, and through-water communications system. Also, be sure you are satisfied with the connection for the lift wire and that the lifting shackle has been properly secured or "moused."

Since each diver's "lock-out" (time spent outside the bell underwater) may last up to four hours or more, you will probably want to take some snacks with you to eat while the bell is in the water, as well as something to drink to help keep yourself hydrated. You may also want to take some paper towels for prepping your mask, cleaning ports, or other applications. Toilet paper isn't a bad idea, either.

Once you're inside the bell, the supervisor will take you through a pre-dive check-list to ensure that everything is operational. When the pre-dive check is complete, the deck crew will then close the outer hatch and the bell will be hoisted over the side.

As the bell is dropped into the water, the outer hatch should seal properly, so that

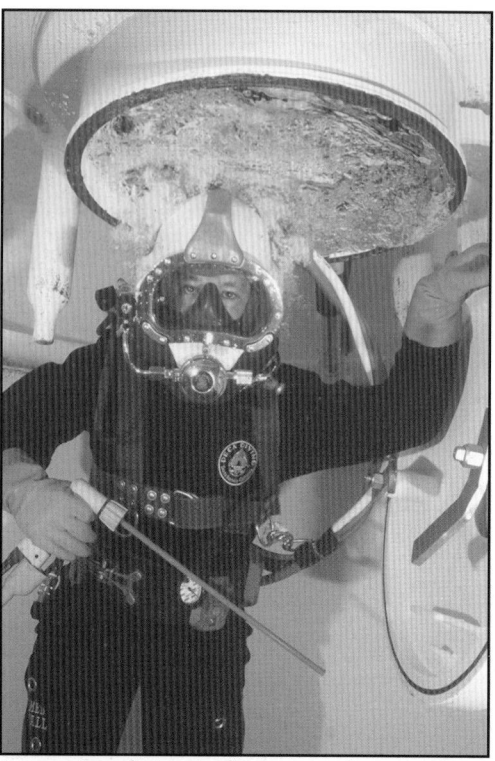

Saturation diving is the most sophisticated type of diving that you can do.

the internal pressure stays the same until you reach the bottom. Brace yourself as the bell goes through the air-water interface to make sure you aren't thrown against the inside of the bell and injured.

If you started your dive with the internal pressure at topside atmospheric pressure, the internal pressure should remain the same throughout the descent. (If you started the dive already saturated in the diving complex, initially, the bell will have an internal pressure greater than the surrounding pressure.)

Once you reach the depth where you will work, the supervisor will have you blow down the bell to the bottom depth. When the pressure inside equals the pressure outside, you'll be able to open the bottom hatch. If you started your bell run already saturated, with the bell on the sat system, you will need to equalize the pressure in the trunk space between the top and bottom hatches. The supervisor will instruct you when it is time to do this.

You'll need to assist your bell-mate in donning his gear. This can be extremely awkward since most diving bells are extremely cramped for space inside. Take extra care not to drop anything through the bottom hatch as it may be lost forever, especially if the bell is in midwater and not close to the bottom.

As the bell "man" (or bell tender) you will need to pay attention to what's going on while your bell partner is in the water. Keep an eye on the bell manifold pressure so you know at all times how much pressure is being supplied to the diver in the water. If you see a sudden drop in the supply pressure from topside, be prepared to switch your partner over to the emergency supply immediately.

Listen carefully to the diving supervisor so you can anticipate your partner's needs. Your mask or helmet should be set up so that you can don it instantly in the event you need to go to the assistance of the diver in the water. If possible, your hose should be connected to your harness and set up so that it will feed out to you if you need to leave the bell to perform a rescue.

Since your bell run may take place at any hour of the day or night, it may occur at a time when you would normally be asleep, or you may have already worked a full shift be-

An individual diver's bell "lock-out" may last four hours or more in the water.

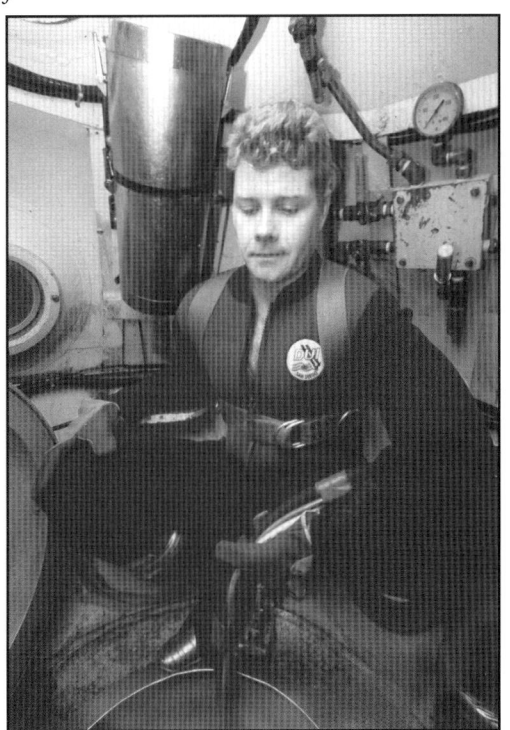

The interior of most diving bells is very cramped.

When you are working out of a bell, you must always know where the bell and you are in relation to the structure you are working on. An offshore oil platform like this one can be a real maze underwater.

fore you are asked to dive without any prior notice. In these situations, it's easy to become drowsy inside the bell. Don't let this happen! If the bell heater is making the bell too warm, turn it off. It's essential that you remain awake and alert throughout your turn as the bell tender.

Pay attention to where the bell is in relationship to any underwater structures. If the bell appears to be moving closer to the structure, let topside know immediately. You don't want to have the bell damage any part of the client's structure, or for the bell itself to be damaged.

Depending on the type of vessel you are working from, the bell may heave up and down in the water column, especially if there is no compensation system to deal with this topside. In this situation, the water level will rise and fall in the bell's trunk, forcing you to equalize continuously. This can be extremely uncomfortable, but there is nothing you can do about it except to grin and bear it.

If there are lights illuminating the work site, and you can see your bell partner, keep an eye on him as much as possible. You want to see if he has any problems and be alert if he needs to be rescued so that you are taking action before topside realizes there is a problem. You would want the same thing done for you.

Once your bell mate has finished his turn in the water, he will return to the bell so that you can trade places. This should be done as quickly and efficiently as possible.

When you first drop into the bell stage, take a moment to make sure that all of your gear is working properly. If the bell is heaving up and down, you may need to brace yourself between the bottom of the bell and the stage to don your fins and secure any tools you need to your harness. Be careful to avoid injury in this situation.

After you leave the stage, you may need to follow the down line to the job site, especially if the visibility is poor or the bell is a long distance from the work site. Be sure not to take a turn around the down line or you will not be able to return to the bell quickly in an emergency.

When you have both finished diving, the supervisor will want you to prepare to leave the bottom as quickly as possible. First, you'll need to close the outside hatch and dog it tight. Next, you'll need to close the inner hatch, taking extra care to make sure nothing is between the hatch and the sealing surface that would interrupt the seal. Take care with your fingers and toes when you close this hatch to avoid injury.

Once you're sure the hatch is closed, the supervisor will start to bring the bell up. Watch the internal depth carefully to make sure you are not losing pressure and notify the dive supervisor immediately if you see that this is a problem. When the bell nears the surface, brace yourself as it moves through the interface again.

After the bell is on deck, it will be mated to the saturation system where you will complete your decompression. When the bell is lifted up for this purpose, be sure to brace yourself to help avoid injury.

With the bell on the entrance lock and the pressure in the trunk equalized, you'll be able to open the top hatch. Carefully, climb down into the entrance lock and transfer any of your personal gear out of the bell as quickly as possible. You need to clear the bell so that the next dive team is able to get inside and start their bell checks as soon as you are able to do so.

Ideally, your crew should be able to "turn the bell around," i.e., bring it up, swap dive teams, and put it back in the water - in under an hour. An experienced dive crew should be able to do this easily.

Once you're back in the sat system and the bell has been put back in the water, you can take your time getting out of your gear and get yourself cleaned up. Your hot water suit and other equipment can be passed out through the medical lock so it can be cleaned up for the next dive.

Emergency Procedures

Accidents are always possible in the commercial diving environment and it's imperative that you think through in advance how you will handle different types of incidents. This doesn't mean that you should spend all your time thinking about morbid events, but you should be clear about how you could respond to emergencies. Probably the most important reason for this type of mental preparation is that different equipment and diving environments may require different sorts of reactions.

Some of the more common incidents to which you may need to respond include a loss of your topside breathing gas supply and the rescue of an unconscious diver. Less common incidents include things like the loss of a diving bell, or the need to evacuate divers who are in saturation aboard a ship that is about to sink.

Loss of the Topside Breathing Gas Supply

It's possible to lose your gas supply due to any number of reasons, including such causes as a compressor failure, a severed hose, or a trapped or crushed hose. You need to consider each of these scenarios and how you might respond depending on where the incident takes place. Unfortunately, there is no one correct response for all situations.

The universal response for losing your topside air supply will normally be to turn on your bail-out bottle and make a direct ascent to the surface. However, if you have a decompression obligation or are making a dive inside a structure like a wreck, or saturation dive, this becomes a much more serious situation.

Probably the most dangerous circumstance in which you could lose your air supply would be if your hose was crushed due to the collapse of a wreck or a fall by an overhead load. If your hose is crushed, but not severed, you must act quickly as you will be trapped at depth. Although you may be able to cut through the diving hose with a knife, it's unlikely you will be able to sever the communications wire this way. In this situation, probably the most efficient way to cut through this type of cable is with a pair of sidecutters.

Recovering an Unconscious Diver

If you ever have to rescue an unconscious diver underwater, be prepared for a physically and emotionally exhausting experience. It's very difficult to move an unconscious diver quickly through the water. Although you may have some assistance from your topside crew, you may have to swim the diver around obstructions without any help from the surface. If you are working out of a diving bell, you will be completely on your own, with no one to help you.

If there is a stage available, getting a diver out of the water is relatively easy, but if the diver must be hoisted up a ladder it can be extremely difficult. Most diving harnesses will have a "D-ring" on them located between the diver's shoulder blades specifically to assist the

Working as a Commercial Diver

crew in lifting an unconscious diver.

Diving bells will typically have a pad eye welded into the top of the bell and a block and tackle or hoist for pulling an unconscious diver inside. If you are working out of a small bell, it can be extremely difficult to position the diver's legs and other gear so that you are able to close the hatch.

Lost Bell

Although it rarely happens, diving bells have at times lost their lift wires and umbilicals. When this happens, the surface crew must take swift action to perform an effective rescue. If the water depth is less than 300 FSW, there's a good chance that the topside crew will send a surface-supplied diver down to attempt to put a new lift wire on the bell. Each diving company will have their own set of procedures in dealing with this type of accident.

In most situations, where a lift wire and umbilical are severed, the accident that will cause this will probably be rather abrupt. The tender inside the bell will need to take immediate action and switch the diver over to the bell emergency gas supply and activate the emergency power system.

Your bell should be equipped with some type of wireless communication system and you should attempt to use this to establish a link with topside. Keep in mind, however, that these systems do not always work. Your bell should be equipped with an emergency pinger/locator and this should be activated promptly. It's important to remember that if you are in this situation, there probably are serious problems with your surface-support vessel and a rescue may be hours away.

If your bell has lost its umbilical and lift wire connection to the surface, there will probably still be a good length of both the umbilical and cable attached to the bell. These wires and hoses may be entangled in any structure you were working on and this would possibly complicate the rescue of the bell.

Even if the torn cable and hoses are not entangled, their weight may prevent the bell from surfacing under its own lift if the ballast weights are ditched. In either case, if topside cannot initiate a rescue, one of you will probably need to lock out to cut away this debris using a hack saw or cable cutter. This is a dangerous situation since you will not have a hot water supply to keep you warm and you will be breathing a heli-ox mix which drains heat away from your body.

You also need to know whether the emergency gas supply and power supply will need to be ditched for the bell to float. Since each company's equipment works differently, this is an important subject that you'll want to discuss with the supervisor and other divers on the job before you ever make a saturation dive. If the emergency gas and power must be ditched, too, there will be an extremely short window during which the bell can be recovered and you would survive.

The first thing that you'll probably want to do, once both of you are back inside, will be to close the bottom hatch and get a seal on it. If you know that surface conditions are good, but there is no rescue operation underway, you'll probably want to try to release your ballast weights and if everything works properly, the bell should float to the surface.

Floating on the surface inside a diving bell can be extremely uncomfortable or even a dangerous situation, especially if surface conditions are rough. Some bells are equipped with restraining harnesses for you to wear in this situation.

If you are unable to drop the weights, or the bell does not surface for some other reason, you'll need to be prepared to wait for a rescue. All bells should be equipped with a lung-powered scrubber system for removing carbon dioxide, and some type of passive heating system for keeping the divers warm in the event of this type of emergency. As the oxygen level in the bell drops, you'll need to either add additional oxygen or flush the bell with fresh mix.

Evacuation by Hyperbaric Lifeboat

Sometimes the topside crew will know in advance that the situation is deteriorating and may prepare to evacuate the divers who are in saturation by putting them in the hyperbaric lifeboat and either transferring it to another vessel or launching it in the ocean. This is a serious decision and not one to be taken lightly. Situations that might require this type of action would include a fire on a vessel or a vessel that was in danger of sinking.

There has been at least one case where saturation divers were evacuated from a drill rig that was on fire by transferring them to the bell and placing the bell on the back of a supply ship. This will never be a simple procedure because there usually won't be time to transfer the bell control van along with the bell. In addition, the crew will have to rig makeshift accommodations to control the temperature in the bell within a safe range.

Reporting Decompression Sickness

Decompression sickness is a risk in all diving and is taken very seriously by most working professionals.

Every diver in the crew should undergo a field neurological exam following the completion of their decompression at the end of each dive or whenever they exit the decompression chamber. This simple test can help to uncover subtle cases of decompression sickness that might otherwise be missed.

Decompression sickness can produce serious permanent disabilities in divers and must always be treated promptly. As a diver, it is your obligation to report any suspected cases of decompression sickness to your diving supervisor immediately. You should never feel as though you are jeopardizing your position within the company for reporting decompression sickness.

Responsibility for Paperwork

As a diver, you will be responsible for completing a wide variety of paperwork for each job. If you are the lead diver on a three-man team, or you are a supervisor of a crew, there will be even more paperwork to which you must attend.

The typical paperwork that must be completed on every job includes dive logs, daily work logs (time sheet), consumables and equipment logs. If you are on an inspection or repair job, you will also be expected to submit reports as to what took place on the job. You will be evaluated on the legibility of your handwriting, the completeness of your paperwork, and the clarity of your writing. Illegible or incomplete documents or unintelligible writing will not advance your career.

The paperwork you submit for your jobs becomes a legal record of what took place. If a customer disputes a charge, or a diver suffers decompression sickness and sues the company, your paperwork will be a central part of the legal proceedings.

Two types of dive logs are used throughout the commercial diving industry. Each diver is expected to maintain a personal dive log which is a record of his personal experience. In addition, a company dive log is normally completed for each dive, which includes specific times, gas mixtures, location, personnel, and similar information.

The daily job log or work log includes a list of the personnel on the job, dives made, hours worked, and progress on the job. This is part of the paperwork that is used to bill the customer. In most situations, a customer's representative will be on hand to sign this paperwork each day.

The consumables log includes all of the

Each diver is expected to maintain his own logbook.

Working as a Commercial Diver

special items that are used for the job and billed to the customer. This form usually has a list of every consumable item that is not considered part of overhead, such as helium-oxygen mixtures, fuel, video tapes, and other special items. Each company handles these items differently, but there are almost always some items in this category that will be billed back to the client.

Equipment logs normally reflect all of the equipment used on the job and may also include mobilization and demobilization charges. In most cases, the office will instruct you in how to complete this paperwork and which items should be billed. Like the job and consumables logs, the equipment log will usually need to be signed by the customer's representative.

Carry a laptop computer with you on the job to keep your paperwork up to date.

Your Mobile Office

As a diver today, it's a good idea to carry a laptop computer and a digital camera with you on every job to which you are dispatched, especially if you are on a small crew or are a supervisor.

Using a laptop in the field will allow you to prepare reports that have a polished appearance, complete paperwork swiftly, and transmit documents electronically back to your office. A digital camera is also highly recommended so that you can photograph conditions topside at the work site and include these in your reports to management.

Moving Up

If you are successful as a diver, perform well and are well-liked, eventually you will be promoted to lead diver. As a lead diver, you will make more money, have the opportunity to go on better jobs, and make the more important (deeper) dives on the jobs you go on. This is an important step in your career.

As you gain experience and maturity, eventually you will almost certainly be asked to supervise, if you have any talents in this area at all. If you're interested in becoming a diving supervisor, be sure to read Chapter 11 on *Working as a Diving Supervisor*.

Interfacing with the Client

If you are the diver that has been sent out as part of a three-man dive team, you will frequently be interfacing with the client's representative directly. It's important that you present a professional appearance at all times, both in your dress and personal conduct.

Nobody expects you to wear a suit and tie to a diving job, but you should have a clean company T-shirt or polo shirt and a pair of jeans in presentable condition for wearing when you go to get your paperwork signed. Be polite and be sure to ask if the client has a moment to speak with you, rather than just barging in and demanding that your paperwork be signed.

Dealing with clients in the oil patch and other construction environments can be difficult, but you must remain calm and always stress safety above all other issues. Author Steve Barsky has shut down drilling rigs operating at thousands of dollars a day when conditions were too dangerous to dive. In all cases, the clients have backed down when the safety issues were explained to them calmly but firmly.

Be sure to have a supply of business cards with you whenever you meet with a client, so that you can hand them one at the start of your meeting. If your company does not supply cards, have some printed up with your name and photograph. You want to have clients asking for you by name if you want to advance quickly in the industry.

True Tales of Commercial Diving from the North Sea

On a typical bell diving job, the ship or barge from which the bell is operating must be anchored to the bottom with a minimum of four anchors to provide the stability and safety needed to conduct the operation. This is a time consuming and expensive process, as it normally takes a separate vessel to run the anchors out and drop them before diving operations can commence. If you could avoid laying anchors, almost a full day of work could be saved.

In order to eliminate the need to lay an anchor spread, naval architects developed ships that operated with "dynamic positioning systems." Dynamically positioned (DP) vessels use a Global Positioning System (GPS) (or other transponders) and multiple thrusters to hover in an extremely tight radius that must not exceed more than a few feet in any direction. These ships were first deployed for diving back in the late 70s.

While the concept of a dynamically positioned vessel is a good idea in theory, they may not always perform as expected, which can cause diving accidents. In 1978, when "DP" ships were a new concept, the Global Positioning System did not exist and DP technology was rather primitive. An incident that happened in the North Sea almost took the life of author Steve Barsky.

I was diving back inside an oil platform at a depth of 100 feet when the diving supervisor told me to work my way back to the down line and prepare to come up. The water was very green and visibility was poor. Although the dive was being terminated after only five minutes, I was not alarmed until the supervisor told me to forget the down line, that the tenders would pull me back to the stage.

I met the stage at a depth of 40 feet and quickly climbed inside, where I was immediately hoisted to the surface. When I reached the deck and removed my mask, the tenders' eyes were wide and they both looked at me and remarked that I had almost been killed. They suggested that I turn around and look at the platform that I had been diving on behind me.

When I looked over my shoulder I saw that the ship was almost 300 feet away from the platform, but when I had entered the water we were only 50 feet from the platform. Apparently, the dynamic positioning system went haywire and the ship began to move rapidly away from the structure. This action alone could have caused me a serious injury, but another problem could have been equally serious or fatal.

A line had been tied to both the ship and the platform so that mail could be lowered to the ship from above. Unfortunately, the line had been tied tight on both ends and when the ship pulled away, the line ripped a 15 foot section of chain link fencing off the side of the platform.

The fencing sailed through the air and landed in the water, apparently just missing me. If it had struck me while I was in the water, it could have killed me on impact, or torn my hose out of the tenders' hands, dragging me to the bottom at 400 FSW. When I went over and tried to lift the line to which the section of fence was attached, I was unable to budge it.

A few days later, the DP system failed again, while a diver was working outside the bell at 400 FSW. The bell crashed into the platform, tilting on its side, partially flooding the interior. Following this incident, we all refused to work from this ship unless an anchor spread was laid.

Steve Barsky

© Bev Morgan. All rights reserved.

Chapter 9
Working with Tools Underwater

If you give a diver three solid stainless steel balls, he will break one, lose one, and try to steal the other one.

As a diver, it is imperative that you are able to work with a wide variety of tools, both topside and underwater. You will be paid for what you can do and how fast you can do it. The more skilled you are in using different tools, the better your chances of success.

Before you take any tool underwater, you need to know how to use it on dry land. While this isn't always possible, it's unrealistic to expect to be able to use a device you haven't seen before and perform well with it. Always take the time to practice with a new tool before you have to use it on the job.

Use the Right Tool for the Job

Another important aspect of proper tool use is to use the right tool for the job. Many accidents have taken place because divers have tried to use the wrong tool rather than taking the time to get the right one. Don't use a wrench as a hammer, or a water blaster in place of a water jet. You're just asking for an accident to occur.

Using an Ascender

Divers sometimes need to rig a means for them to work on the underside of structures so that they can hang there effortlessly while they do the work. If you are using a dry suit, this is a relatively simple matter, because you can adjust your buoyancy with the suit to hold yourself in position.

When you are wearing a wetsuit or hot water suit, without buoyancy control, then rigging a means of holding yourself stable while hanging beneath a corner joint or

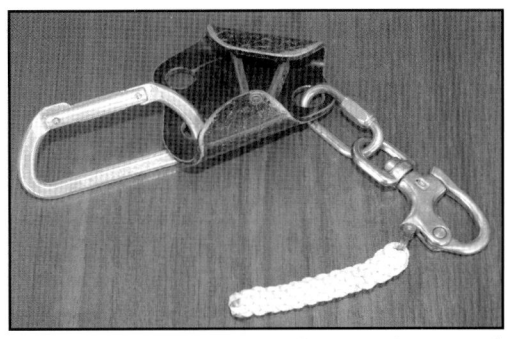

An ascender properly rigged can make it much easier to work when you must be suspended in midwater.

"node" on a platform becomes much more difficult. Although some divers tie themselves in, using manila line, this can be a hazardous procedure if your line is difficult to release and you have an emergency where you must leave the bottom quickly.

We've found that a better method of rigging is to use what is known as an "ascender," which is a device used by rock climbers. These devices are normally used by mountaineers to go up a cliff face using a rope. The ascender is spring loaded and only allows the rope to be pulled through its jaws in one direction. When a load is applied to the rope in the opposite direction, the ascender "bites" down on the line.

The beauty of the ascender for diving is that the line can also be released from the jaws almost instantaneously, and because they are built for outdoors use, most designs will not rust. It can be quickly tightened or loosened as required to position your body where you need it. The ascender should be further enhanced by using a snap shackle with a lanyard as your main release point and stainless steel quick link or a carabiner to fasten the rig to your harness.

To use the ascender and snap shackle together, you'll need a length of manila with an eye splice in one end and a back splice in the other. The line must be long enough to go around the object you'll be working on with two to three feet of additional slack.

Connect the eye splice to the spinnaker snap shackle, take the line around the structure, and pass the running end of the line through the jaws of the ascender. You can tighten or loosen the line through the ascender to position yourself exactly where you need to be. In the event you need to release yourself quickly, pull the lanyard on the spinnaker snap shackle and the eye will pop free.

Lines for Tools

Most smaller tools will be rigged with a line on them to attach them to your harness. This is an accepted procedure, although it does cause some drag when you are swimming, and anything hanging off of you creates a risk of entanglement.

Any tools that you hang off your harness should be attached with as large a clip or snap hook as practical to make it easy to disconnect if you need to remove it quickly. The lanyard that attaches to the tool and the clip should be neatly braided and wrapped with waterproof electrical tape to help prevent it from unraveling.

Hand Tools

The most basic tools you will use underwater are hand tools and these include items such as hammers, wrenches, drift pins, and cable cutters. While you may use hydraulic or pneumatic tools for heavy construction, hand tools are still used in many instances. It takes skill to use these items properly.

Since very few tools are truly designed to go underwater, you will need to pay particular attention to maintenance for these items. While hammers and box end wrenches have no moving parts, it's still a good idea to spray these items with a coating of a corrosion inhibitor, like WD-40® to help prevent them from turning into a ball of rust.

Hammers

It's been said that the four-pound hammer is the working diver's best friend, and in many cases, this may be true. The hammer may be needed to loosen valve handles, drive drift pins through bolt holes for aligning flanges, and for smacking the face of a hammer wrench (also known as a "slugging wrench" or in the UK, a "flogging spanner"). It may also come in handy when there's just a bit of "slag" holding together two pieces of metal, after you've cut them with a burning torch, to knock them apart.

It takes skill to use a four-pound hammer effectively underwater and it's fatiguing if you have to do this for very long. Although this tool is not as widely used today as it was in the past, you'll still find one on almost every diving job, as a back-up if nothing else.

Wrenches

While open or box-end wrenches are rarely used to tighten bolts on pipelines or other structures where heavy torque values are required, they may be used on smaller structures. However, hammer wrenches are a better choice if you must put any real muscle into tightening a connection and power tools are unavailable.

Adjustable wrenches should never be used in situations where any substantial torque must be applied to a nut. They may slip and round the nut or cause an accident.

Box-end wrenches are frequently used as a backup wrench to secure the head of a bolt while the nut is tightened with a power tool. Take care not to get the wrench jammed, or to catch your fingers between the wrench and the flange when power is applied to the impact wrench.

Hand Powered Hydraulic Cable Cutters

There may be occasions where you need to cut heavy cables underwater and a cutting torch is unavailable. In situations like this, a hydraulic cable cutter is an invaluable tool for cutting thick wire rope.

Most hydraulic cable cutters work by pump action. They normally will have two

The Simple Guide to Commercial Diving

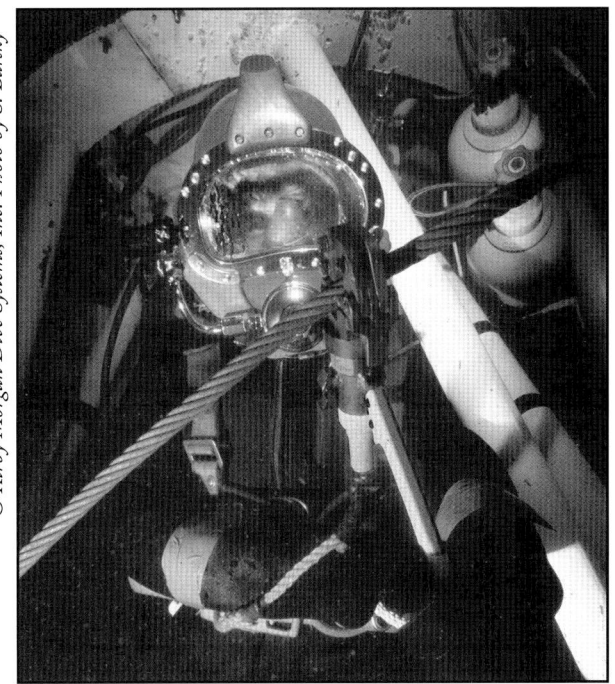

Hydraulic cable cutters are simple to use, but you must think about where you make your cuts, if there is a lot of wire in the water.

cylinders or chambers, and like other hydraulic tools, they will have a bleed valve to transfer fluid from one chamber to the other. You can cut wire rope that is quite thick with these devices pretty easily.

Come-Alongs and Hoists

It's not uncommon to use both come-alongs and chain hoists underwater. These devices may be used for lifting or dragging items along the bottom.

Come-alongs or heavier duty Tirfors have a variety of applications underwater. We've used them to move large gratings and other debris lying inside of a platform at depth when a crane was unavailable and the items were too heavy to move by hand.

Chain hoists are sometimes used with small A-frames to help align the ends of two pipes so they can be bolted together. This technique is usually much safer than using a crane from the surface, and is essential if you are trying to align pipes inside a dry "welding habitat" on the sea floor.

It's essential not to exceed the rated capacity of these tools to help avoid accidents. Watch for frayed wires ("meat-hooks") on come-alongs and Tirfors that can catch on your gear and cut your skin.

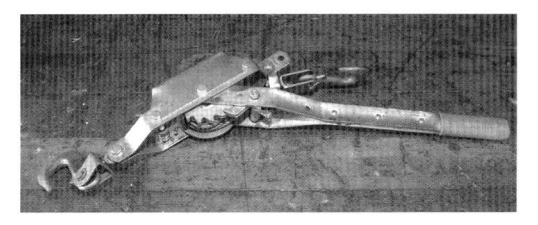

Come-alongs and hoists are common tools on commercial diving jobs.

These devices are not designed to go underwater in the marine environment, so maintenance and lubrication are essential whenever they are used in the ocean.

107

Working with Tools Underwater

Courtesy of Chicago Pneumatic

Pneumatic wrenches work well in shallow water, but they do require proper maintenance to keep them operational in salt water.

Pneumatic Tools

Pneumatic (air powered) tools are commonly used underwater, although they are not the best choice in most situations. The advantages of pneumatic tools are that they are less expensive than hydraulic tools, they are usually lighter weight, and they operate with a single, reasonably flexible hose.

The disadvantages of pneumatic tools are that they may not be as powerful as comparable hydraulic tools, they require lots of maintenance, they can become clogged with sand or other debris, and they have a depth limitation of 100 FSW due to the fact that they operate on compressed air. They also discharge their exhaust bubbles underwater, which can interfere with visibility. Pneumatic tools require a high volume, low-pressure compressor topside to provide them with the power they need.

Most people who use pneumatic tools underwater use some type of in-line lubricator to help reduce maintenance on these tools. However, you'll almost always need to tear these tools down after they have been used in salt water. Be sure to use only an EPA approved oil for lubrication.

We've used pneumatic impact wrenches and jackhammers underwater and these tools can be very useful in the right circumstances. As with any power tool, you must be very careful that the tool is correctly positioned and engaged before you pull the trigger so that it does not fly off the work and strike your body.

Hydraulic impact wrenches generate lots of torque and are crucial for bolting clamps and flanges together at deeper depths where pneumatic wrenches are ineffective.

Hydraulic Tools

Hydraulic tools are very popular for underwater use due to their power and reliability. However, these features come at a cost, which includes a higher purchase price, greater weight, and the bulk of the hydraulic hoses which can be awkward to maneuver underwater. Hydraulic systems are also more complex to maintain than pneumatic gear, and the hydraulic power units are quite large and much noisier. Your choices in hydraulic tools will also be more limited.

We've used hydraulic impact wrenches, saws, cutters, and jack hammers on a variety of jobs. For bolting up large pipelines underwater, special hydraulic "jacks" are used

© Kirby Morgan Dive Systems, Inc. Photo by S. Barsky

The Simple Guide to Commercial Diving

Hydraulic saws are frequently used to cut concrete underwater.

to tension the bolts to very precise measurements.

One of the most difficult things about using hydraulic tools underwater is that they tend to be much heavier than pneumatic tools of similar size, due to the higher internal pressures at which they operate. For this reason, you must be clever about how you work with these tools so you do not wear yourself out.

Hydraulic tools have tremendous power and can easily injure you if you use them carelessly. Take care and make sure you do not have any loose folds of your suit, lines or other equipment that could become entangled in the tool when you pull the trigger.

If you're using a hydraulic wrench, it's also important to be sure that the wrench does not develop more torque than is called for by the nuts and bolts you are fastening together.

An example of a job where several different types of hydraulic tools were used involved the removal of old conductors (steel pipes carrying oil up from the sea bed) at a depth of

This hydraulic reciprocating saw is used to cut pipe underwater.

200 FSW. Each conductor had several successively smaller pipes inside of it, with cement filling the empty space between each pipe.

To cut the conductors, first the outer layer was cut by a hydraulic cutter which walked around the pipe's circumference to make two horizontal cuts three feet apart. The cutter worked like a milling machine, removing small chips of metal with each pass until the concrete layer was reached. Next, another cutter was fastened to the conductor to make two vertical cuts on opposite sides of the conductor between the two horizontal cuts. This split the sleeve into two semi-circular pieces which fell away, exposing the concrete below the outer layer.

With the concrete exposed, a hydraulic jackhammer was used to remove the cement filling the space, exposing the next pipe underneath. A hydraulic reciprocating saw was then fastened to the pipe to cut through the final layer.

Burning Gear

Of all the skills you can possess as a diver, being a good "burner" is one of the most important. It takes real skill to cut steel underwater effectively with an oxy-arc torch and it's important to know how to do it right.

You will need sufficiently long cables to reach the job site with both the ground clamp and the torch. Just getting the cables to the site can take a lot of time, especially if the wa-

Working with Tools Underwater

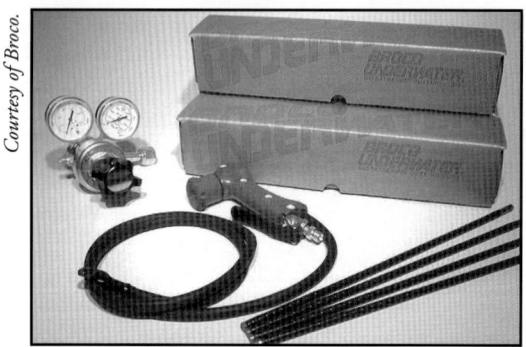

Courtesy of Broco.

For cutting you will need a torch, an oxygen regulator, and plenty of rods.

ter is deep. The further the distance from the welding machine, the heavier the cables must be to handle the electrical load. Check to be sure that the tenders have set up the welding station properly before you enter the water. Inspect the insulation on the cable to be sure it is in good condition and that the torch head is well insulated. Be sure that your gloves do not have holes in them.

Before you begin any burning job you should have a plan of the order in which you will make your cuts. It's usually a good idea to make the most difficult cuts first and save the easier ones for the end of your dive when you are tired, although this may not always be possible. Besides completing the job quickly, your goal is to be sure that anything you cut will fall away from you and not on your body or your hose.

On steel structures that extend above the water line, the ground cable can be attached to a clean area on the surface. Otherwise, the ground cable will need to be attached underwater.

If you have to attach the ground underwater, you'll need to clean the area where you plan to attach it. Use your scraper and brush to make sure you have a clean contact. This should be as close to where you want to make the cut as possible. You'll also need to clean the area where you plan to make your cut. Although this is time consuming, it's more time consuming to try to burn through a bunch of barnacles and other marine growth.

Underwater cutting or "burning" takes both physical skill as well as knowledge and careful planning. Diving is as much a mental game as a physical one.

110

Loosen the torch head and insert a rod into the collet with the bare end of the rod entering the torch first. Tighten the torch head until it is snug. Check to be sure that the oxygen is flowing out of the rod and not at the torch head itself.

You body needs to be in a stable position with both hands free to hold the torch whenever you are cutting underwater. When you're ready to start your cut, hold the tip of the rod a quarter of an inch or so away from the surface from where you want to make your cut, pull the trigger to start the flow of oxygen and tell topside to, "Make it hot!" When you've finished your cut or need to change rods instruct topside to, "Make it cold!" and await their confirmation before removing the rod stub from the torch. Never burn the rod stub less than two inches in length to avoid damage to the torch.

Once you have an arc and you can see that you are starting to burn through the metal, move the torch slowly in the direction you want to cut. The tip of the rod should be aimed at a slight angle forward in the direction of your intended travel. Keep the rod moving smoothly forward as long as you are making progress through the metal. If you are cutting on a ship or similar structure, your cut may slow at times if there are other pieces of metal welded behind the piece on which you are working.

Remember that it is extremely dangerous to burn on or inside a closed compartment, or anywhere the hydrogen gas liberated by the electrolytic process may collect in a pocket. You must take the time to properly vent any closed area so that the hydrogen cannot collect along with any unburned oxygen and explode. If you fail to do this, it may be the last burning job on which you ever work.

Hydrogen gas can also accumulate when you're burning on metal that has packed mud, clay, sand, or concrete behind it, such as burning on what's known as "sheet pile" which is commonly used to reinforce ship channels. Be sure to cut a generous number of vent holes above where you are burning on this type of material to allow any gas to escape. This will take extra time, but it is an essential step.

Never allow any part of your body to get

Always be sure to have topside open the knife switch before you change rods.

between the ground clamp and torch. This could be a painful if not fatal experience.

Use a cutting guide of some type whenever possible to ensure you cut the straightest possible line and the shortest possible distance. You can use a piece of manila rope tied around the structure if it's not too large, but stiffer material is better. Divers have used stiff rubber gasket material, webbing, or other materials and attached them with bungee cords or similar devices to maintain tension.

You will get minor shocks from time to time as you burn, whether it's due to holes in your suit or gloves, or accidentally touching the rod against your helmet when the visibility is poor and you're working with your face close to the work. Divers who do lots of burning usually end up wearing the chrome plating off their masks or helmets. We've also heard divers who wear full-face masks complain that they've had the fillings in their teeth consumed over time due to the electrical current. Whether this is true or not is unknown, but it sure makes a good story…

If you can see the light of the arc through the "kerf" behind the cut, and you have held a continuous arc without interruption, you can pretty much assume that you have burned through the work completely. If this is not the case, or you are unsure, pass a thin blade, like a hacksaw blade or a kitchen knife, through the cut, to check your work. If slag builds up in the cut you can be assured that you have not made an effective pass and there are "hangers" that will prevent the metal from separating.

On jobs where there is a lot of metal to burn, you have to think about the order in which you want to make your cuts to ensure your safety. It's common for divers to leave a "hanger" to be burned away after all of the rest of the cutting is complete, for the "final cut." If you don't know where these hangers are, you can end up looking pretty foolish when the piece you've finished cutting won't separate from the rest of the work. It's a good practice to take the time to make sure that all of your cuts are "hanger free" with the exception of the portion you've left for your final cut. Watch your "kerf," i.e., the channel made by the torch for fusion or "slag" (burned metal) that will create a hanger between the two pieces. It's amazing how small a hanger it takes to prevent even a large piece of metal from separating from another piece. Practice whenever you get the chance.

It takes most people time to become a good underwater "burner" and it takes regular practice to maintain this skill. Good burners know how to watch for "landmarks" in the direction they are cutting, such as weld seams, scribe marks, or other features, so they know where they are on a cut, particularly on a large piece of work. Make sure that you are in a safe position whenever you do your final cuts, so that there is no danger that the piece you are cutting will fall on you or your hose.

There are other systems for cutting underwater, such as the Petrogen® system, but the arc-oxygen arrangement remains the most popular.

Working Underwater with a Crane

There will probably be many times during your career that you will need to work with a crane to lift or place things while you are underwater. Since you will not be communicating with the crane driver directly, but will need to communicate through the person running your communications box topside, you will need to be extremely precise in your instructions, taking into account the lag time for your instructions to be transmitted.

When you give instructions to the crane operator, be sure to state exactly how much movement you want. For example, instead of saying, "Come up on the load," you would want to say, "Come up on the load three feet and all stop."

Keep in mind that if the crane is on a ship or barge, the load at the end of the crane will be moving up and down as the vessel heaves up and down in the seas. It can be very tricky to time the movement of the load, especially if the visibility is poor.

Welding Underwater

Electric arc welding is performed regularly underwater and it takes skill to do it right. There are probably fewer skilled underwater welders than there are underwater burners.

Underwater welding may be performed either "dry" or "wet." Dry welding is usually the preferred method for any "serious" welding, such as repairing a pipeline or platform structural member. It is a complicated proce-

There are systems for burning underwater that are completely self-contained that carry cylinders of oxygen and batteries to ignite the rod.

Working with a load suspended from a crane can be very tricky when you are underwater. The load will move up and down with the movement of the barge. Some of the cranes used in the offshore industry are truly massive, like the ones used here during the installation of an offshore platform.

dure that requires lots of support equipment.

To perform dry welding, a specially constructed watertight habitat is placed over the structure to be repaired and all of the water is pumped out of the habitat. These dry habitats may be large enough to enclose the diver's entire body, or just his upper torso. They are large, bulky pieces of equipment that must be carefully positioned in order to prevent any damage to the structure to be repaired.

Once the habitat has been "dewatered" and filled with gas, the diver enters the structure and preps the surface to be welded. This may require cutting away any damaged material and usually involves a significant amount of brushing with a hydraulic brush and grinding with a hydraulic grinder to remove marine life and bevel the surface. The diver may wear a lightweight full-face mask inside the habitat to help prevent him from breathing the fumes from the welding process. Once the repair is complete, the habitat must be removed and brought back to the surface.

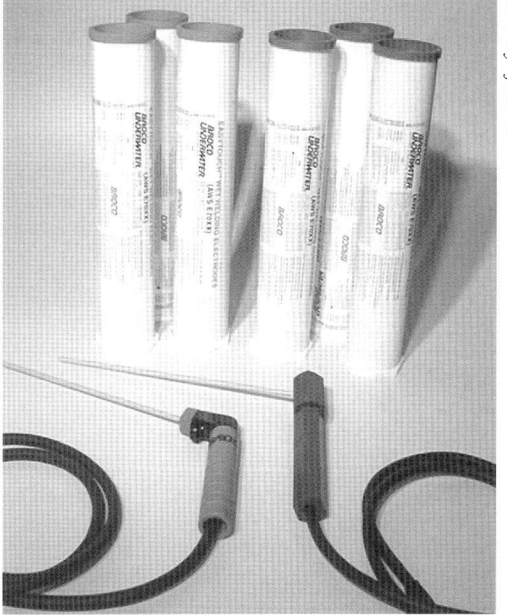

Special rods and torches or "stingers" are used for wet welding underwater.

Working with Tools Underwater

Highly skilled habitat welders are normally certified to strict standards and having this certification can be an important asset in obtaining work. There are only a small number of people who can do this type of job.

Wet welding is also used and the quality of the welds that are possible has greatly improved over the years. However, the big problem with most wet welding is that the water "quenches" (cools) the weld quickly which tends to make it brittle.

Water Blasters

High-pressure water blasters are used to remove "stubborn" marine growth such as barnacles and encrusting worms, from underwater structures when inspections and repairs must be performed. As mentioned previously, these tools develop 10,000-20,000 p.s.i. of water pressure at their tip, depending on the model.

Most blasters will have a front nozzle as well as a rear discharge that also releases pressure. The rear discharge balances the considerable thrust of the device and makes it easier for a diver to control it. Never allow any part of your body to be positioned in front of either of these orifices. Be sure to always wear foot protection when you use these tools, and never use them in place of a water jet for digging a trench in the bottom or moving mud.

The hoses that supply the water pressure to these blasters are heavy and difficult to handle. They also are subject to drag when there is a current.

In most cases, you'll need to let topside know when you want pressure to the blaster when you are on the site and ready to start work. You must be in a position where you have excellent stability to use this equipment with any degree of safety and efficiency.

© Bob Evans. La Mer Bleu Productions.

Water blasters develop tremendous pressure, and can cause serious injuries if you are careless. This diver is using a blaster to clean marine growth from an underwater platform.

To use the blaster, hold it within an inch or two of the surface you need to clean until you can see that it is having the desired effect. You may also want to slowly sweep it back and forth across the surface you are working on so that you can see how much growth has been removed without the need to actually stop work for inspection purposes. The type of growth you are working on, and how tenaciously it is attached will determine the best

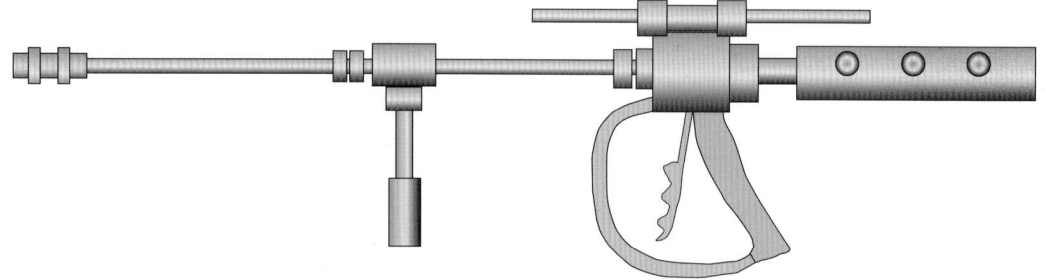

Water blasters have both a front and rear discharge. This type of gear is used on many different types of jobs.

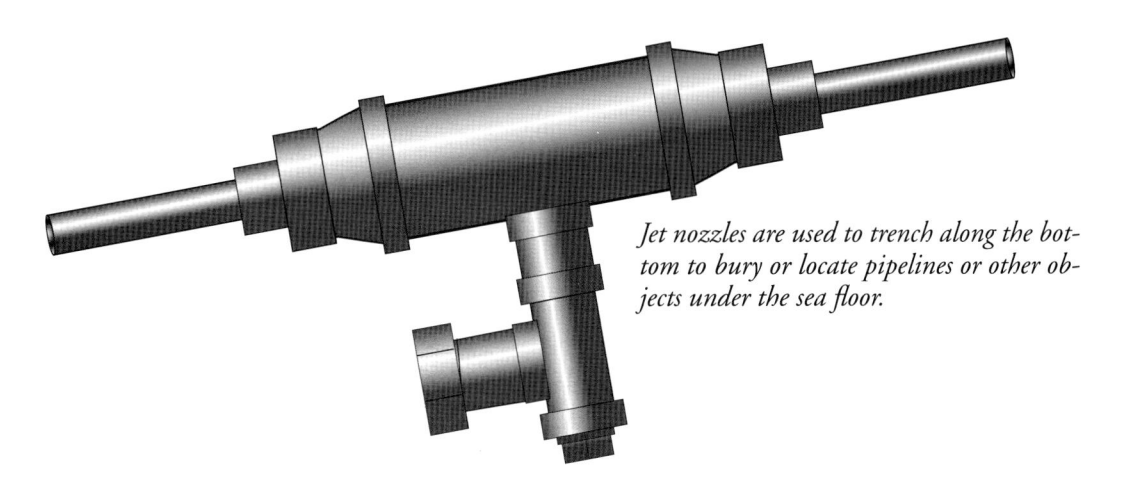

Jet nozzles are used to trench along the bottom to bury or locate pipelines or other objects under the sea floor.

technique. This is a fatiguing tool to use.

If you are injured by a water blaster and your skin is broken, it is essential to seek immediate medical assistance. Even though the wound may not look like much, there can be serious internal injury, and the chance of infection is extremely high.

In some circumstances, you may be required to use a blaster that delivers a fine grit for removing paint. These devices are appropriately known as grit blasters.

Using a grit blaster is identical to using a water blaster, with the exception that the grit blaster's residue will end up almost everywhere, including inside your wetsuit or hot water suit and inside the hood of your full-face mask. You'll want to be sure to clean your gear thoroughly after you have been working with a grit blaster.

Jet Nozzles

If you are working on a pipeline installation, you will probably be required to "jet the pipe down" at various points in the job. Although most pipe will be buried by a "jet sled" operated from the barge, there will be times when this work must be done by hand.

A water jet is a relatively low-pressure (200-300 p.s.i.) device that delivers a large volume of water to wash away mud or sand on the bottom. The nozzle will normally be "T" shaped so that there is a front discharge and a rear "retro-jet" to stabilize the gun.

Before you dive, find out how deep your trench should be for the pipe. This will normally be specified in the description of the work from the client.

Once you've reached the job site underwater, you'll need to let topside know that you need power to the jet. To use the jet nozzle, kneel on the bottom next to the pipe so you are in physical contact with it and point the nozzle to the area immediately next to the pipe. You'll need to excavate the area to the side of the pipe first before you can get underneath it. As you wash away the bottom under the pipe, it should slowly drop into the ditch.

Jetting can go very quickly or be extremely tedious work, depending primarily on the composition of the bottom. For example, some types of sand are easy to move, but tend to run back into the hole as soon as it is excavated. This can make the work go quite slowly. Similarly, clay bottoms may literally need to be cut up into "chunks" that must be lifted out of the hole a piece at a time.

Explosives

In the early days of commercial diving, it was quite common for divers to work with explosives underwater in the offshore environment. Today explosives are rarely used offshore, but you may encounter them if you work inshore or on foreign operations.

For you to handle these materials with any degree of safety, it's important for you to understand the risks in using explosives and in being near an underwater explosion. If at

Working with Tools Underwater

Explosives like this shaped charge are rarely used in the marine environment in the U.S. today.

Photo by Jack Drake. Courtesy of Doug Smith.

all possible, you should take an explosives course before you ever work with explosives. You don't need to be an expert, but you do need to have an understanding of the basic rules in dealing with explosives and how these tools work.

Explosives are most commonly used in the salvage of underwater structures, although they may also be used in construction. They're also used in exploratory drilling to cut off drill "stem" during the "plug and abandon" phase on a "dry" well. They can be used to effectively cut materials very quickly. Unless you become an expert in explosives, your job as a diver will primarily be to place explosives prepared by other crew members or technicians. If you have the opportunity to work with a person who is knowledgeable in this area, be sure to take advantage of it and learn everything that you can about this specialty area.

Explosive charges to be used underwater will normally be detonated with an electric blasting cap, and possibly some Primacord®, which is used to set off other explosives that may be connected to the main charge. A blasting machine is normally used to generate the power used to set off the blasting cap.

One of the most important things you must understand about explosives is that you must never be in the water when an explosive charge is detonated. Even if you are not right next to the charge, the shock wave from an underwater explosion can kill you if you are in the vicinity of the blast.

In some circumstances, explosives may be lowered down inside an oil well casing by the rig crew and will be used to cut off the casing at or below the mudline. In this situation, it will be the diver's job to inspect the site after the blast to ensure that the casing was properly severed.

Digital Still Cameras

Still and video cameras are used extensively in underwater inspection work to document the condition of platforms, pipelines, and other structures. They may also be used to monitor your progress as you work, which some divers may find rather intrusive.

Although film may still be used in some applications, digital photography is the best way to go for the commercial diver. Digital photography allows you to more easily store, catalog, and retrieve images than ever before. In addition, digital images save time, money, and the environment, since they eliminate the chemicals used in photo processing. Besides making prints, digital images can also be used for computer-projected presentations, on web sites, and of course, they can be instantly transmitted via e-mail.

To produce optimal photos of platform nodes, pipelines, or pier pilings underwater, you will need a camera with a wide-angle lens.

There are many excellent digital camera housings for producing high quality photos.

© Light and Motion. All rights reserved.

Wide-angle lenses allow you to get close to your subject when the visibility is low. Even in relatively clear water, a wide-angle lens is still desirable to get the most detail and vibrant colors in your photos.

Most digital cameras, unfortunately, do not provide as wide an angle as you need to take photos of large subjects like wrecks, platform nodes, or pipelines. This is due to the fact that the chip in all but the most expensive digital cameras reduces the lens image to a fraction of what the lens sees. In situations where wide angle is crucial, you'll need either a lens adapter for the camera, or a lens adapter for your camera housing.

Check to see if some type of macro adapter is available for either the camera or the housing. Close-up shots are essential if you need to provide inspection photos of welds, or cracks in concrete.

You'll want a camera that allows you to manually override the automatic settings so that you can make adjustments to the exposure settings for underwater use. In most cases, the settings for the camera will have been worked out prior to your dive, so all you will need to do is set the camera to the proper lens opening (aperture) and shutter speed, position yourself at the correct distance, and take the picture. Make sure you understand how to adjust the settings on the camera and position the flash before you go underwater.

One of the greatest things about shooting digital underwater is the ability to see your results instantly. The housing will undoubtedly have a window that allows you to see your results while you are still underwater. This enables you to tweak the camera's settings if your exposures aren't perfect. While you may be tempted to use this feature to allow you to see which pictures you may want to delete, it's usually wise not to delete any of the photos until after the dive when you have had a chance to view them on a computer screen. Many times you'll find that you'll be able to correct some, if not all, of the problems with a particular photo by manipulating it in your computer by using a photo-retouching program like Adobe Photoshop®.

You'll want a camera and housing combination that allows you to turn off the camera's built-in flash, and use one or more external underwater flash units that connect to the housing through a waterproof bulkhead connector. Unfortunately, the built-in flash units that come with most digital cameras are

Underwater photography is an important tool used to document work and the condition of the job site.

© Kirby Morgan Dive Systems, Inc.

Working with Tools Underwater

worthless underwater, and you'll need an electronic underwater flash to properly light your subjects.

Be sure to check the depth rating of the housing. Good housings will generally go to at least 200 feet, and many will perform at deeper depths.

Some housings feature a lens system that will allow you to change external lenses underwater, so you can switch between wide angle and close-up. By changing lenses, you can shoot an overall photo of a weld and a defect in the weld on the same dive.

To obtain the best results as an underwater photographer, you'll want to take at least an introductory course in underwater photography. This is the best way to improve your skills in the shortest time span possible. These types of courses are frequently offered through sport diving stores, but may also be offered through professional photography schools, or even community colleges.

It's also important to read and study the manuals for all of the equipment you are using, including the camera, the housing, and the underwater flash system. Like any tool you might use while diving, before you take any photos underwater, you need to be familiar with how the camera operates topside.

The key to producing good underwater still images is to get as close as possible to your subject before you take your photograph. You want the subject to fill the frame of the camera as much as possible without cutting anything off. If the subject is a horizontal object (i.e., longer than it is tall) such as a pipeline, then the subject should be photographed horizontally. If the subject is a vertical subject, such as an underwater oil wellhead or "Christmas tree" then the camera should be turned on its side and the image should be a vertical.

Unless the water is extremely clear, the flash(es) should never be pointed directly at the subject, but turned slightly out towards the side. This will eliminate the illumination of the particulate matter or "backscatter" in your photos.

Underwater Video

Underwater video is a powerful tool that goes hand in hand with underwater still photography. Video is especially effective for documenting large subjects and to help give the viewer a perspective on the relative distances between objects. Underwater, most video cameras see better than the human eye. For most people, it's easier to produce good video than it is good underwater stills. Video also allows you to document subjects in very low light without supplementary lighting.

TV cameras are frequently mounted on the diver's helmet with the image transmitted to topside via a wire bundled into the diver's umbilical.

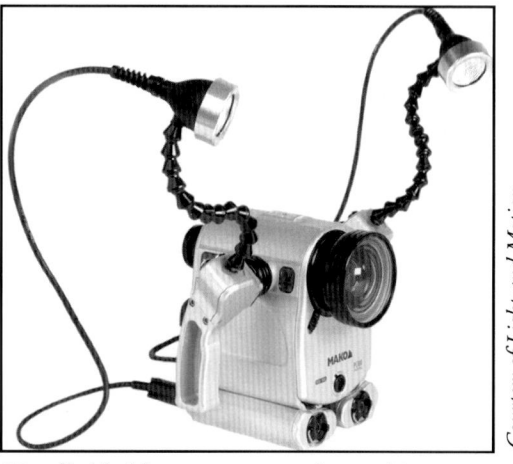

Handheld video cameras are also used in certain situations.

There are two different types of underwater systems that are commonly used underwater. Helmet mounted video cameras are usually exceptionally compact and are frequently mounted on the handle of your diving helmet. A cable transmits the images to topside and allows the diving supervisor to see essentially the same view as you do. These systems require no adjustment or handling on your part, however, the image quality may not match that produced by a separate camera in a housing.

Video cameras in underwater housings generally produce the best possible images in terms of clarity and color rendition. Of course, they require more effort to use and swim underwater.

Once you understand how your camera works, and have mastered the controls for the housing, the key to producing good video is to get close to your subject and move slowly. People watching your video will not be able to follow what's happening if your camera movements are quick and/or jittery. The camera must be very stable, must move at a leisurely pace, and must focus on any important subject for a long enough time for the viewer to absorb and understand what they are seeing.

Be sure to get as close to your subjects as possible. It's important to give perspective so that your viewer understands what they are seeing in the frame. For example, if you are trying to show damage to a welded joint or "node" on a platform, where several structural members meet, it's important to show a wide angle shot first to establish where the damage is located, followed by a medium shot (closer still) and ultimately, a close-up shot of the damage itself.

Ideally, you don't want to deliver "raw" footage to the client, but should instead produce a finished, edited program with titling, graphics, transitions, and all of the elements that reflect a polished presentation. With today's desktop computers it's possible for any diving company to deliver this type of product to the customer without an undue amount of effort. If you take the time to learn how to do this work, it will make you much more valuable and distinguish yourself from all of the other divers on the job who don't have these skills.

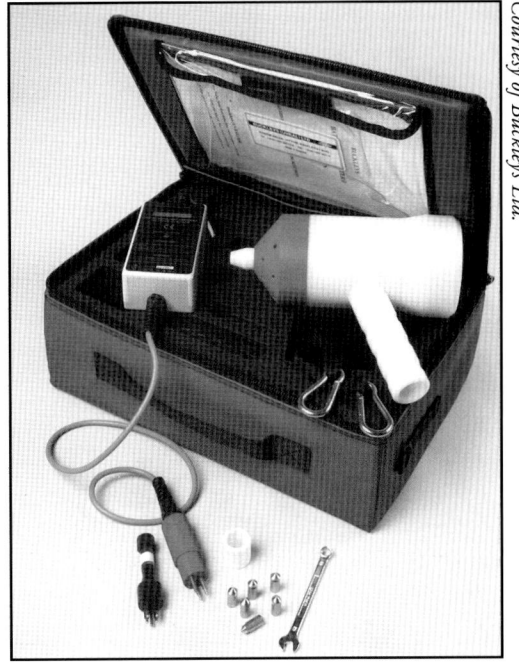

This bathycorrometer is used to measure corrosion on steel structures underwater.

Courtesy of Buckley's Ltd.

Non-Destructive Testing

Underwater structures in the ocean, such as bridges, platforms, and pipelines, are continuously subjected to the unrelenting power of the sea and the corrosive effects of salt water. To help ensure that these structures do not fail, causing human injury and environmental damage, regular inspection of these objects is essential. An important part of these inspections is a variety of procedures formally known as "non-destructive testing" or "NDT."

There are many different instruments and procedures that are used for non-destructive testing, including corrosion meters (also known as "cathodic protection meters," "CP probes," or "bathycorrometers"), ultrasonic thickness meters, and magnetic particle inspection (MPI). Each device and technique has its own application.

Corrosion meters are used to measure the deterioration of steel structures underwater. They record the electrochemical potential of the structure being inspected against its own internal reference electrode. As a diver, it's

Working with Tools Underwater

Author Steve Barsky performs magnetic particle inspection on a platform in the Gulf of Mexico. Note the electromagnet he is using to do the job.

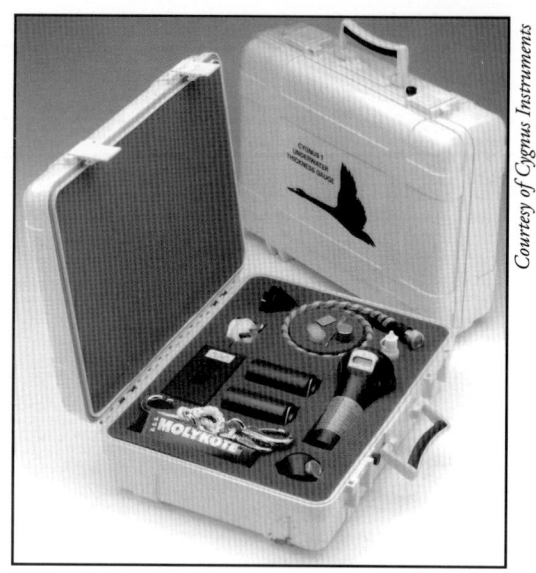

This ultrasonic thickness meter is used to measure the remaining thickness of a steel platform at strategic locations where corrosion may affect the integrity of the structure.

your job only to use the instrument and take measurements, not to interpret the results, which is a job for a corrosion engineer. The information provided tells the engineer whether there is sufficient cathodic protection (usually "sacrificial" zinc anodes) to protect the object from deterioration. Corrosion meters are used to inspect all types of steel structures, including platforms, drilling rigs, pipelines, ship's hulls, and other edifices.

Using a corrosion meter is simple. The device has a stainless steel tip that is jabbed against an area that is clean of marine growth and a reading appears on the digital display on the back of the unit. Zinc and magnesium blocks are normally supplied to provide a reference reading to be sure the meter is reading correctly.

An ultrasonic thickness meter is a device used to measure the wall thickness of the metal on a platform leg, pipeline, or similar item, where it is impossible to use a thickness gauge or a Vernier caliper. The ultrasonic thickness meter bounces sound waves within the metal, and based on the time it takes them to return provides a highly accurate reading of the thickness of the steel.

Magnetic particle inspection is a technique used to inspect defects in welded steel joints that might otherwise be difficult to spot. The site of the weld is magnetized using a powerful electromagnet, and a fluorescent ink containing magnetic particles is sprayed over the weld. If there are cracks in the weld, the particles will line up in the crack making it much easier to see and photograph. To properly perform magnetic particle inspection requires training and practice.

120

True Tales of Commercial Diving from the North Sea

In 1977, the North Sea was at the height of the oil boom in that region as new wells were drilled and new platforms were installed. Commercial diving operations were being conducted for sustained periods at unprecedented depths, and saturation divers were making fortunes.

I had arrived in Aberdeen, Scotland in the summer of 1976 to work for a company called SubSea International, which was one of the largest commercial diving firms in the world. That year, SubSea had 50 people working offshore, but by the following year they had almost 300 people working offshore. Anyone who could dive was quickly promoted from tender to diver.

I was finishing my first year as a tender and working on a saturation system that was performing platform inspections from a ship in the Forties Field, one of the first producing oil fields in the North Sea. It was a sunny day, and while the divers were working out of the bell at 400 feet, I was on deck painting some equipment with several other crew members. One of the other tenders on the job approached me and said, "Hey Steve, go get your stuff, you're going into saturation." Since I had a relatively low number of dives, and as far as I knew, I hadn't been promoted, I ignored the instructions I had been given, thinking it was a joke.

About 20 minutes later, one of the diving supervisors came up to me and asked me what I was doing, and why I was painting. I started to give him a smart aleck reply when I realized that I was really supposed to be preparing to go into saturation. Half an hour later, I was in the entrance lock to the sat system, pressurizing down to the storage depth of 200 FSW. Two hours later, I was climbing up into the diving bell in preparation for making a bell dive to 275 FSW.

Five hours later, after tending my bell mate during his dive, I made my first bell lock-out at 275 FSW. As I dropped down into the bell stage, I was simultaneously exhilarated and scared to death. Conditions were rough on the surface, and the diving bell was heaving up and down, at least eight feet through the water column, like a giant wrecking ball.

I swam over to the platform we were inspecting and looked back at the bell, which looked like a Christmas tree ornament 300 feet away. I took photographs of the structure, made measurements, and gave verbal reports to accompany the video I was transmitting topside, during a dive that lasted almost four hours. The whole time I was in the water I kept thinking about what would happen if my umbilical was severed and I could not make it back to the bell.

By the time the bell got back to the surface, and locked onto the sat system, I was exhausted, but I couldn't sleep. I was still frightened by what I had experienced. I asked to speak to the diving supervisor over the intercom and when he came on the line, I explained to him that I was scared and didn't know whether I could make another dive. He did not ridicule me or chide me about my fears, but suggested that I think it over carefully, because if they brought me out of saturation, it would be unlikely I would ever get the chance to dive again. I thought it over and agreed to try it again.

Thirty-six hours later, I made another dive, this time to 410 FSW and stayed in the water for four hours and 46 minutes. I was completely comfortable during the dive and went on to continue my career as a diver for another six years.

Everyone who dives has moments of fear underwater. It's natural and understood. As the saying goes, commercial diving is made up of hours of interminable boredom punctuated by moments of sheer terror…

Steve Barsky

© Bev Morgan. All rights reserved.

Chapter 10
Rigging for the Commercial Diver

Please don't tell my mother I'm a diver, she thinks I'm a piano player in a whore house!

All commercial divers must be knowledgeable in the use of a wide variety of lines, splices, knots, slings, and rigging tools. In the diving field, you will work with lines every day, and you must be able to select the correct type of line for the job you need to do.

You will be expected to know how to fasten equipment down to the deck of the ship and how to rig a load for lifting underwater. You must know how to select the proper line for specific applications and how to tie it off so it won't come undone accidentally, but can be rapidly removed when you are ready to do so.

You must be able to perform your rigging quickly, and underwater you may be forced to do it by feel. You need to know which knot or hitch to use in a particular situation so that you don't have to stop and ponder which method is correct or remember how to fasten the line.

This chapter is intended to provide you with a basic introduction to rigging to give you some idea of the importance of this skill and what you need to know to be a successful rigger. For more detailed information on rigging, we recommend that you pick up a copy of the *Handbook for Riggers* by Newberry. This pocket guide is inexpensive and indispensable for divers.

Safe Working Loads

With any rope, whether it is fiber rope, wire rope, or a flat strap made from synthetic fiber, you must know the safe working load of the material and any associated rigging. If the rope has obviously been abused, if it is dam-

You must know the safe working load for all the lines and ropes you use.

aged in any way, you cannot depend on the rope to safely lift a load at the stated capacity of the material. In addition, if there are knots or splices in the rope, this will reduce the safe working load.

Probably the single most important rule that you must remember as a person working in the commercial diving industry is that you must never be underneath any load that is being lifted. If the load should fall, you could be seriously injured or killed.

Fiber Rope

There are many different kinds of fiber rope, but the two main categories of fiber

Rigging for the Commercial Diver

Left to right: manila, nylon, and polypropylene lines.

ropes are natural fiber ropes, such as manila, and synthetic fibers such as nylon and polypropylene. Each type of rope has its advantages and disadvantages which make it suitable for a particular usage.

Manila

Manila is the most widely used natural fiber rope. It is relatively inexpensive yet has reasonable strength. As a natural fiber (made from organic material) manila does not have the life that synthetic ropes have, and it deteriorates over time.

When manila first becomes wet it contracts and is difficult to use. Any manila that will be used underwater by a diver should be wetted down and stretched prior to use. If this is not done, it balls up into a knotted mess. Manila sinks quickly when it is wet, and it does not stretch.

Use manila in situations where you may want to discard the line underwater and where great strength is not needed. For example, manila is frequently used as a "weak link" at the end of a down line, because it will break when a load is put on it, rather than sending a diver down to unfasten the line at the end of the job.

Polypropylene

Polypropylene is a good line for rigging on deck, but is not used underwater very often because it floats and is difficult to work with when you are on the bottom. Most of the "polypro" you will encounter will be either yellow or white. It's instantly recognizable by its shiny appearance and slippery feel.

Polypropylene will stretch but not to the extent that nylon does. It also has good strength, but again is not as strong as nylon of the same diameter. It is resistant to most chemicals and it will not rot like natural fiber rope, but does not stand up well to exposure to the sun.

It's appropriate to use polypro for making rope slings and securing loads, for tag lines to prevent heavier loads from spinning, and similar applications. Polypropylene is not the best line for fastening knots due to its slippery nature. It is commonly used for mooring lines because it floats and as the downline for the diver to travel to and from the job site underwater.

Nylon

Nylon is generally a more expensive rope than polypropylene, but it has more capabilities. It is stronger, absorbs shock well, and has excellent elasticity. It also has good abrasion resistance and it does not float.

Like polypropylene, nylon resists rotting and mildew, but is more resistant to sunlight, as well as exposure to oil and gasoline. However, it has poor resistance to acids.

Nylon is widely used in the marine environment for many applications. In diving, it's sometimes used for the down line to the job site. It has a relatively long service life when compared to other synthetic ropes.

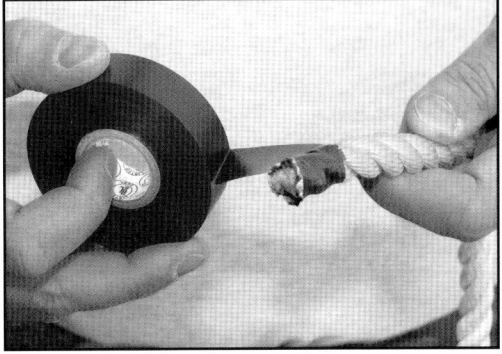

The simplest way to whip a line is with electrical tape.

Whipping

Whenever you are working with a piece of rope, the end of the line must be "whipped" to help prevent the ends from coming apart or "unlaid." There are several ways this can be done.

The simplest method of whipping a line is to use waterproof electrical tape and tightly wrap it around the line no more than 1/8 inch away from the end. Be sure to stretch the tape to ensure you get good adhesion.

If you are using synthetic line, the end of the line should always be melted or burned whenever it is cut. Avoid breathing the fumes as these are unhealthy. However, even if you have burned the ends it's still a good idea to whip the end with electrical tape, or a synthetic twine if you have the time to do so.

Both natural and synthetic fiber ropes can be whipped with a small diameter twine. The procedure is very simple. Lay a 5-6 inch loop of twine against the line lengthwise with the loop closest to the end of the line you are whipping. Do not cut the twine off the reel.

Wrap the twine as tightly as possible around the rope, starting about two inches from the open end of the loop. Each wrap of twine should be tight against the prior wrap. Continue to wrap the twine around the rope until there is about a half-inch of the loop sticking out from the whipping. Cut the twine off the reel with about two inches to spare.

Insert the end of the twine you have just cut off through the loop closest to the end of the rope. Grab the tail of the line sticking out from the other end of the whipping and pull it until the loop and the end of the line disappear under the whipping. Cut off the loose ends of the twine from the whipping as close as possible to your wraps around the rope without damaging the wraps.

If you have the skill and a few spare minutes, you may want to "back-splice" the end of the line, as discussed in the next section. A back-splice is a very neat way to finish a line, but it does increase the diameter substantially and may not be desirable in all situations.

You can also whip a line using waxed linen.

Every line you work with should be whipped.

125

Rigging for the Commercial Diver

Splices

There are two very common splices that you will use on a regular basis as a diver. These are the back splice and the eye splice.

The back splice is used whenever you want to finish off the end of a rope neatly or if you are low on electrical tape and don't want to use it to whip the end of the line. Once you have practiced splicing a few times, you will be able to perform this skill very quickly.

The most commonly used splice is the eye splice and it's easy to make. You need to be able to quickly create an eye splice, as you will constantly need lines with eyes in the end of them. You will use lines with eye splices to bundle diving hoses after they have been coiled, to secure tarps over equipment, to make lanyards for tools, and a thousand other applications. It's essential that you learn how to make a proper eye splice

Eye splices are used to attach lines to tools, to secure tarps, and for many other applications.

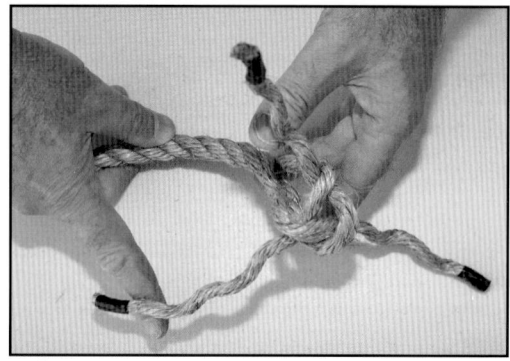

When you splice with natural fiber rope you must make three tucks with each strand of the line. This is the start of a back splice.

An eye splice is used whenever you want to put a permanent "eye" or loop in the end of a line.

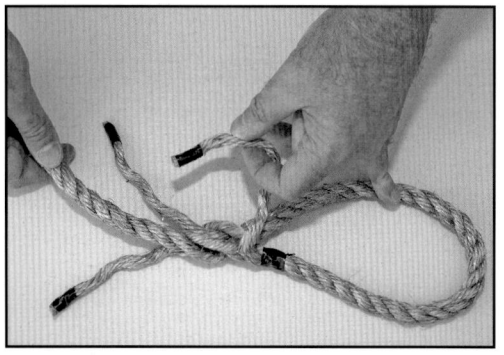

The back splice is a neat way to finish a line, but it does produce more bulk than if you just whipped the line. Normally the tails would be cut flush with the end of the splice and the entire splice would be whipped.

Before you do any splicing, you'll need to whip the ends of the line so it does not come unlaid.

The Simple Guide to Commercial Diving

Knots

The most commonly used knot that you will tie is the bowline, and it is indispensable. It will not slip and is easy to untie.

One method that you can use to help secure any knot so that it will not come undone is to unlay the "live" part of the line and tuck the "bitter end" of the line through it. When there is tension on the line it will tightly grip the end of the line so it can not slip out.

Round turn and two half hitches

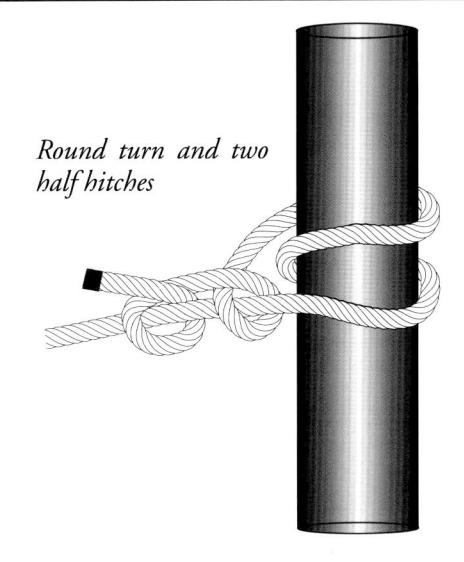

A bowline is the most commonly tied knot used by divers.

Hitches

There are many different hitches that are used to secure lines around a variety of objects. Hitches are often used to lift a piece of pipe or secure a vessel.

The simplest application for a hitch is to secure a vessel by "making the line fast to a cleat." Nothing is more embarrassing, and potentially dangerous, than to tie a vessel off and have the line slip and the ship float away. This is a fundamental skill that you must know how to perform.

Another simple hitch is the round turn followed by two half hitches. This is a simple technique for securing a line to a stationary object.

The clove hitch and the constrictor hitch are very similar and are both used to secure a line around a piling or a railing. Of the two, the constrictor hitch is the preferred method to use in this application. It's extremely secure, but easy to release when you need to do so.

The timber hitch is a good method to secure a line around a single piece of pipe or a

A clove hitch is an effective way to fasten a line around a timber.

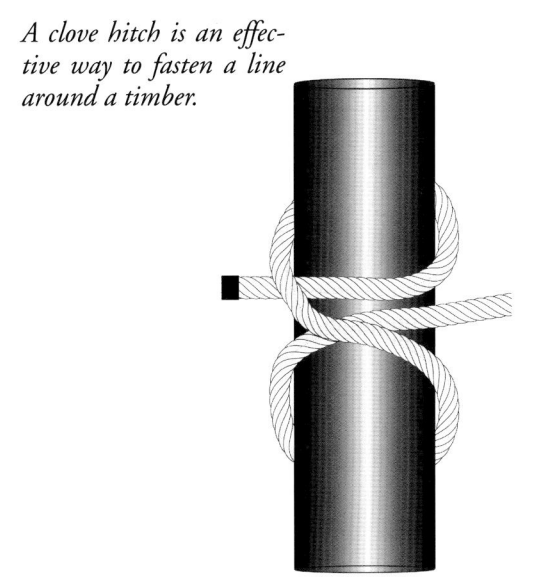

Every diver must be able to make a line fast to a cleat.

Rigging for the Commercial Diver

The constrictor hitch is an extremely secure method for making a line fast to a timber or stanchion.

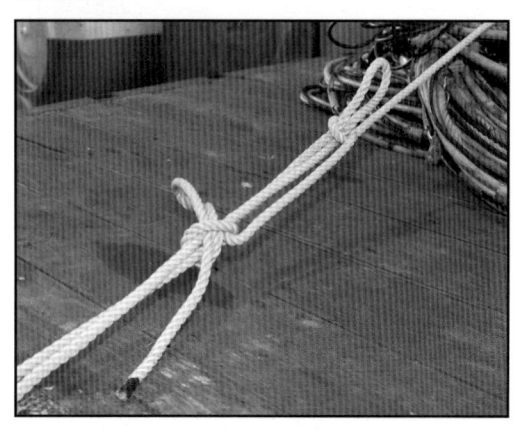

Use the trucker's hitch for tying a diver's hose or other equipment down on a truck.

piling that needs to be lifted out of the water. We've used this technique to recover a length of drill "stem" (pipe) that was dropped over the side of a rig. The important thing to remember is that the line must be kept under strain so that it does not slip.

One of the most useful methods for tightening up a line to secure a load on a truck or a ship is to use a trucker's hitch. This hitch produces a mechanical advantage, much like using a block and tackle.

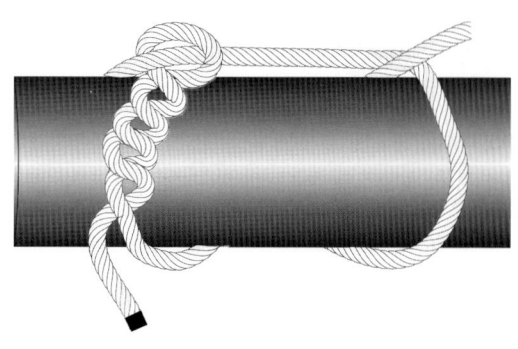

A timber hitch provides a secure method for lifting a piece of pipe.

Wire Rope

Wire rope is obviously much stronger than any fiber rope, and is used for all heavy lifting in the offshore environment. As a diver, you will frequently work with wire rope and you should be familiar with its characteristics and how to use it. You should also know how to perform a basic wire rope splice, called a "Molly Hogan," as well as how to apply wire rope clips.

Wire rope is specified by its diameter and by the number of bundles in the rope and the number of strands in each bundle. It is also specified by the material in the core of the rope. For example, 6X19 wire rope has six bundles of wire with 19 individual strands in each bundle. The center or "core" of the wire rope may be either a fiber core, or what is known as "IWRC," which stands for an Independent Wire Rope Core. Any wire rope that is used in the marine environment must be galvanized.

Wire rope is, of course, much stronger than any comparably sized fiber rope, but it is always much heavier. Flexibility is not a characteristic of wire rope, and large wire rope slings can be extremely difficult to handle.

Wire rope can really chew up your hands if you are not careful, especially if there are damaged strands or ends, commonly referred to as "meat hooks." In addition, new wire rope may have some lubrication on it and older ropes may have rust. For all of these reasons, it is essential to always wear gloves when handling wire rope, both topside and underwater.

Wire rope is widely used in the offshore

environment. Any time a nongalvinized rope goes underwater, it will start to rust from the inside out and may part unexpectedly. Slings of this type should be tagged or discarded after use.

Beware of slings that are heavily rusted or that have been kinked. They may fail without warning.

Wire Rope Eye Splices and Slings

Whenever possible, use a thimble when you are performing a wire rope splice. The purpose of the thimble is to add strength and mechanical protection to the splice. It's difficult to use a thimble when you are performing a splice in wire rope by hand.

OSHA (Occupational Safety and Health Administration) regulations and the American National Standards Institute (ANSI) no longer permit the use of wire rope clips to fabricate wire rope slings. According to OSHA, any sling must be fabricated with a mechanical splice.

Divers must splice lines all the time, and in at least one case, the divers spliced the anchor wire on a 250-foot supply vessel in the North Sea when the boat's crew was incapable of doing the job.

One simple method of making an eye in wire rope is to "perform" a "Molly Hogan" as shown here. To finish your Molly Hogan, you'll want to apply wire rope clips. There must be sufficient "tail" to the splice (or "turnback") to apply the proper number

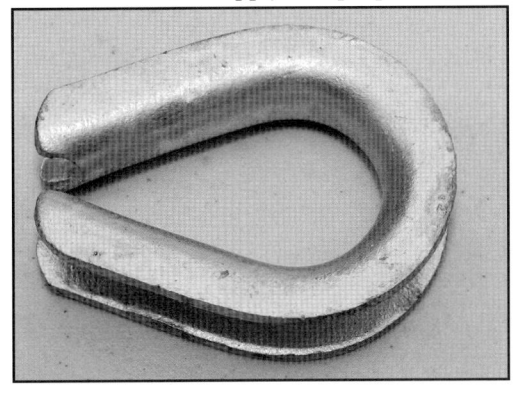

Whenever possible, use a thimble to add strength to any eyesplice in wire rope.

To perform a Molly Hogan, the rope must be unlaid.

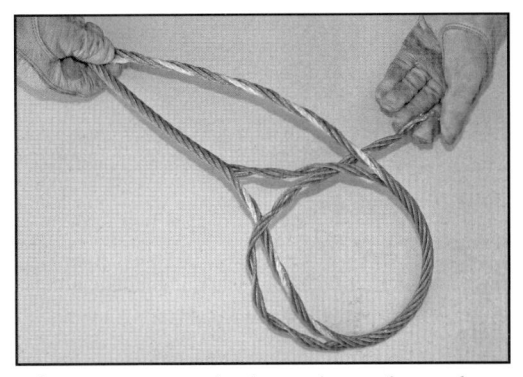

The rope is woven back together to form a loop.

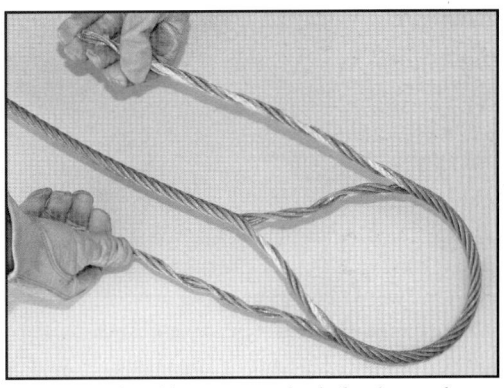

The rope should "nest" perfectly back together.

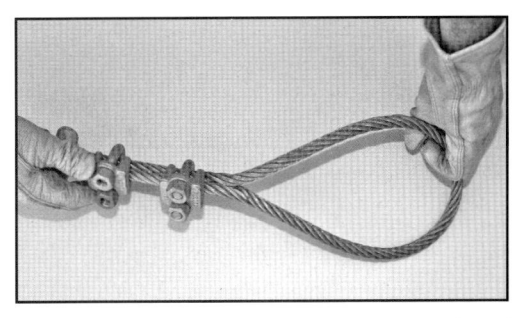

Wire rope clips must be properly applied and spaced on the wire rope.

The Simple Guide to Commercial Diving

129

Rigging for the Commercial Diver

The crane in this photo is lifting a flotation sphere that was used to float this platform out to its location in the North Sea. Divers had to rig the sphere for lifting with wire rope slings at a depth of almost 400 feet before they cut off the struts attaching it to the platform, using underwater cutting torches. To get some idea of the size of the sphere, take a look at the tug (on the left side of the photo) which is over 50 feet long.

Wooden fids are especially useful when you are splicing large diameter fiber rope.

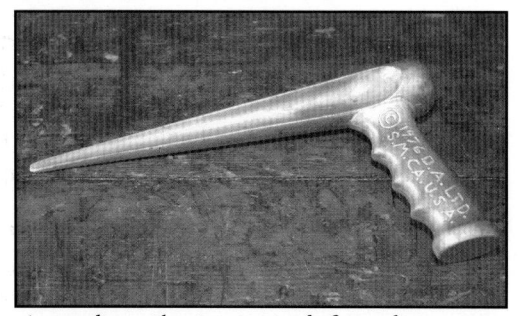

A marlinespike is required for splicing wire rope.

of wire rope clips with the proper spacing, according to the diameter of the wire.

Rigging Tools

The most common tools you will use for rigging include a marlinespike, a "fid" (which is like a large marlinespike), a cable cutter for cutting wire rope, and a socket wrench for making up wire rope clips. A "hot knife," which is a knife with a heated blade, is extremely useful for searing the end of synthetic lines as they are cut, rather than using a match or lighter.

Rigging Hardware

The most commonly used piece of rigging hardware is a shackle. Shackles are used to connect chain to anchors, to fasten slings to loads, and for other applications in the offshore environment.

Although there are many different types

of shackles, the most commonly used shackle in the marine environment is the "screw pin shackle," which has a threaded pin which is used to fasten the device. The size of the shackle is determined by the diameter of the metal in the "bow" or curved section of the shackle. Just as there are safe working loads for fiber and wire ropes, there are safe working loads for shackles, which are usually printed right on them.

When you use a shackle you want to take two important precautions. First, you never want to position the shackle so that a load pulls on the pin at an angle at either end of the pin. Secondly, you never want the pin positioned so that there is a possibility it could unscrew itself.

You will frequently find yourself fastening and unfastening shackles both topside and underwater. When a shackle is corroded or if another person has screwed the pin into the shackle with great force, it can be extremely difficult to unscrew the pin. For this reason it's always important to carry some type of device with you to help turn the pin, especially if you know that a shackle has been underwater for an extended period. A marlinespike is a good tool for this job. We've also known divers who have taped a welding or burning rod against their leg, inside their hot water boot, especially for this purpose.

Hooks

Whenever you are working with a crane you will be using a hook on the end of the crane wire to connect whatever load you are lifting. While in most cases this isn't something that you will have the option of changing, you need to be familiar with the different types of hooks and the correct method for attaching a load.

Snap hooks with a spring-loaded closure are the preferred type of hook for lifting a load in the marine environment, as the spring loaded "tongue" will help to prevent the load from jumping out of the hook. You must take extra care when working with this type of hook not to get your fingers or hand caught in the hook. It can take a bit more time to release a load from a hook of this type, too.

Always position the hook so it is cen-

Shackles come in many different sizes and some of them are truly enormous.

tered over the load. Use a tag line when lifting things on deck to help prevent them from swinging and to control or position the load.

Chain

Chain is used in many cases to fasten gear down on the deck of a ship or for transporting equipment by truck. Chain is generally stronger than wire rope, and less subject to abrasion, although it is usually much heavier when compared to wire rope of the same length. It's rare for devices to be rigged for underwater use with chain, other than anchoring equipment.

When chain is used to fasten gear down to the deck of a boat or on a truck, the chain is normally secured with what is known as a "chain binder." This is a tensioning device with a "cam" action that produces mechanical leverage and helps to tension the chain and immobilize the object being secured.

If the chain is heavy or there is minimal slack to be tensioned up, a short section of pipe is usually slid down over the handle of the chain binder to add sufficient leverage to swing the lever on the binder over the top of the cam. Once the handle on the binder

Rigging for the Commercial Diver

Changing out a propeller requires expert rigging to get the balance just right so the load hangs properly, as demonstrated by diver Mark Wimberly. This photo was shot by Kevin Peters of Miami Divers.

swings past the center it will usually snap closed forcefully. If you are not using a pipe for leverage, or not wearing gloves, your fingers could be badly pinched.

When the handle is locked down, it's a good idea to secure the handle with a bit of line by tying it to the chain itself. This is extra insurance to help prevent the load from popping the binder open.

Chain binders are used to secure equipment to truck beds for transport and on the deck of a ship.

True Tales of Commercial Diving from the Santa Barbara Channel

The majority of my working diving experience was in "heavy gear," the old hardhat gear that was in vogue for a very long time. This incident happened while using one of the early commercial recirculator heavy gear helmets on a HeO2 mix. A recirculator helmet is designed to reuse as much expensive helium-oxygen mixture as possible by filtering out the carbon dioxide (like a rebreather) and adding a small but continuous flow of additional fresh gas.

The site was a floating drill ship sitting over a well in progress in about 250' of seawater. The base plate was on the bottom as was the blowout prevention stack (BOP) and the guide wires were all in place. The job was to jet mud away from the base of the BOP.

I was briefed, dressed-in and went into the water through the "moon pool", that hole in the center of a floating drill ship through which all drilling activity takes place.

The customary method used on a surface dive using gas was to go to 40' on air, switch to gas, and when the gas comes through go into the recirculation mode and head for the bottom. Descent was as rapid as possible because time of descent was part of a diver's working bottom time.

I arrived at 40', stopped and asked for gas, checked out my equipment and when the gas came in headed for the bottom like the proverbial rock. Upon hitting bottom and acknowledging same to topside, I realized that I was getting very wet through one arm. My suit was literally starting to flood through a badly ripped cuff. This was very bad for several reasons; my potential productivity was zilch, I was losing both gas and buoyancy, and the water was very cold. Even with a minimal decompression commitment the cold was a serious problem.

The only reasonable solution was to hold the ripped cuff low and closed as best as possible and head up. At about 120' the switch was made from gas to air and the situation improved considerably. A short decompression was necessary before hitting the surface, but oh boy, did the surface look good! The worst part of this whole episode was my lack of productivity and the subsequent embarrassment. Also, situations such as this do nothing for a diver's reputation.

Bob Christensen

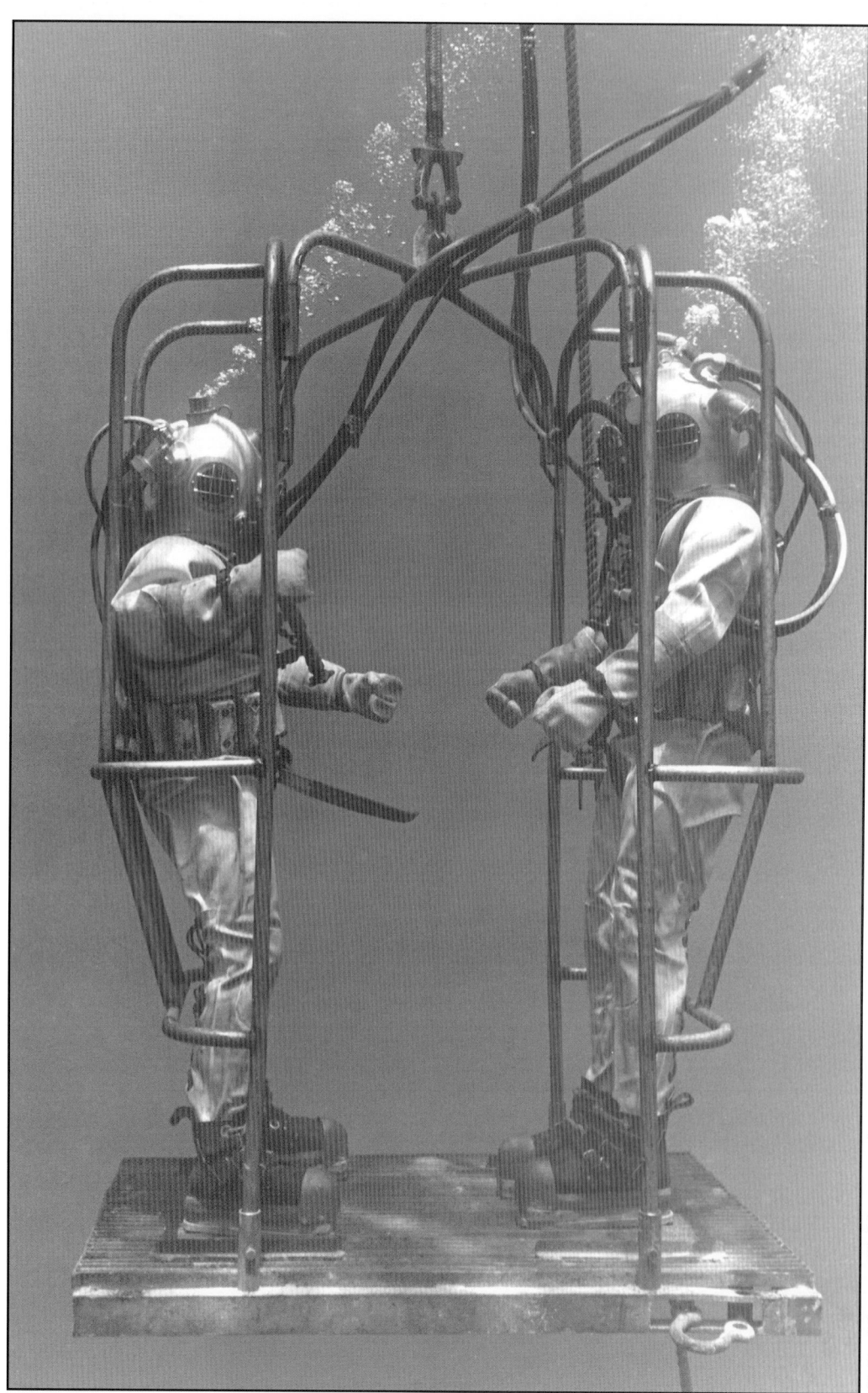

© Bev Morgan. All rights reserved.

Chapter 11
Working as a Diving Supervisor

We're only going to send you out to this job for a "couple of days"... (yeah, right...)

Once you have achieved success as a diver, it's only natural for the company you work for to approach you to act as a diving supervisor. Although some divers are able to decline this responsibility, if you have any leadership ability, you'll be pressured by the company to accept this job, at least part of the time you work offshore.

Make no mistake, working as a diving supervisor imposes serious responsibilities on anyone who accepts this position. You are responsible for the lives of everyone who works under you, and if you make the wrong decisions, people can be seriously injured or killed. We have known supervisors who have been in this position when divers have been killed, and even though it wasn't necessarily their fault, they have had to live with the memories of these events for the rest of their lives. It wasn't pleasant. If you don't think you can cope with this type of situation, or you have a difficult time dealing with stress, then you must decline to take this job.

From Diver to Management

Once you are promoted to diver, there are many paths you can follow to further your career. It's an industry where there is a place for everyone, no matter where your talents may lie.

As soon as you break-out as a diver, you will probably have the opportunity to supervise air diving jobs. As an air diving supervisor, you will be supervising jobs down to 165 FSW. If you like responsibility, being a diving supervisor is a good way to make yourself more valuable to the company.

Divers who gain solid experience in mixed-gas diving can expect to find themselves offered the chance to supervise mixed-gas operations, especially if you have already demonstrated leadership ability as an air diving supervisor. As a mixed-gas supervisor you will be running a crew with as many as twelve divers.

Although you will make more money on an hourly basis as a supervisor, you will not make as much money as if you dive. Many divers decline to supervise for this reason, opting to remain diving and making more money with less responsibility. This is a personal decision, but if you have supervisory abilities and don't use them, most diving companies will not look on you favorably. However, if you're smart, you can trade time spent supervising against the guarantee of a certain amount of diving the rest of the year.

Once you've gained experience as a bell/saturation diver, you will undoubtedly be asked to assist the diving supervisor with running bell dives, and eventually be asked to run a shift on a saturation job. Again, if you are a good supervisor, the company will usually be willing to reward you with a certain amount of diving on other operations.

"Saturation superintendents" are the highest paid diving supervisors working offshore. As a superintendent, you may oversee multiple diving jobs at the same time, with several supervisors reporting to you.

Talents of the Diving Supervisor

As a diving supervisor you must be on your toes at all times, but especially whenever you have a diver in the water. You must always

Working as a Diving Supervisor

It takes real skill as a supervisor to hold a crew together when they have been offshore for weeks or even months at a time. Divers on this barge often spent 90 consecutive days or more working offshore.

put the welfare of the diver at the end of the hose first, because he is totally dependent on you. Safety must always be your number one priority. You must never let a client or management put you or your crew in a situation where your people are at risk. Never sacrifice safety for speed.

You must have the ability to remain cool when things are going badly if you expect to be effective in a supervisory role in a diving company. Multi-tasking, the ability to deal with more than one issue at a time, is also an essential ability. You've got to think clearly and logically when you are under stress and be able to maintain an even disposition when things are grim. If there is an accident, you will be held accountable and there is nothing worse than having to face the family of a diver who is injured or killed, or having to testify in court as a defendant in a case like this.

To be effective as a supervisor, you must have experience doing the types of jobs you are asking your crew to do in the water. They need not be the exact same type of work, but similar enough that you can understand the problems and foresee any difficulties or dangers that might arise. You can't pay lip service to safety. You also must be able to empathize with your divers.

Diving supervisors always need to be thinking several steps ahead in regards to where the job is at the moment and what is coming up. You must be proactive so that you can anticipate what tools your people will need to complete the work and what you need to do to help them. You don't want to be "reactive" when unexpected situations arise.

People skills are especially important for the diving supervisor, in dealing with customers, management, and your crew. You must be able to make the customer feel he is important and that you understand and are meeting his needs, yet you must have a clear picture of the importance of safety in your operation. We've never met a customer who insisted that we make a dive that we felt was unsafe.

You've got to keep the customer informed, so that he has a good idea of what you are doing to keep the work moving forward. If things aren't going well, you shouldn't lie to the customer, but should explain what the problems are and what steps you are taking to correct the difficulties and get things back on track.

Communicating with management on a regular basis is crucial to your success as a diving supervisor. You must be organized and methodical and get your paperwork into the office on time, since this is how the company bills the customer. You need to remember that your company is in business to make a profit so it can stay in business (and you will have a job!).

You need to make yourself available for pre-job meetings with the client and be able to offer ideas about how to make the job successful. You need to go the extra mile in filing reports and offering suggestions for improvements that will make the company more efficient and profitable, without compromising quality or safety.

To gain the loyalty of your crew, you must show them that they are the most important part of any job, and that you are willing to help them achieve their personal goals in their profession as divers. You must lead by example, and help train the tenders even as you lend your expertise and knowledge to the divers. If you have the loyalty and support of your crew, there is almost no job that you can't complete.

Take the time to get to know each member of your team, their likes and dislikes, their strengths and weaknesses, and what their ambitions are for themselves. If you know your crew, you'll understand when they have distractions ashore that may be diverting their full attention from their work and how to speak with them to avoid any problems their concerns may provoke.

Challenge your crew and give them assignments based on their strengths. Know who your lead diver is and make sure he understands you expect him to help train the divers and tenders under him. Talk to the tenders and be sure they understand what you expect of them.

If you have a diver who makes a mistake on a job, don't chew him out while he is in the water. Remain calm and take him aside to discuss his performance privately with him. Rather than tell him what he did wrong, discuss ways that he can ensure that the problem does not occur again.

At every opportunity you should be an advocate for the divers who work for you. If they do a good job, let the office know about it, and if they deserve a promotion, recommend them in writing. Your support of the divers with whom you work will be appreciated and in turn they will do everything they can to support you when you need it.

You need to be firm, fair, and consistent in your dealings with the people who dive under your supervision. Let them know what you expect from their performance and reward them when they do well. Don't play favorites, but treat each person equally. As the saying goes, "what goes around comes around."

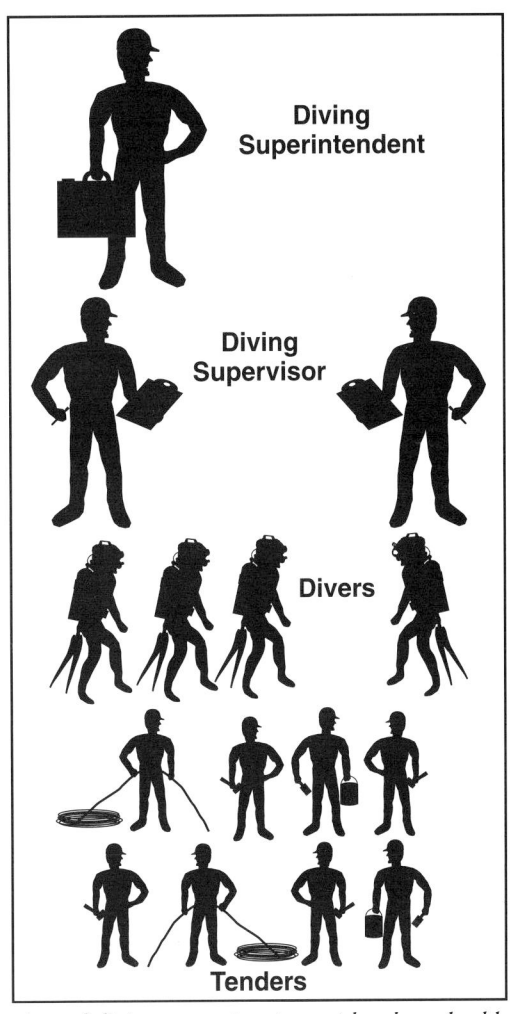

A good diving supervisor is considered a valuable asset by most diving companies. In the long run, becoming a supervisor often makes good sense.

Company Politics

There are politics in every job. However, we've always found it best if you deal with people in a fair and equitable manner, and avoid situations where you may find yourself pitted against one group or another.

Most companies have people who tend to gripe and complain about everything. They choose sides to advance their own agenda, rather than do what's best for the divers in the field or the company itself. If you can politely avoid these people and the situations surrounding them you will generally be better off.

Divers always want to know why they didn't get to go on a particular job or why another person advanced in pay or title ahead of them. Deal with the people who work for you as fairly as you can, and you will generally find yourself well-liked and able to get things done more quickly because you will have the cooperation of the people who do the work.

Moving Into Management

Most divers and supervisors find that they get tired of the diving lifestyle after working offshore for many years, and for those who are interested, there are usually opportunities in management. There are positions for people who want to be project managers, operations managers, and other executive slots. However, if you want to work directly with divers, you'll probably be interested in a position such as an "operations manager" or a safety officer.

The operations manager is in regular contact with the divers in the field, and helps to support their jobs with the manpower, equipment, and supplies that they need. He is the person who assigns divers to a particular job and handles hiring, firing, and promotions. This is a difficult position and requires a person who has exceptional "people skills."

You need to realize that at the lower levels of onshore management in a diving firm, your pay will not be as good as that of a successful diver working offshore. Of course, you won't be working seven days a week, in the middle of the night, or taking the same risks, either.

If you can make the transition to upper management you can expect to make a salary that starts to approach what a successful diver might earn. Of course, a business education would be desirable if you hope to take this path.

Careers Beyond Diving

Many divers who have had a successful career in the industry make the decision to no longer work underwater or even onshore for a commercial diving firm. They may choose to go to work for a commercial diving equipment supplier, as a consultant to the industry, as a teacher at a commercial diving school, or in an entirely unrelated field.

Most people find that many of the job skills and the work ethic they have developed as a commercial diver are not wasted if they decide to pursue other types of employment. There's no substitute for a person who has a "can-do" attitude and who will be relentless in getting the job done, no matter what the job entails.

True Tales of Commercial Diving from Alaska

While working in Alaska, I got a call out to fly down to the Cook Inlet to a sea going tug that had backed down over its tow wire. My tender and I had to travel light, so we took a band mask and cutting gear with a couple of scuba bottles for the air supply.

The cable was a heavy two inch wire that went from the reel on deck over the rail into the water. I dressed in and went into the water which had zero visibility. I followed the wire around the curve of the hull., under a deep skeg, and up three or four feet where it made a couple of turns around the shaft before taking a turn in the propeller and falling away into the depths.

I was concerned about the tension in the wire and what might happen when it parted. Would it snap towards me when I cut it? My plan was to cut the wire between the skeg and the shaft while positioning myself on the section leading back to the surface. I would be using burning gear to make the cut.

As I burned I could hear and feel the strands snap as they were cut, but it didn't seem to be dangerous. When the final strand parted, I "fell" away while still clinging to the section of wire leading to the surface.

An inspection of the results of my work revealed that there were still two turns of wire around the prop and shaft, but it was much looser than when I started the job. Back on deck, I had the tug crew put the gears into reverse. Two rotations of the shaft in reverse with the jacking gear cleared the wire and we were home free.

Bob Christensen

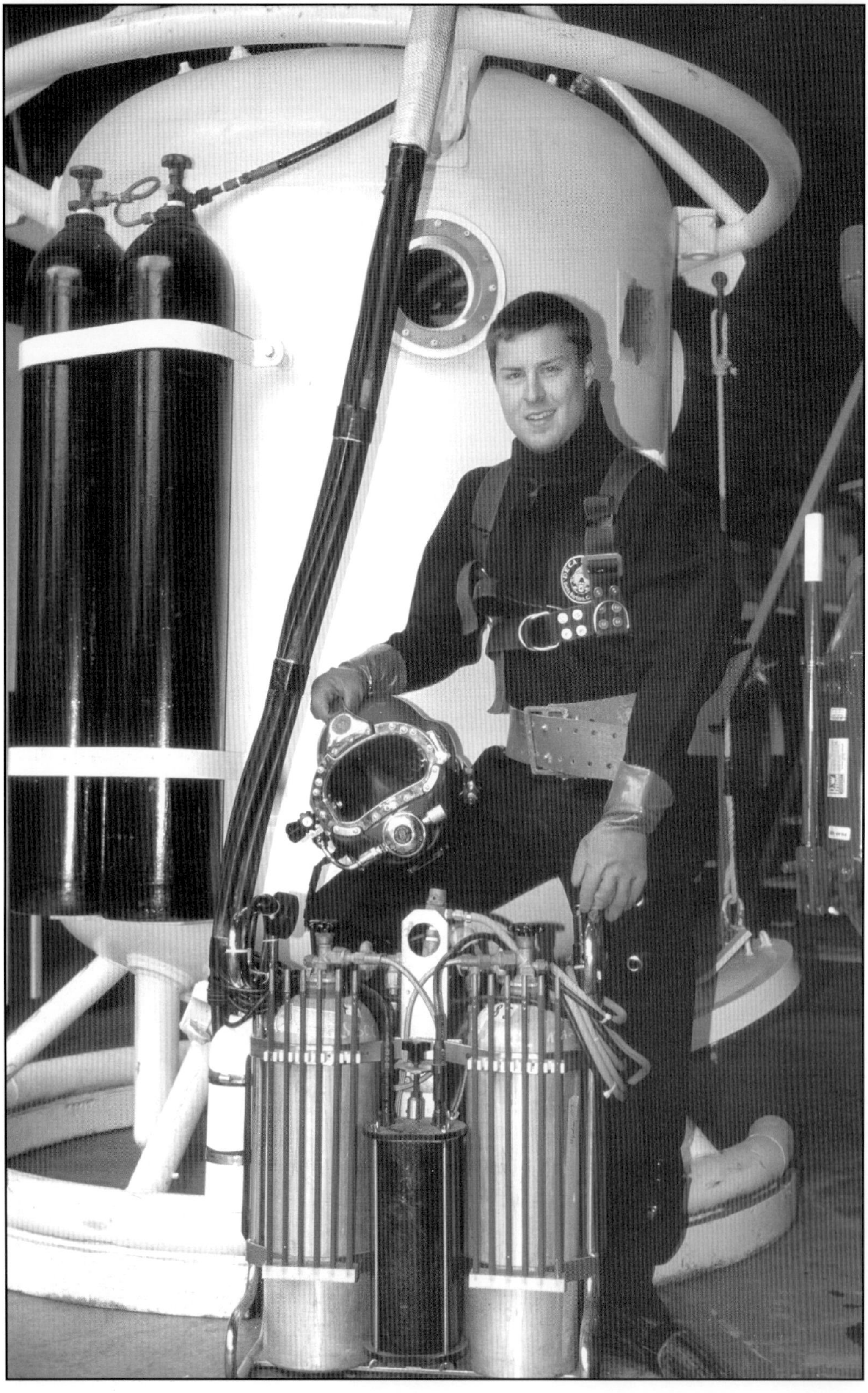

Chapter 12
The Future of Commercial Diving

In Morgan City, Louisiana or Aberdeen, Scotland, if you meet a girl in a bar and tell her you're a diver, she'll probably ask you, "Which kind? Air or "sat?"

The commercial diving industry has changed greatly during the past fifty years, and we have moved from an era of heavy gear divers, like the ones in the photos at the start of many of the chapters in this book, to robotic vehicles and sophisticated one atmosphere suits. The industry has grown and become more sophisticated, and divers have had to adapt to these changes.

Twenty years ago, when remotely operated vehicles came on the market, many people predicted the end of the diving industry. Yet, today, there are still divers working underwater, and although our numbers are smaller than they were, there are still lots of people working in the commercial field. ROVs are capable of performing more jobs now than they ever could in the past, as more subsea production equipment is adapted to the capabilities of these undersea vehicles. They're also working at depths that far exceed what a diver can safely reach.

While we will undoubtedly see even more changes in the next fifty years, there will probably always be a need for human beings to go underwater. There will always be tasks that require the human eye and the human touch, that can't be duplicated by the most sophisticated robotics.

Helping to Ensure Your Employment

The best thing that you can do in the diving industry to help ensure your continued employment is to never stop learning. In your off hours, take any courses you can that will help you in your job. Especially useful are ad-

As long as there are jobs to be done underwater, there will be a need for divers.

The Future of Commercial Diving

ditional courses in electronics, welding, computers, and any other mechanical skill that can be used in the offshore environment.

With the rapid changes in technology today, the more diverse your skills are, the better your chances of staying employed. Don't get lazy just because you are successful.

Your Future

We hope that you have enjoyed this book and have found it useful in deciding whether or not to pursue a career in commercial diving. If after reading this book you decide that the commercial field is not for you, that's okay. This is not a career that everyone will enjoy, and hopefully we've helped you reach the decision that is right for you.

If you do go on in the diving field, we wish you the best of luck and hope your career is successful. It's a serious career decision that can affect your health, safety, and lifestyle. The decision to be a diver is one that only you can make, and should only be made after careful thought and consideration.

Sunrise in the Santa Barbara Channel, home of some of the earliest offshore platforms.

True Tales of Commercial Diving from the Gulf of Mexico

I was working on a drill rig in the Gulf of Mexico, just prior to Christmas one year, where we had just installed a bell diving system and I was due to make a 580 foot bell dive. When we finished installing the hot water machine that heated the water for our suits we fired it up and tested it, only to find that the relief valve on the machine would not function. Without a properly working relief valve, if the machine got too hot it would explode and we would lose all of our hot water. The drill crew told us that we would not be diving right away and that we probably wouldn't dive until after the New Year's holiday, so they sent us back to shore.

On New Year's eve afternoon I was at home, newly married at the time, when the phone started to ring. My wife told me not to answer it, but after half an hour of nonstop calls, I decided I had better pick it up. Of course, it was the diving company telling me to get down to the shop to pick up some gear so we could fly out by helicopter that evening to make the dive.

I drove down to the shop and met the other members of the dive team there. Working from the list of supplies we needed for the diving system, I picked up everything we had identified as needed and threw it all in a cardboard box.

Out on the drill rig we hurried to get ready for the dive. I had just put on my hot water suit when my bell partner reminded me that we still needed to install the relief valve on the hot water machine. I pulled the valve out of the box of supplies and suddenly realized that I had selected a 3000 p.s.i. service valve for a hydraulic power machine rather than a 300 p.s.i. service valve for a hot water heater. This was a big mistake.

My bell partner and friend was visibly upset as he had visions of us not making this high-paying dive. I told him to relax, and took the valve and placed it in a vice to disassemble it. With the valve apart, I took the spring from inside the valve, cut it in half, reassembled the device, and installed it in the machine. We fired up the machine, but when the pressure reached 300 p.s.i. the valve still did not release pressure.

Once again, we shut the machine down, removed the valve, and disassembled it. This time I cut about another third of the spring away and put the whole thing back together once more. This time, when the hot water machine reached 290 p.s.i., the valve opened and we were ready to go.

We made the dive, almost without incident (but that's another story!), and successfully completed the job, cheating death once again! The money wasn't too bad, either…

Steve Barsky

An offshore oil platform starts on its journey from the shipyard to offshore. Note the size of the automobiles relative to the size of the platform.

Bibliography

Association of Diving Contractors International. *Consensus Diving Standards*. Best Publishing, Flagstaff, AZ, 2003.

Barsky, Steven M. *Diving in High-Risk Environments, third edition*. Hammerhead Press, Ventura, California. 1999.

Krieger, Michael. *All the Men in the Sea.* Free Press, New York, 2002.

Supervisor of Salvage and Diving. *U.S. Navy Divers Manual*. U.S. Government Printing Office.

Newberry, W.G. *Handbook for Riggers*. Newberry Investments Co., Ltd. Alberta, Canada. 1967.

About the Authors

About the Author - Steven M. Barsky

Steve Barsky started diving in 1965 in Los Angeles County, and became a diving instructor in 1970. His first employment in the industry was with a dive store in Los Angeles, and he went on to work for almost 10 years in the retail dive store environment.

Steve attended the University of California at Santa Barbara, where he earned a Masters Degree in Human Factors Engineering in 1976. This has greatly assisted his thorough understanding of diving equipment design and use. His master's thesis was one of the first to deal with the use of underwater video systems in commercial diving. His work was a pioneering effort at the time (1976) and was used by the Navy in developing applications for underwater video systems.

His background includes being a commercial diver; working in the offshore oil industry in the North Sea, Gulf of Mexico, and South America. He worked as both an air diving supervisor and a mixed-gas saturation diver, making working dives down to 580 feet.

Barsky was marketing manager for Viking America, Inc., an international manufacturer of dry suits. He also served in a similar position at Diving Systems International, now called Kirby Morgan Dive Systems, Inc., the world's leading manufacturer of commercial diving helmets. At DSI, Barsky worked very closely with Bev Morgan, a diving pioneer.

Steve is an accomplished underwater photographer. His photos have been used in numerous magazine articles, catalogs, advertising, training programs, and textbooks.

A prolific writer, Barsky's work has been published in *Sea Technology, Underwater USA,*

Steven M. Barsky

Skin Diver, Offshore Magazine, Emergency, Fire Engineering, Dive Training Magazine, Searchlines, Sources, Undersea Biomedical Reports, Santa Barbara Magazine, Selling Scuba, Scuba Times, Underwater Magazine, and many other publications. He is the author of the *Dry Suit Diving Manual, Diving in High-Risk Environments, Spearfishing for Skin and Scuba Divers, Small Boat Diving, Diving with the EXO-26 Full Face Mask, Diving with the Divator MK II Full Face Mask, The Simple Guide to Snorkeling Fun,* and a joint author with Dick Long and Bob Stinton of *Dry Suit Diving: A Guide to Diving Dry.* Steve has taught numerous workshops on contaminated water diving, dry suits, small boat diving, spearfishing, and other diving topics. With his wife Kristine, he wrote *California Lobster Diving* and *Careers in Diving* (with Ronnie Damico).

In 1989 Steve formed Marine Marketing and Consulting, based in Santa Barbara, California. The company provides market research, marketing plans, consulting, newsletters, promotional articles, technical manuals, and other services for the diving and ocean industry. He has consulted to Dräger, AquaLung/U.S. Divers Co., Inc, Zeagle Systems, Inc., Diving Unlimited Intnl., Diving Systems Intnl., DAN, NAUI, and numerous other companies. He also investigates diving accidents and serves as an expert witness in dive accident litigation. He has taught specialized diving courses for organizations like Universal Studios, the U.S. Bureau of Reclamation, the City of San Diego Lifeguards, the National Park Service, the Canadian Defense Forces, and the American Academy of Underwater Sciences.

In 1999, Steve and his wife Kristine formed Hammerhead Press to publish high quality diving books. Both Marine Marketing and Consulting and Hammerhead Press operate under the umbrella of the Carcharodon Corporation. Hammerhead Press published the book *Investigating Recreational and Commercial Diving Accidents* by Steve and Dr. Tom Neuman in 2003.

In 2001, Steve wrote and produced four books for Scuba Diving International; *Deeper Sport Diving with Dive Computers - Wreck, Boat, and Drift Diving - Easy Nitrox Diving -* and *Underwater Navigation, Night, and Limited Visibility Diving.*

Steve is also a partner in Scuba-Training.Net, one of the first on-line distance training programs in the scuba industry. The web site provides the academic portion of diver training including text, photos, animations, and full-motion videos. Both quizzes and exams are administered and graded instantly on the site.

Steve has produced several video projects including a CD-ROM for Viking dry suits and DVDs on *California Lobster Diving, Dry Suit Diving in Depth*, and *The Simple Guide to Boat and Wreck Diving*. All of these projects were produced by Hammerhead Video.

Steve lives in Ventura, California, with his wife Kristine, and they regularly dive at the Channel Islands.

About the Author - Robert W. Christensen

Bob Christensen moved to Santa Barbara, California as a young teenager in the summer of 1941 and immediately became enamored with the ocean. He enjoyed swimming and body surfing in the ocean while attending junior and senior high schools in Santa Barbara. After graduation from Santa Barbara High he worked for three years primarily in auto mechanics before attending the University of Southern California in Los Angeles. In 1953 he graduated from U.S.C. with a B.S. degree majoring in Pharmacy.

Immediately after graduation from U.S.C. the military draft prompted Bob to seek the greenest military pastures and he joined the U.S. Navy with an appointment to Officer Candidate School in Newport, Rhode Island. While at O.C.S., future schools and assignments were explored in depth and Bob applied for Underwater Demolition Training. He reported to UDTRA Class 11 in Coronado, California in April 1954, graduated and was assigned to Underwater Demolition Team Eleven the following July.

At that time, all dive training using breathing apparatus was done in the teams, so shortly after joining Team 11 Bob was trained in both open and closed circuit scuba. He also took U.S. Navy Second Class Diver training aboard the dive ship *U.S.S. Coucal* while on temporary assignment in WesPac (Japan). Second Class Diver training consisted of air diving to a maximum 150 feet on air using the standard Mark 5 heavy gear. An introduction to shallow water diving gear (Jack Browne) was included.

In 1957, after discharge from active duty, Bob returned to Santa Barbara and a fulltime white-collar job as a pharmacist. He actively

Bob Christensen

© Bev Morgan. All rights reserved.

pursued sport diving and soon began teaching scuba classes through the local dive shop. He obtained instructor certification from NAUI, YMCA and NASDS.

The offshore oil industry had moved into the Santa Barbara area and was creating a need for commercial divers. In 1960, Bob got a call from a friend in the diving industry seeking a qualified scuba diver to work on an offshore pipeline installation. The pipeline was assembled on shore and was to be pulled offshore to connect with an offshore well head. The diving required was to swim a messenger line from the pulling barge to the beach and then standby to ride the sled on the head end of the pipeline as it was pulled over the nearshore reefs. Regular inspections and reports were made during the pull. This job was the spark that ignited Bob's desire to become a commercial diver.

Although scuba divers had a very poor image in the commercial industry this was Bob's forte. He survived by diving scuba, tending heavy gear and working in the shop doing gear maintenance.

In 1963, Bob and a crew of four worked on a lengthy diving job bolting split pipe protectors around a transpacific telephone cable near Morro Bay, California. Work was started on the beach wearing only wetsuits, continued through the surf zone using scuba and evolved to using scuba and hookah as the depth increased. As the job was to go to the 80-foot depth, Bob and crew successfully petitioned to use hookah and heavy gear to allow increased bottom times. They assembled a set of heavy gear and proceeded to self-train on the job, diving alternately heavy gear, and hookah. This was well received by the diving crew and work went well.

Since Bob was now a heavy gear diver, he was given a weekend training dive in HeO2 heavy gear from a barge anchored in 240 feet of water off Santa Barbara. This HeO2 heavy gear helmet had a scuba second stage regulator installed between the lower edge of the face port and the top of the neck ring. Dives were started on air on open circuit and switched to demand mode by breathing through the internal regulator mouthpiece when on gas. Communication was accomplished by briefly going off the mouthpiece to talk. This gas-training dive moved Bob onto the list of gas divers.

Shortly after this training dive and while Bob was still working five days a week on the Morro Bay job, he got a weekend callout to fill out a gas diving crew on a drill ship in an emergency. Bob was to be the third diver. He would dress in and stand-by with no expectation of getting in the water. The underwater task was to repair a broken hydraulic pipe on a riser at 360-foot depth. The first two divers made good progress but did not quite complete the job, so Bob's first working gas dive was to complete cutting a thread on the pipe, screwing on a quick connect fitting and snapping on a hydraulic hose. This was carried off successfully and the number three diver was solidly on the gas diver list.

In 1965, working with Ocean Systems, Bob was an experimental subject during the development of HeO2 decompression tables at the Linde Laboratory in Tonawanda, New York. In this capacity he made several bounce dives in a compression chamber up to 600 feet. A final saturation dive to 650 feet culminated this series of tests.

September 1965 saw the completion of the test dives and a call to work in the Cook Inlet of Alaska on a pipeline laying operation. Bob liked Alaska and worked there seasonally for several years.

In 1969, Santa Barbara City College was starting the second year of the two year long Marine Diving Technician Program and Bob was invited to apply as an instructor. He ultimately taught in this program for 16 years, retiring in 1985. One of the many highpoints in Bob's activities at City College was meeting and working with the author of this book, Steve Barsky. Steve was an inspired student, a very hard driver and best of all has become a long time good friend.

After a few years enjoying a variety of activities in retirement, Bob started working part time with Kirby Morgan Diving Systems, Inc.. He has worked in several capacities there over the past 14 years and is still associated with them.

Appendix
Field Neurological Exam

The following examination should be conducted whenever a diver surfaces from a no-decompression dive or after the diver exits the chamber. If the diver exhibits any behavior that is not normal for that person, a diving medical physician should be consulted as soon as possible.

Alertness - Does patient seem to be aware of what is going on and able to communicate appropriately?
Orientation - Does patient know who they are, how old are they, where they are, what date/day it is, what have they been doing?
Memory - Ask patient to remember three objects, then later in the exam ask the patient to recall the objects.
Calculation - Have patient count backwards from 100 by sevens
Cranial Nerves:
Eyes - Can patient see, is vision normal, is eye movement normal?
Hearing - Can patient hear equally in both ears, is hearing normal?
Smell - Can patient smell (coffee, peppermint, etc.)?
Facial Muscles - Is the face equal in muscle tone and control? Have patient smile.
Tongue - Can patient control tongue movement? It should stick straight out.
Gag Reflex - Does the "Adam's Apple" move when patient swallows?
Facial Sensation - Can patient feel light touch equally on both sides of their face?
Shoulders - Can patient raise their shoulders equally against resistance?

Muscle Strength against resistance (using 0-5 scale):
Arms:
Lift arms away from side
Push arms towards side
Pull forearm towards upper arm
Push forearm away from upper arm
Lift wrist up
Push wrist down
Squeeze examiner's finger
Pull fingers apart
Squeeze fingers together

Legs:
Lift legs up
Push legs down
Pull legs apart

Push legs together
Pull lower leg towards upper leg
Push lower leg away from upper leg
Push feet away from legs
Pull feet towards legs

Sensory (have patient close eyes while checking sensory perception):
Light Touch - Can patient feel light touch equally on both sides of the body?
Sharp/Dull - Can patient distinguish between a sharp or dull object on both sides of the body?
Hot/Cold - Can patient distinguish between a hot or cold object on both sides of the body?

Coordination (on any test requiring a patient to stand make sure someone is there to support them):
Have the patient touch their nose with their index finger of each hand with eyes shut
Have the patient rapidly slap one hand on the palm of the other, alternating palm up and then palm down - test both sides
Have the patient walk heel to toe in a straight line - forwards and backwards
While standing, have the patient touch the heel of one foot to the knee of the opposite leg, and while maintaining this contact, have them run the heel down the shin to the ankle - test each leg
With eyes closed, have the patient stand with feet together and arms extended to the front, palms up

This examination is based on information from the USC Catalina Hyperbaric Chamber and the following contributors:

The Standard Neurological Examination
- Gordon Boivin

A Broad Outline of the Neurological Exam
- Dr. Jeff Sipsey

Patient Assessment Overview
- NAUI Workbook

Neurological Examination
- US Navy Diving Manual

Index

A

A-frame 107
Aberdeen, Scotland 6, 121
abrasion 131
accident 37, 41, 100, 106, 107, 136
acid 125
ADCI 29, 76, 89. *See also* Association of Diving Contractors International
address 70
adjustable wrench 85, 86, 106
Adobe Photoshop 117
air-water interface 35, 97, 98
air break 82
air compressor 11
air control panel 76
air diving 76, 135
air filter 54
air flow 48
air pressure 30, 55
air sample 33
air supply 38, 54
alcohol 21
alkaline 63
anchor 103, 130
anchor line 10
annual physical exam 21
annual testing 33
anodes 94
anxiety 38
aperture 117
apprentice 4, 9
arc 80, 91, 111
arc-oxygen cutting torch 41
arc welding 112
arthritis 25
ascender 105, 106
ascent 82, 93
aseptic bone necrosis 25, 39
asphyxiation 38
Association of Diving Contractors International 29, 76, 89
asthma 21
atmospheric pressure 96, 97
attitude 73, 76

automatic settings 117

B

backscatter 118
back problem 21
back splice 106, 125, 126
bacteria 42
bail-out bottle 30, 38, 39, 49, 50, 77, 81, 89, 99
ballast weights 100
barge 3, 10, 29, 44, 63, 75, 76, 84, 96, 112, 115
barnacles 110, 114
bathycorrometer 119
beeper 70, 71, 84
bell heater 98
bell manifold pressure 97
bell mate 97, 98
bell port 35
bell stage 98
bell system 33
bell tender 97
benefits 69, 70
bilge 75
biological hazard 42
black water 10, 94, 96
blasting machine 116
block and tackle 61, 100, 128
blood vessel 39
blowout preventer stack (BOP) 19
boat handling 14
bolt 106, 109
bolt hole 106
bone 39
bottom depth 97
bottom hatch 61, 97, 100
box end wrench 106
brass 79, 85
break-out diver 89
breaking out 86, 89
breathing gas 30, 54, 61, 99
breathing gas control manifold 30
bridges 119
briefcase 86
brush 110
Built-In Breathing System (BIBS) 58, 81

built-in flash 117
bungee cord 111
bunk 63
buoyancy 52, 105
buoyancy compensator 52
buoyancy control 105
burning gear 41
burning rod 41, 111, 131
burning torch 106
business card 102
business education 138

C

cable 94, 109, 119, 139
cable cutter 100, 106, 130
camera 117
car 71, 83
carabiner 106
carbon dioxide 61, 62, 63, 64, 65, 100, 133
cardio-pulmonary resuscitation 39
career 101, 102, 142
cathodic protection 120
cathodic protection meters 119
cellular phone 3, 70, 71, 84
chain 9, 131, 132
chain binder 9, 131
chain hoist 107
chamber heating 25
chemicals 116
chemical pollutant 51
chrome 111
cigarette 81
circulation 39, 82
cleat 127
client 94, 102, 136
clipboard 82
clove hitch 127
coastal area 42
collet 79
come-along 9, 107
commercial diving company 18, 21, 138
commercial diving equipment 16
commercial diving school 9, 15, 17, 69, 71, 138
communications 48, 50, 55, 58, 61, 64, 65, 81, 83, 91, 92
communications box 60, 76, 112
communications wire 30, 56, 99
community college 16
company management 91
compressed air 108

compression 25
compressor 24, 38, 48, 54, 76, 81, 82, 99
computer 12, 13, 70, 142
computer-projected presentation 116
computer screen 117
concrete 109, 117
condensation 82
conductor 109
confidence 14, 76
constrictor hitch 127
construction 41, 43, 49, 74, 116
consultant 138
consumables log 101, 102
contaminant 30, 42, 48
contaminated water 48
control van 61, 64
convulsion 22
copper tubing 63
corrosion engineer. 120
corrosion inhibitor 106
corrosion meter 119. *See also* bathycorrometer
coveralls 51
crane 10, 43, 44, 78, 107, 112
crane accident 38
crane driver 112
credit card 85
cross-over valve 81
current 30, 51, 92, 94
curriculum 16
customer 137
customer's representative 101, 102
cutting 10, 11, 78, 91
cutting guide 111
cutting rod 79
cutting torch 79, 80
cylinder 50

D

D-ring 49, 50, 65, 77, 99
daily planner 84
dam 1, 41, 69
davit 58
day crew 73
DCS. *See decompression sickness*
death 4, 38, 43, 45
decompression 22, 23, 24, 33, 61, 63, 81, 82, 99, 101
decompression chamber 11, 22, 24, 33, 39, 54, 57, 58, 63, 76, 78, 80, 82, 83
decompression dive 50, 57

Index

decompression obligation 99
decompression schedule 82
decompression sickness (DCS) 4, 23, 24, 39, 57, 82, 83, 101
decompression stop 22, 39, 81
deep air diving 76
deep dive 39
delta-P 39
demand helmet 48, 50
demobilization 83, 102
depth 21, 50, 62, 64, 82
depth gauge 55, 96
depth limitation 108
depth pay 73
depth rating 118
Desco 48
diesel-fired burner 24
diesel engine 9, 11, 54, 65
differential pressure accident 38, 39
digital camera 102, 117
digital photography 12, 70, 116
disability 4
dishwashing soap 77
ditch 115
Divator MKII 49
diver-tender 86
dive log 101
dive profile 23
dive station 76
diving bell 33, 35, 61, 62, 65, 76, 78, 96, 98, 99, 101, 100, 103
diving company 72, 74
diving contractor 19
diving gear 29
diving helmet 42, 47, 49, 63
diving hose 126
diving rotation 91
diving supervisor 6, 24, 35, 54, 78, 82, 94, 97, 135, 137, 138
diving support vessel 65
divorce 45
dock 2
doctor 83
double-lock chamber 57
down line 78, 92, 93, 98, 124
drag 94
Drager gas detection tube 65
drift pin 106
drill rig 38, 45, 53
drill ship 87
drinking water tank 1

drop weight 62
drowning 38, 39, 41
drug-free work place 21
drug screen 21
dry glove 42
dry suit 24, 42, 47, 51, 52, 85, 105
duct tape 51, 56, 77
duffle bag 85
dynamically positioned vessel (DP ship) 103
dynamic positioning system 103
dysbaric osteonecrosis 39. *See also* asceptic bone necrosis

E

ear drum 42
ECU *See environmental control system*
Ekofisk Field 66
electrical current 35, 41
electrical shock 80
electrical tape 85, 106, 125, 126
electricity 9
electric arc welder 10
electric blasting cap 116
electrochemical potential 119
electrocution 4
electromagnet 120
electronics 9, 13, 142
electronic locating pinger 63
e-mail 116
emergency 25, 50, 62, 93, 98
emergency breathing gas 38
emergency gas supply 61, 96, 97, 100. *See also* bail-out bottle
emergency pinger 100
emergency power supply 61, 96, 100
emergency repair 74
emergency valve 50
emotional stress 45
EMT 70
engine mechanics 9
entanglement 50, 106
entrance lock 35, 61, 63, 75, 99
environmental control system (ECU) 33, 61, 63
environmental regulations 42
EPA 108
equipment log 101
exhaust bubbles 108
exhaust system 42
exhaust valve 92
EXO-26® 49

expense report 13
experience 4
exploratory drilling 2
explosion 4, 38, 41, 115, 116
explosives 42, 115, 116
explosive decompression 39
explosive mixture 41
eye 30, 39, 93, 118
eye protection 64
eye splice 106, 126

F

family 45
family crises 70
fear 86
feet 25, 84
fiber rope 10, 123
fid 130
field neurological exam 82, 101
    (also see Appendix of book - page 150)
figure eight 57
film 116
filter 12, 78
filtration system 54
fins 47
fire 81, 101
flange 41, 106
flash 117
flash arrestor 79
flight 85
flogging spanner 106
fluorescent ink 120
foam padding 48
foot guards, 89
foot protection 114
Forties Field 6, 26
foul-weather gear 85
four-pound hammer 79
four-wire communications system 55
frame grab 12
free-flow helmet 48
free-flow valve 92
front nozzle 114
FSW 1
full-face mask 30, 38, 41, 47, 49, 50, 111, 113, 115
fumes 113
fungal infection 25, 52, 63

G

galley 78
gas-bottle key 85
gasket material 111
gasoline engine 11
gas cylinder 33, 60
gas mixture 24
gauge 96
gauge calibration 33
gauntlet glove 52
generator 6
Global Positioning System (GPS) 103
gloves 53, 64, 77, 80, 85, 110, 111, 128, 132
government regulations 29, 30
Great Britain 26
grit 115
grit blaster 115
ground cable 110
ground clamp 79, 109, 110. 111
Gulf of Mexico 38, 41, 45, 69, 71
gutter 43

H

habitat welder 114
hacksaw blade 79, 111
hack saw 100
half-mask 58
hammer 105, 106
hammer wrench 106
hand 25, 52, 131
hand tools 86, 106
hanger 112
hanger checker 79
harbor 1, 42, 43, 69
hard hat 84
harness 30, 49, 51, 53, 77, 81, 91, 96, 97, 98, 106
hatch 62
hazard 37, 89
head 48
head injury 84
head protection 49
hepatitis 26
hearing test 21
heart 38
heart attack 45
heart defect 21
heat 100
heater 61, 62

Index

heavy gear 87, 133
heavy gear diver 141
heli-ox mix 100
helicopter 38
helium 23, 24, 33, 59
helium-oxygen mixture 48, 52, 60, 102, 133
helium ear 60
helium speech 60
helium unscrambler 60
helmet 30, 38, 41, 91, 92, 96, 97
helmet handle 48
HeO2 139
high-pressure cylinder 30, 48, 54
high-pressure regulator 59
high-pressure water blaster 89. 114. 115
High Pressure Nervous Syndrome (HPNS) 25
high school 70
hitch 123, 127
hoist 58, 100
hose 26, 38, 50, 54, 59, 61, 76, 77, 92, 96, 99, 108, 112, 136
hose clamps 50
hot knife 130
hot water 53, 61, 64, 100
hot water hose 24, 33, 56, 93
hot water suit 24, 25, 33, 47, 52, 53, 63, 96, 105, 115
housing 12, 73, 118
Houston, Texas 71
HPNS. *See also* High Pressure Nervous Syndrome
humidity 25, 33, 63
hurricane 44
hydraulics 65
hydraulic brush 113
hydraulic cutter 106, 109
hydraulic grinder 113
hydraulic hose 108
hydraulic impact wrench 108
hydraulic jack 108
hydraulic power unit 108
hydraulic pump 11
hydraulic tools 11, 106, 108, 109
hydraulic wrench 109
hydroelectric firm 4
hydrogen 41
hydrogen gas 111
hyperbaric chamber 63 *See also* decompression chamber
hyperbaric lifeboat 63, 100
hypothermia 4, 44

I

impact wrench 106
in-line lubricator 108
income 4, 73
Independent Wire Rope Core 128
industrial environment 37
industry standard 30
inert gas 23
infection 54, 115
injury 43, 99, 119
inner hatch, 98
inner lock 57, 81
inshore 1
inspection 12, 74, 101
inspection work 24
insulation 24, 52
internal depth 98
internal injury 115
internal pressure 97
International Marine Contractors Association (IMCA) 29
interview 72, 73
IWRC 128

J

jackhammer 108
jeans 102
jellyfish 53
jet sled 115
JHR 89
JIM 60
Job Hazard Analysis (JHA) 89
Job Hazard Review (JHR) 89
jocking system 48

K

kerf 111, 112
Kirby Morgan Band Mask 49
Kirby Morgan Dive Systems, Inc. (KMDSI) 48
kitchen knife, 111
knife 53, 84
knife switch 78, 80
knot 10, 123, 127

L

ladder 30, 58
lake 42
lanyard 53, 85, 105
laptop computer 102

launch system 65
leadership ability 135
lead diver 102, 137
leather work gloves 53
legal record 101
lens adapter 117
letters of recommendation 70
leverage 3, 131
life-support equipment 47
lifestyle 3, 138
life support system 65
life support technician 60, 65, 76
life support van 64
lift 96
lift wire 62, 63, 65, 96, 100
light 48
lighting 94, 96
line 84, 94, 109, 123
load 78, 123
long bone 25
long term disability 43
loss of appetite 25
Louisiana 71
low-pressure air compressor 30, 108
low-pressure air supply 59
loyalty 137
lubrication 107
lung 38
lung-powered scrubber 35, 100

M

machine shop 14
macro adapter 117
magnesium 120
magnetic particle inspection (MPI) 119
maintenance 33, 49, 107, 108
management 83, 102
manifold 54, 59, 61, 62
manifold operator 55
manila 10, 77, 93, 105, 106, 111, 124
manipulator 94
manual 118
manual dexterity 61
marine growth 114, 120
marine life 113
marine life injuries 38, 41
marlinespike 53, 130
meals 73
meat hook 107, 128
medical assistance 115

medical decision 83
medical lock 33, 63
messenger line 78, 93
metatarsal guards 89
metering valve 59
military training 70
mixed-gas diving 48, 59, 69, 135
mixed-gas diving system 33, 59
mixed-gas manifold 33, 59, 64
mixing manifold 24
mobilization 102
moisture 30, 63
Molly Hogan 128
monel bolt 41
money 4, 73, 86, 96, 102
mooring line 124
Morro Bay, California 87, 139
motion compensation system 65
motorcycle 84
mudline 116

N

natural fiber rope 124
nausea 25
Navy Seal Team 19
neoprene 51
New Iberia, Louisiana 71
night crew 73
nitrile 54
nitrox 23, 81
node 105, 117, 119
non-destructive testing (NDT) 14, 26, 70, 119
non-point source pollution 43
non-return valve 38
North Sea 44, 66
nylon 92, 124, 125

O

Occupational Safety and Health Administration (OSHA) 30
Oceaneering International 60
oceanography 14
office 72, 102
offshore 1
offshore environment 74
offshore oilfield 2, 26
offshore platform 3
oil 11, 54
oilfield 42
oilfield diver 69

Index

oil company 4
oil patch 69, 102
oil platform 84, 94, 103, 105, 107, 116, 120
oil well casing 116
one atmosphere suit 60, 61, 141
open bottom bell 33, 60
operations manager 16, 72, 138
organizational ability 14
OSHA. *See also* Occupational Safety and Health Administration
Otic Domeboro 25
outer hatch 96, 98
outer lock 57, 81
over-pressure relief valve 58
oxy-acetylene torch 11
oxy-arc torch 109
oxygen 22, 23, 33, 38, 41, 57, 58, 59, 62, 63, 64, 78, 79, 80, 81, 82, 100, 111
oxygen analyzer 65, 78, 82
oxygen cylinder 78
oxygen enriched air 23

P

pad eye 100
pager 3
painting 78
paperwork 101, 102, 137
particle mask 64
particulate matter 118
passive heating system 100
passive thermal protection 24
penetrator 58, 61
perforated tube 25
permanent disabilities 101
personal business 76
personal conduct 102
personal digital assistant (PDA) 84
personal dive log 101
personal pride 17
personal problem 45
personnel 101
personnel basket 44
Peterhead, Scotland 83
Petrogen® 112
photography 12
photo processing 116
physical condition 21
physiology 21
pier 2, 69
pier piling 116

piling 127, 128
pipe 29, 115, 128, 132
pipefitting 9, 11
pipeline 2, 11, 41, 56, 94, 106, 108, 112, 116, 117, 118, 119
pipe fitting 11
planning 14
platform 44, 94, 119
pliers 79, 86
plumbing 57, 61
pneumatic tool 11, 106, 108, 109
pneumofathometer 30, 54
pneumofathometer hose 56
polarity 79
politics 138
pollutants 42
polluted water 42, 48, 51, 53, 54, 56
polypropylene 92, 124, 125
positive terminal 79
power 96
pre-dive check-list 96
pre-employment physical exam 21
pre-job meetings 137
pressure 98
pressure pay 73
pressure related injuries 38
Pressure Vessel for Human Occupancy (PVHO) 58
Primacord® 116
privacy 3
private trade school 15
professional photography school 118
project manager 138
promotion 74, 86
propeller 29, 94
prophylactic 25
public college 15
puncture 24, 54
push-to-talk 55

Q

quick link 106
Quincy air compressor 54
quiver 79

R

random drug screen 21
rebreather 64
reciprocating saw 109
recirculator 133

recreational diving 9
reference electrode 120
regulator 50, 54, 80, 89
regulator diaphragm 48
relief valve 62
Remotely Operated Vehicle (ROV) 94, 141
report 12, 13, 70, 101
reputation 86
rescue 99, 100
reserve 30
respect 87
responsibility 55, 80, 89, 135
restraining harness 100
resume 70, 72
retirement 69
retro-jet 115
rig 3
rigging 9, 123
rigging tool 123
rig fire 45
risk 4, 24, 30, 37, 39, 52, 106, 115
river 42, 51
robotic arm 94
rod 41
rod stub 111
rope 9
round-robin 55
rubber glove 79
rust 106, 128

S

sacrificial zinc anode 120
safety 23, 37, 78, 81, 94, 102, 136
safety diver 91
safety equipment 89
safety officer 138
safety record 37
safe working load 123, 131
salary 4, 73, 75, 138
salvage 1, 2, 10, 41, 43, 116
Santa Barbara Channel 19
saturation 73
saturation chamber 61
saturation diver 101, 135
saturation diving 23, 39, 69, 70, 75, 76
saturation diving system 33, 35
saturation superintendent 135
saturation system 23, 25, 59, 61, 64, 78, 96, 97, 98
scraper 79, 110

screwdriver 48, 86
scrubber 61
scuba 9, 29, 30
seal 98, 100
sea conditions 30
sewage spill 43
sewer outfall 1, 51
sexual discrimination 3
shackle 9, 92, 93, 96, 130
shark 41
sheet pile 111
ship 3, 38, 63, 76, 78, 84, 96, 112
ship repair 1
shock wave 42
shop 74
shorty wetsuit 52
shoulder blades 99
shoulder straps 51
shower 63
shutter speed 117
sidecutters 53
side hatch 61
silent bubbles 39
skiff 139
skin 25, 43, 52, 115
slack 77, 92, 94
slag 106, 111, 112
sleep 82, 83
sling 123, 124, 128, 130
slugging wrench 106
smoke inhalation 45
snap hook 53, 131
snap shackle 77, 105, 106
socket wrench 130
Sodasorb® 63, 65
software 12
spark 41
speaker 91
spider 77
splice 10, 123, 129
sport diver 47
spouse 45
squeeze 38
stage 26, 30, 33, 58, 92
standby diver 91
steel-toed boot 80, 84
stinger 29
stock 69
stopwatch 82
storage yard 74
straight polarity, electrode negative 79

159

Index

strand 128
strength 21
strength member 56
stress 135, 136
SubSea International 6, 121
subsea production equipment 141
SuperLite® 48, 49
supervisor 37, 73, 75, 91, 92, 97, 100, 102
supplementary lighting 119
supply ship 26, 76
supply valve 82
sur-d-O2 *See surface decompression on oxygen*
surface-decompression on oxygen 22, 57, 81
surface-supplied diving 22, 29, 30, 49, 58, 65
surge 13
surrounding pressure 97
symptoms 82
synthetic fiber 124
synthetic line 10, 125

T

tables 23
tag line 131
team player 73, 75
technical report 12, 15
technician 116
teeth 111
telephone 70, 76
television cable 56, 61
television camera 48
temperature 33, 63, 82, 101
tender 4, 6, 18, 39, 65, 71, 73, 74, 75, 76, 77, 80, 83, 85, 87, 89, 92, 96, 100, 110, 137
terrorist act 43
tether 94
Texas 71
thermal protection 24
thermal underwear 52
thimble 129
three-man dive team 102
through-water communications system 96
thrusters 94
timber hitch 127
time sheet 101
Tirfor 107
titling 119
toggle switch 55
toilet 63, 75
tools 47, 76, 78, 89, 93, 94, 98, 105
tool box 86

topside air supply 30
top hatch 35
torch 41, 111
torch head 111
torque 109
toxic chemical 42
toxic dinoflagellate 42
trade school 16
trade skills 15, 16
training 1, 12, 42
transportation 83
travel 70, 85
treasure hunting 1
treatment 24
treatment tables 83
trench 115
trigger 108, 111
trucker's hitch 128
trunk 62, 97, 98, 99
tubing 11
tug 76
twine 125
twisted umbilical 56
two-wire communications system 55

U

ultrasonic thickness meter 120
umbilical 33, 56, 62, 63, 65, 74, 93, 94, 100
unconscious diver 99, 100
underwater cutting torch 11
Underwater Demolition Team 19
underwater flash 117, 118
underwater photography 12, 24, 118
underwater video 118
United States Coast Guard 30

V

vacation 70
valve 41, 52, 55, 62, 64, 96
valve handle 106
van 33
ventricular fibrillation 38
vent hole 41, 111
vessel 10, 30, 35, 98, 112, 127
video 12, 13
videography 12
video camera 94, 116, 119
video editing 12
video tape 102
virus 42

visibility 11, 14, 37, 92, 94, 108, 117
vision 80, 91
volume tank 30, 54

W

WASP 60
watch 82, 85
waterman 13
waterproof bulkhead connector 117
water blaster 105
water jet 105, 114, 115
water pollution 43
water stop 23, 81
WD-40® 106
weak link 93, 124
weather 37
web site 116
weight belt 50
weld 118, 120
welding 9, 10, 91, 142
welding habitat 11, 107, 113
welding lens 79, 91
welding machine 6, 79, 110
welds 117
weld seam 112
wetsuit 24, 51, 85, 105
wet welding 114
whipping 125
wide-angle lens 116, 118
wire 56
wireless communication system 100
wire brush 79
wire rope 106, 128, 131
wire rope clip 10, 128
wire rope splice 10
women 3
work ethic 138
work log 101
work site 93, 96, 98, 102
wreck 41, 99, 117
wrench 48, 105, 106
writing 101

X

x-ray 21

Y

yoke 42

Z

zero visibility 10
zinc 120